"Katherine Vessenes has traveled these roads as a planner and a lawyer. **Follow the map and you won't get lost**."

VICTOR J. PRYLES
Vice President
Investors Financial Group

"There are two types of financial planners: **Those who read this book**, and those who are committed to learning the hard and painful way."

MYRA SALZER
Money Strategies, Inc.

"Well-organized and practical"

JAN WALSH
Academic Associate
National Endowment for Financial Education

"This book is a practical guide to a subject of paramount importance to registered reps, broker-dealers and managers. **Katherine Vessenes has clearly communicated technical compliance information in a format that is easy to apply** to your practice. **We have ordered a copy for each of our registered reps**."

LAWRENCE J. RYBKA, JD, CFP
President
ValMark Securities

"The definitive guide on the subject."

STEWART H. WELCH, III, CFP,
CHFC, AEP
The Welch Group

"Katherine Vessenes underscores the most important element of successful financial planning: **When you keep your clients happy, you keep your clients**. Whether you've been a financial planner for years or are new to the profession, **you'll find *Protecting Your Practice* an essential addition to your professional library**."

THOMAS W. JOHNSON
Executive Editor
Financial Planning

"**A voice of authority and knowledge that comes from years of dealing with these issues**."

ROBERT CLARK
Editor-in-Chief
Dow Jones Investment Advisor

"Katherine Vessenes . . . is **ahead of the pack in providing clear and concise text, real-life situations, and action items** that can be incorporated into the successful planner's practice. . . . **A must read for serious financial professionals**."

JEFFREY H. RATTINER, CPA, CFP
Director of Professional Development
and Corporate Sponsorship
Institute of Certified Financial Planners

"***Protecting Your Practice* is a continuation of Katherine Vessenes's valuable contribution to the financial planning profession**. We don't like to think about it but **we must take appropriate steps to ensure the continuation of our practice** for our own protection and that of our existing clients. **This book tells us how to do it**."

LINDA S. LUBITZ, CFP
Woolf, Lubitz and Folders

"Its no-nonsense approach...provides **practical solutions for avoiding the various legal and regulatory pitfalls** of the financial services industry."

> RICK YOUNG
> Director of Compliance
> *FSC Securities Corporation*

"**An excellent resource for compliance officers, financial planning practitioners, and investment advisers**. Katherine Vessenes's suggestions show how compliance can *and should* become an integral part of your day-to-day activities—without causing 'sales prevention.'"

> NANCY J. JOHNSON, CFP
> Vice President
> *Cambridge Investment Research*

**... and praise for her previous book,
The Compliance and Liability Handbook for
Financial Planners and
Financial Service Professionals
by Katherine Vessenes
in cooperation with the IAFP**

"**We require all our representatives to read Katherine's practical and insightful book**. Our group works with high-producing independent agents who need to know specifically what they must do to protect their business. **Her marketing ideas on how to grow your business are invaluable**. Combined with her legal viewpoint on how to avoid litigation, every detail is worthwhile."

> LAWRENCE J. RYBKA, JD, CFP
> President
> *ValMark Securities*

KATHERINE VESSENES

PROTECTING
YOUR
PRACTICE

Also available from
The Bloomberg Professional Library

Best Practices for Financial Advisors
by Mary Rowland

Swap Literacy:
A Comprehensible Guide
by Elizabeth Ungar, Ph.D.

An Introduction to
Option-Adjusted Spread Analysis
(Revised Edition)
by Tom Windas

And from
The Bloomberg Personal Bookshelf

Smarter Insurance Solutions
by Janet Bamford

Investing in Small-Cap Stocks
by Christopher Graja and Elizabeth Ungar, Ph.D.

A Commonsense Guide to Mutual Funds
by Mary Rowland

BLOOMBERG PROFESSIONAL LIBRARY

KATHERINE VESSENES

PROTECTING YOUR PRACTICE

IN COOPERATION WITH THE
INTERNATIONAL ASSOCIATION
FOR FINANCIAL PLANNING

BLOOMBERG PRESS
PRINCETON

Books are available for bulk purchases at special discounts. For information, please write: Special Markets Department, Bloomberg Press.

This publication contains the author's opinions and is designed to provide accurate and authoritative information. It is sold with the understanding that the author, publisher, and Bloomberg L.P. are not engaged in rendering legal, accounting, investment-planning, or other professional advice. The reader should seek the services of a qualified professional for such advice; the author, publisher, and Bloomberg L.P. cannot be held responsible for any loss incurred as a result of specific investments or recommendations made by the reader.

First edition published 1997
1 3 5 7 9 10 8 6 4 2

Vessenes, Katherine

    Protecting your practice / Katherine Vessenes. - - 1st ed.

      p.   cm. - - (Bloomberg professional library)

    Includes index.

    ISBN 1-57660-053-X (alk. paper)

    1. Financial planners- - Legal status, laws, etc.- - United States-

-Popular works.   2. Financial planners- - Malpractice- - United States-

-Popular works.   I. Title.   II. Series.

KF2921.Z9V473   1997

332.6'068 - - dc21   97-25544

                                         CIP

Permissions credits on page 472.

Book design by Don Morris Design

*This book is
dedicated to the
Creator of Truth
and Integrity*

— K.V.

CONTENTS

Acknowledgments

THIS BOOK WOULD NOT have been possible without the help of many generous people. I am especially grateful to Laurie Grover, Todd Wilson, Carey J. Gifford, Robin L. Bellinson, Dale E. Brown, Barbara Diez, Jared Kieling, Patricia A. Taylor, Priscilla Treadwell, and my review committee: Ed Morrow, John McGovern, Dennis Kaminski, Nancy Johnson, John Simmers, Janet McCallen, and Rick Young. The following people kindly allowed us to include copies of their forms and documents: Arnie Abens, Alexandra Armstrong, J. Floyd Swilley, Nancy Johnson, Ed Morrow, Fred Haiker, Richard Young, Linda Lubitz, Norman Boone, and Lawrence J. Rybka.

Without the unselfish support of my husband, Peter, and my children, Peter, Ted, and Sarah, I could never have completed this manuscript. To all of you, my most heartfelt thanks.

INTRODUCTION

PROTECTING YOUR PRACTICE

NOTHING HIDES SIN like a bull market. When stock prices are soaring, the last thing on most clients' minds is regulation violations. In a prolonged bear market, however, even your favorite clients may be phoning you from their attorneys' office.

When I first started in the business, my mentor taught me to do certain things that were actually felonies. He was not trying to make me a criminal. He was just handing on to me the same overzealous sales practices that had made him a lot of money. In the years since then, the field has become so competitive and complex that even experienced financial professionals will find new things in this book to improve their practice and keep them out of trouble.

The first step in building a successful practice is knowing what business you are in. Forty years ago, proprietors of drive-in restaurants thought they were in the hamburger business. McDonald's Corp. founder Ray Kroc understood something his competition did not: he was really in the speed and clean-restroom business. That knowledge made him a billionaire.

You need to know what kind of business you are in. What is really motivating clients to seek your advice?

Believe it or not, we are in the peace-of-mind business. Whenever I lecture on choosing an adviser, an investment, or even a broker-dealer, I counsel the audience to first look at the character of the people at the top. If people of good character are running the operation, they will work hard to save even the worst deal. On the other hand, leaders with poor character at the helm can destroy even the best deal.

Character is critical. Trusting a financial adviser to behave ethically when no one is looking is the single most important factor on a consumer's mind. Clients are begging for someone they can trust. We can build that good faith and reliance by showing

them that our integrity is beyond reproach.

I believe in doing what is right by the

client. I believe this not just to appease

regulators and avoid lawsuits but also

because it builds business.

This book is about the "how" of doing

the right thing.

K . V .

KNOWING THE
ALPHABET

THE FINANCIAL SERVICES industry has

more than its fair share of acronyms. To

make this book as user-friendly as possible,

it was decided to include all widely used

acronyms in this front material. These

acronyms are presented below in alphabeti-

cal order. Whenever you see an acronym in

the text and are not sure what it stands for

or means, just refer to this listing for a brief definition.

In general, acronyms specific to one subject matter and appearing in only one chapter are not included here. Thus, ADR or Alternative Dispute Resolution is not listed below as it is described solely in Chapter 18. However, both ADR and Alternative Dispute Resolution appear as entries in the Index.

AICPA (AMERICAN INSTITUTE OF CERTIFIED PUBLIC ACCOUNTANTS) Based in New York City, AICPA has 328,000 members throughout the country. Although only 1,650 accountants have earned its PFS designation, the Personal Financial Planning Membership Section of AICPA has 7,000 members.[1]

CFA (CHARTERED FINANCIAL ANALYST) This designation, awarded by the Association for Investment Management and Research, is described in Chapter 4.

CFP (CERTIFIED FINANCIAL PLANNER) The CFP and Certified Financial Planner designations are two separate federally registered service marks, which are for the use of individuals who have completed the requirements established by the CFP Board. Approximately 31,500 people are currently licensed to use the CFP mark.[2] This is discussed in Chapter 5.

CFP BOARD (CERTIFIED FINANCIAL PLANNER BOARD OF STANDARDS, INC.) This is a private, not-for-profit, professional regulatory organization which sets standards for CFP credentials, including education, examination, work experience, and ethics.[3] These standards are discussed in Chapter 5.

ChFC (CHARTERED FINANCIAL CONSULTANT) This educational designation, described in Chapter 5, is granted by The American College, Bryn Mawr, Pennsylvania. The American College was founded to serve the life insurance industry by the American Society of CLU and ChFC, a national association for life insurance and financial services professionals also headquartered in Bryn Mawr. Approximately 15,300 members of the society have been awarded the ChFC designation.[4]

CLU (CHARTERED LIFE UNDERWRITER) This educational designation, described in Chapter 5, is granted by The American College, Bryn Mawr, Pennsylvania. The American College was founded to serve the life insurance industry by the American Society of CLU and ChFC, a national association for life insurance and financial services professionals also headquartered in Bryn Mawr. Most of the 34,000 members of the society hold the CLU designation.[5]

CPA (CERTIFIED PUBLIC ACCOUNTANT) This designation, awarded to accountants after a prescribed course of study and experience, is described in Chapter 4.

E&O (ERRORS AND OMISSIONS COVERAGE) Chapter 17 is devoted to this form of liability insurance.

ERISA (EMPLOYER RETIREMENT INCOME SECURITY ACT OF 1974) Regulation of pension plans is included within the scope of this Act.

IAFP (INTERNATIONAL ASSOCIATION FOR FINANCIAL PLANNING) This is a professional membership association dedicated to advancing the financial planning process. Founded in 1969, IAFP is the oldest and largest nonprofit organization of its type in the world. The IAFP represents more than 16,500 individuals and institutions in all 50 states and abroad who are committed to furthering the financial planning process as the foundation for smart decision making. Its members, primarily financial advisers, are from all backgrounds and disciplines.

IARFC (INTERNATIONAL ASSOCIATION OF REGISTERED FINANCIAL CONSULTANTS) Headquartered in Chesterfield, Missouri, this professional association has more than 1,000 members. It provides practice management support services, hosts educational conferences, and awards the RFC designation to those who have earned it.[6]

ICFP (INSTITUTE OF CERTIFIED FINANCIAL PLANNERS) Headquartered in Denver, Colorado, this is a membership association for the Certified Financial Planner professionals who have qualified for the license prerequisites set by the CFP Board of Standards, Inc., the professional regulatory body also located in Denver. ICFP has 11,000 members.

IPS (INVESTMENT POLICY STATEMENT) This written document verifies a client's investment philosophy, financial goals, and the specific strategies for attaining these goals.

NAIC (NATIONAL ASSOCIATION OF INSURANCE COMMISSIONERS) Created by state insurance regulators in 1871 to address the need to coordinate regulation of multistate insurers, NAIC membership includes commissioners from all states, the District of Columbia, and the four U.S. territories. NAIC helps regulators fulfill their obligation of protecting the interests of insurance consumers and provides a forum for the development of uniform policy.

NALU (NATIONAL ASSOCIATION OF LIFE UNDERWRITERS) This is a federation of approximately 950 local life underwriters associations affiliated with 50 state associations; together, the local and state associations make up the national organization. There are 120,000 sales professionals in life and health insurance and other financial fields that belong to the local associations. To fulfill its mission, NALU develops programs in communications, education, ethical conduct, government relations and advocacy, member associations, public relations, and community service.

NAPFA (NATIONAL ASSOCIATION OF PERSONAL FINANCIAL ADVISORS) With more than 575 members and affiliates, NAPFA is the largest association for fee-only financial planners. It is headquartered in Buffalo Grove, Illinois, and seeks to improve and promote comprehensive fee-only financial planning as well as to increase public awareness of the financial planning field and fee-only financial planners. The association has three membership categories: member, provisional member, and sustaining member. NAPFA affiliates are fee-only professionals in financial services and related industries who are not otherwise candidates for any category of NAPFA membership. Compensation based on commissions, rebates, bonuses, finder's fees, or other types of compensation based on financial planning recommendations cannot be accepted by members.[7]

NASAA (NORTH AMERICAN SECURITIES ADMINISTRATORS ASSOCIATION) The oldest international organization devoted to investor protection, NASAA is the voice of the 50 state securities agencies responsible for grass-roots investor protection and efficient capital formation. Its standing committees are organized into four sections, one of which is in the area of broker-dealer and investment adviser regulation. Uniform national model codes and guidelines developed and adopted by NASAA are made available for adoption by individual states.

NASD (NATIONAL ASSOCIATION OF SECURITIES DEALERS, INC.) Subject to SEC oversight, NASD is the nation's largest self-regulatory organization and has responsibility for the Nasdaq Stock Market as well as the vast over-the-counter securities market and the many products traded in it. Its membership includes virtually every broker-dealer that does a securities business with the public.

P&C (PROPERTY AND CASUALTY INSURANCE) This form of insurance includes homeowner and automobile policies. As discussed in Chapter 12, it is rarely reviewed by financial planners.

PFS (PERSONAL FINANCIAL SPECIALIST) This is

a professional designation that has been created by AICPA for CPAs who want to specialize in financial planning. It is described in Chapter 5.

RFC (REGISTERED FINANCIAL CONSULTANT) This designation, described in Chapter 5, is awarded by IARFC.

RIA (REGISTERED INVESTMENT ADVISER) A financial services industry person or firm who gives investment advice about securities and is registered with the SEC and/or state securities administrator(s).

RR (REGISTERED REPRESENTATIVE) A broker or sales representative of a broker-dealer.

RR/RIA Registered Representatives who are also Registered Investment Advisers.

SEC (U.S. SECURITIES AND EXCHANGE COMMISSION) This is an independent, nonpartisan, quasi-judicial regulatory agency with responsibility for administering federal securities laws. The SEC also regulates firms engaged in the purchase or sale of securities, people who provide investment advice, and investment companies.

SIA (SECURITIES INDUSTRY ASSOCIATION) This is a trade association representing the business interests of more than 700 member securities firms throughout North America. SIA represents members' interests in Washington and serves as a liaison between the industry, the regulators, and the exchanges; offers a broad range of services, enabling its members to operate more effectively; and serves as a medium through which member ideas, experience, and information can be exchanged.

UPIA (THE UNIFORM PRUDENT INVESTOR ACT) This model act updated trust investment law and trustees' responsibilities in recognition of the many changes that have occurred in modern investment practice.

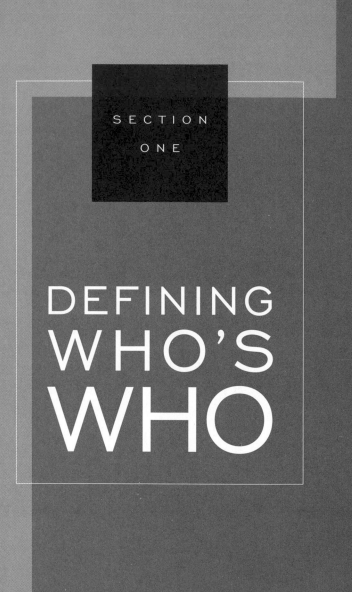

SECTION

ONE

DEFINING WHO'S WHO

ESTIMATES INDICATE that there are hundreds of thousands of you managing many billions of dollars of assets. Yet, you exist in a legal limbo. Your professional duties can subject you to lawsuits in one state but not in another. Statutes and organizations vary widely in the way they do or do not distinguish among financial planners, financial advisers, and investment advisers. You can tell clients you are an insurance agent and yet, in some states, legally be held responsible as a financial planner. The first step, then, in protecting your practice is to determine what exactly you do and what you are legally entitled or required to call yourself.

CHAPTER

THE

FINANCIAL PLANNER

1

FINANCIAL PLANNERS and advisers find themselves on their own, trying to figure out how to describe their services accurately and how to play fair. Many follow the lead of their professional organizations in simply describing a financial planner as a person whose business is personal financial planning. While federal and state regulations are often excruciatingly more specific, they may not agree.

Not only is it hard to define who is a financial planner, it is difficult to determine what laws and rules apply to the profession. Unfortunately, there is no significant body of law to use as guidelines regarding standards for financial planners and advisers. Because the financial planning profession and the statutes regarding the profession are so new, few cases have been tried under these laws; fewer still have been appealed and therefore reported as authority.

To protect your practice, you need to be aware of the nuances various legal entities and professional organizations incorporate in their definitions of what constitutes financial planning activities and who qualifies as a financial planner. In general, the various definitions are anchored in one of two basic precepts: "holding out" (i.e., title used) or "in the business" (i.e., services provided). As explained below, the federal government, the various state governments, and your own professional organizations are not consistent in which approach they use.

SEC Definition

AT THE FEDERAL LEVEL, the SEC uses the services provided approach to define financial planning in these terms:

> Financial planning typically involves providing a variety of services, principally advisory in nature . . . regarding the management of . . . financial resources based upon an analysis of individual client needs. Generally, financial planning services involve preparing a financial program for a client based on the client's financial circumstances and objectives. This information normally would cover present and anticipated assets and liabilities, including insurance, savings, investments, and anticipated retirement or other employee benefits. The program developed for the client usually includes general recommendations for a course of activity, or specific actions, to be taken by the client. For example, recommendations may be made that the client

obtain insurance or revise existing coverage, establish an individual retirement account, increase or decrease funds held in savings accounts, or invest funds in securities. A financial planner may develop tax or estate plans for clients or refer clients to an accountant or attorney for these services.

"The provider of such financial planning services in most cases assists the client in implementing the recommended program by, among other things, making specific recommendations to carry out the general recommendations of the program, or by selling the client insurance products, securities, or other investments. The financial planner may also review the client's program periodically and recommend revisions.[1]

To summarize, the SEC defines a financial planner as a person who does business in the following manner:
◆ Provides advisory services regarding the management of financial resources
◆ Provides analysis of individual client needs
◆ Prepares a financial program based on the client's financial circumstances and objectives, including:
— present and anticipated assets and liabilities
— insurance
— savings
— investments
— retirement and employee benefits.
The SEC staff believes most financial planners also:
◆ Provide special recommendations for client action
◆ Assist the client in implementing the recommendations
◆ Periodically review the program and recommend revisions.

State Definitions

STATE DEFINITIONS OF financial planners vary considerably and utilize either or both of the two basic precepts: holding out and in the business.

Maine seems to use both the holding out and the in the business concept by defining a financial planner as "a person who provides a variety of services, principally advisory in nature, to consumers with respect to management of financial resources based upon an analysis of individual consumer needs."[2] Under this definition, "financial planner" includes, but is not limited to, persons "who designate themselves financial analysts, advisers, consultants or planners, financial management advisers, securities or investment analysts, estate planners or other such terms."

Maryland, on the other hand, uses only the holding out definition. It requires all who hold themselves out, among other things, as "financial planners" to register as investment advisers.[3]

Minnesota also uses a holding out approach, and its regulations and statutes incorporate a very broad definition. In this state, a financial planner is any person who indicates he or she is a "financial planner, financial counselor, financial adviser, investment counselor, investment adviser, financial consultant, estate planner, or any other similar designation."[4] Thus, financial planners are all who hold themselves out using one of these magic words on their business cards, letterheads, signage, or yellow page advertisements.

Some years ago, a large brokerage firm in Minnesota took the position that its registered representatives were stockbrokers and did not provide financial planning services. As a result, the firm did not consider them financial planners. This analysis may have been correct under SEC regulations or the IAFP's definition discussed below. However, those definitions did not apply to the state's law. Because the brokerage firm was calling its registered representatives financial consultants, the Minnesota Department of Commerce found those representatives were indeed financial planners, whether or not they actually did financial planning. Not only were these brokers miraculously transformed into financial planners, suddenly they also had a statutory duty to act as fiduciaries rather than just sales representatives. The firm also received a $30,000 fine for failing to provide certain paperwork to its clients, another state requirement of financial planners.[5]

The vast majority of insurance agents in Minnesota believe they are plain-vanilla life insurance agents. However, almost all of them provide estate planning services. After all, the two purposes of insurance are to build an estate and to preserve an estate. It would make sense that anyone selling this kind of insurance would be an estate planner. However, "estate planner" is a magic phrase under the Minnesota definition of financial planners. Most life insurance agents are surprised to find they are considered to be financial planners because they do estate planning.

Although Minnesota life insurance agents often find themselves classified as financial planners under their state's specific law on that subject, those living elsewhere should be aware that their state's insurance laws may also define financial planning. Generally, these statutes describe whether or not an agent qualifies as a financial planner.

What about persons who do not practice financial planning but have the designation "Certified Financial Planner," "Chartered Financial Consultant," or "Personal Financial Planner" even if they are not actually in the business of planning? One might argue that any one of these titles makes them a financial planner in Maryland even though they are not actively in the business of doing planning. That is the interpretation made by Jacqueline H. Hallihan, President, and Robert Stirling, Associate, of National Regulatory Services, Inc.[6] According to them, two states, Maryland and Washington, have gone further than the SEC and have stated that simply using the CFP licensee designation after one's name is "holding one's self out" as providing investment advice.[7]

What are the laws in your state? It can make a big difference in how you practice your profession. Call or write your state departments of securities and insurance to request a copy of their statutes and rules on financial planners and advisers. Specifically ask them how they define financial planners and whether there are any special legal requirements. You might be surprised to discover how your state departments of securities or insurance define the term "financial planner."

Industry Definitions

GIVEN THE DISPARITY IN legal definitions of financial planners, it is not surprising that consumers are confused. As Bill E. Carter, President of Carter Financial Management, Inc., sums up the situation, "Many consumers cannot distinguish what it is that makes someone a financial planner as opposed to another type of financial services provider."[8] This confusion is not good for the profession.

In an attempt to clarify these issues, the IAFP established this definition: "[t]he financial planning process involves assessing an individual's current situation and setting financial and personal goals before implementing financial decisions. It includes identifying financial problems and providing a written plan. The final steps involve implementing the plan and periodically reviewing and revising it."[9]

The IAFP also holds "[a] financial adviser is a financial services professional who helps people achieve their financial goals based on their individual condition, resources and capabilities. IAFP encourages advisers to use the financial planning process."[10]

The CFP Board of Standards, on the other hand, defines financial planning as "[t]he process of determining whether and how an individual can meet life goals through the proper management of financial resources." It defines the "financial planning process" as typically including, but not limited to, "the six elements of data gathering, goal setting, identification of financial issues, preparation of alternatives and recommendations, implementation of client decisions from among the alternatives, and periodic review and revision of the plan."[11]

NAIC takes a much broader approach and declares a financial planner is an individual who has competence and expertise in numerous financial products and their legal framework.[12]

DILEMMA

A FEW OF US are old enough to remember a popular television show in the fifties and sixties, in which people would stand on a stage while four astute panelists would have to deduce what they did for a living. Now picture if you will the Financial Planner Game. Four people are standing on a stage. While they are all in the financial services industry, they are not all financial planners. You as a panelist must decide who the financial planners are.

◆ SUSIE STOCKBROKER is a registered representative for a large brokerage firm. She also has an insurance license. Susie specializes in clients over the age of 60 and emphasizes municipal bonds. Her business card reads: Registered Representative, Life Insurance Agent.

◆ LARRY LIFE INSURANCE SALESMAN is an agent for a large insurance company, who occasionally brokers with other companies. He specializes in buy-sell arrangements. His card reads: Insurance Executive.

◆ IVY INVESTMENT ADVISER has securities and insurance licenses and is a registered investment adviser. She charges a fee for services and specializes in pension benefits. Her card reads: Pension Consultant.

◆ CHARLIE CPA has no insurance or securities licenses and is not a registered investment adviser. He advertises himself as a financial planner who specializes in estate planning and tax reduction strategies. His card reads: CPA, Estate, Tax, and Financial Planning.

Question: As a panelist, how many of the four do you believe should remain seated because they are financial advisers and not really financial planners? As they would say on the old TV program, "Will the real financial planner please stand up?"

Answer: Charlie CPA stands up. Although on the surface Charlie looks like a regular certified public accountant, his business activities need to be analyzed more carefully. There is no question that providing tax reduction strategies is part of the business of being an accountant. What about his financial plans? If his activities fit into the definition established by the SEC, he is also a financial planner on the federal level. In many states, merely by holding himself out as a financial planner as he did on his business card, he becomes a financial planner whether he is actually doing planning or not. In this case we know that Charlie is indeed doing planning and he is holding himself out as a planner. Consequently, Charlie, much to his surprise, is more than a CPA; he is also a financial planner.

Susie Stockbroker remains seated because she holds herself out as a registered representative and insurance agent who does no planning. If Susie was performing planning activities as defined by the SEC or state laws, she would be legally labeled a planner no matter what she calls herself.

Larry Life Insurance Salesman can use the same analysis as Susie and remain seated. Does Larry do financial planning as defined by state law or the SEC? Larry is not doing detailed written asset allocation models or estate planning projections. Instead, he simply analyzes the buy-sell arrangement and makes an insurance recommendation.

Ivy Investment Adviser's registration as an investment adviser will not alone make her a planner. It is true she does have to be registered in order to charge for investment advice, but is she a planner under the SEC's definition? If she is limiting her advice to pension plans, but not performing planning as defined by the SEC, she is not a financial planner. Ivy, who thought she was a financial planner, may feel a bit bewildered, but should remain seated too.

One of the things that made those old television shows so enjoyable was how challenging it was to choose the correct person. Although the challenge may be great fun for game shows, it is not much consolation to a financial planner who is trying to practice ethically and legally.

It is sometimes extremely difficult for even experienced professional compliance officers to determine whether a person is a financial planner or a product salesperson. The following test has been created to help you determine your status. It utilizes a three-tier concept. The first tier consists of insurance agents and registered representatives who give product advice and are compensated by commissions. The second is comprised of investment advisers whose service goes beyond product information and includes ongoing

Financial Planner Test

First Tier

1 Do you limit your business to advice about securities and/or insurance, *and all* of your compensation is commission based?

_____ YES   _____ NO

If yes, go to next question. If no, go to 3.

2 Do you call yourself a registered representative, insurance agent, or some other financial professional term other than "financial planner?"

_____ YES   _____ NO

A yes answer here does not automatically mean you are only a registered representative, insurance agent, or other financial adviser. Go to next question.

3 Do you refrain from calling yourself a financial planner?

_____ YES   _____ NO

If no, this does not automatically make you a planner. Go to next question.

4 Do you limit your advice on insurance and securities to the traditional subjects covered by brokers and agents?

_____ YES   _____ NO

If you scored four yes answers here, you can be comfortable with a registered representative or insurance agent label.

Second Tier

5 Do you give advice about securities for which you are compensated by a fee?

_____ **YES**   _____ **NO**

No matter what your response, go to next question.

6 Does your advice about securities go beyond that of a typical broker?

_____ **YES**   _____ **NO**

A yes answer to either 5 or 6 will make you an investment adviser who needs to be registered with the SEC and most states. You are still not necessarily a financial planner.

Third Tier

7 Do you perform the business of planning as defined by the SEC?

_____ **YES**   _____ **NO**

If yes, you are a planner for the purposes of the SEC and many states, no matter what you call yourself.

8 Do you hold yourself out as a planner, using it as a marketing tool, but really function as a registered representative, insurance agent, or pension consultant?

_____ **YES**   _____ **NO**

If yes, you may trigger financial planner status in some states where they have a holding out or title statute to define a financial planner. This holds true even if you gave a no answer to 7.

portfolio management and advice. These people are typically compensated by charging a fee for assets under management, although some may charge an hourly rate or flat fee. They may also receive commissions on specific product recommendations. The final tier of service is provided by financial planners, who may be compensated by fees, commissions, or both. In addition to asset management, financial planners provide a detailed strategy for achieving financial goals.

TO FURTHER DETERMINE if you are a financial planner, take the following two steps. First, look at your business activities, comparing them to SEC Release IA-1092. If your activities match the definition, you are a financial planner. Second, if you are not providing financial planning, look to your state statutes and rules for a holding out provision. You may be a planner just because you hold yourself out as one.

If you are indeed a planner, and this may be a shock to some financial advisers and professionals, you might as well call yourself one. You will be bound by the rules affecting planners regardless of how you label yourself. This will put you squarely under the SEC and state rules and regulations, which endeavor to make sure the public is not misled. Consequently, the SEC staff and state securities departments smile upon financial advisers who give fair and honest disclosure about their true business activities.

If you cannot tell if you are legally a planner, get a written opinion from your insurance company's home office, broker-dealer, or an attorney who specializes in this area. In some cases you may want to contact the SEC or your state securities department directly for a no-action letter to clarify your position.

Finally, if you are not providing planning services, do not call yourself a planner: it may trigger unnecessary rules, requirements, and obligations.

CHAPTER

THE

INVESTMENT ADVISER

2

ONE OF THE MOST complicated, confus-

ing, and misunderstood subjects in the

financial services industry is the role, regis-

tration, and regulation of the investment

adviser. Whether your firm is a large orga-

nization managing assets for multiple

mutual funds or a one-person investment

consultant on Main Street, many of your

responsibilities and liabilities are deter-

mined by whether or not you or your firm

are legally required to be registered as an

investment adviser.

There are many benefits to being an RIA.

It is the only way you can legally charge fees,

whether an hourly rate, a flat fee, or a percentage of assets under management. It allows you legally to provide a wider range of services and financial planning recommendations, which can increase your revenues and market penetration. Finally, this license can be a big advantage when it comes to attracting more sophisticated and upscale clients.

The confusion starts with how to spell adviser. English teachers have long favored the use of "advisor." Then, in 1940, Congress opted for adviser with its passage of the Investment Advisers Act. Over the next half century, a dual spelling system—adviser vs. advisor—fought it out in the legal and popular press. In the end, many journalists yielded to Congress. Bloomberg Press style now conforms to that of Congress and uses only the adviser spelling. As Congress has yet to pass an "advisery" rule, that word remains true to its original form and is spelled "advisory."

This chapter makes the whole subject more clear and offers strategies for avoiding common but dangerous land mines. Look for two main things in this chapter and how their application will affect you and your practice:

1 The definition of investment adviser on both federal and state levels. Does your firm fit that definition, or are you and your firm exempt or excluded from having to register?

2 If your firm is an investment adviser, are you responsible to the SEC, your state, or both for oversight? The 1996 Investment Advisers Supervision Coordination Act created a distinction between large RIAs, which must be registered with the SEC, and smaller firms, which must be registered with state securities administrators. How does this legislation affect your practice?

Firm and Individual Registration

IT IS IMPORTANT TO DIFFERENTIATE at the outset between firm and individual registration. Large investment advisers are typically corporations who retain individuals who are investment adviser representatives or associated persons. These are the people who are actually meeting with clients and giving investment advice. Sometimes an RIA is an unincorporated sole proprietor. Both the large corporate entity and the unincorporated sole proprietor are considered to be the RIA or the "firm." However, only when a sole proprietor is registered as an RIA is the individual person an RIA. This distinction is frequently misunderstood and used erroneously in the industry where it is not uncommon to hear individuals say they are RIAs when in fact it is their corporation that is the RIA and the individuals are technically representatives or associated persons of the firm. In this book, when using the phrase "registering as an RIA," it means either the individual must register as an RIA or affiliate with an RIA.

The distinction between individual and firm registration becomes important under recent legislation which requires large RIAs, typically corporations managing institutional assets, to register solely with the SEC. Smaller RIAs and individuals who are RIA representatives must register with state securities administrators. This legislation was designed to eliminate the old system of dual state and federal registration for firms. However, as you will see later in this chapter, it is possible to own a firm or be part of a firm that is registered with the SEC, but be an individual who is required to be registered with a state as an RIA representative.

Penalties for failing to register with the SEC as an investment adviser are horrifying. In addition to fines of up to $10,000, there is also the felony penalty of up to five years in jail.[1] These penalties apply per case. Simultaneously violating state investment adviser laws can increase the fines and jail time. Failing to register can also make all contracts advisers have with their clients void and unenforceable. This means clients do not have to pay the fees owed to the adviser, and the adviser may have to refund fees previously paid.

Definition

IN 1940, CONGRESS ENACTED the Investment Advisers Act and authorized the SEC to regulate a business that then consisted primarily of advising institutional investors. Since the Act has not kept up with the current business climate, one of the problems financial services providers have today is applying retail situations to definitions that were designed for institutional advisers and their clients.

Use the following brief summary and chart as your guideline. You, or your firm, must register with the SEC if you meet the definition of Investment Adviser, have more than $30 million of assets under management, and are neither excluded nor exempted from registration.

The term "investment adviser" is defined in Section 202(a)(11) of the Advisers Act to mean:

> [A]ny person who, for compensation, engages in the business of advising others, either directly or through publications or writings, as to the value of securities or as to the advisability of investing in, purchasing, or selling securities, or who, for compensation and as part of a regular business, issues or promulgates analyses or reports concerning securities; but does not include:
>
> A) A bank or any bank holding company as defined in the Bank Holding Company Act of 1956, which is not an investment company,
>
> B) Any lawyer, accountant, engineer, or teacher whose performance of such services is solely incidental to the practice of his profession,
>
> C) Any broker or dealer whose performance of

You must register with the SEC if:

◆ You meet the definition of Investment Adviser[2], *and*

◆ You have more than $30 million of assets under management, *and*

◆ You are not among the following who are excluded from the Definition:[3]

    — banks

    — broker/dealers, lawyers, accountants, teachers, and others whose advice about securities is incidental to their business

    — certain publishers, *or*

◆ You are not among the following and others who are exempted from registration:[4]

    — Your principal place of business is in one state, *and* you give no advice regarding securities on a listed national exchange

    — Your clients are limited to insurance companies

    — You had fewer than 15 clients in the preceding 12 months *and* do not hold yourself out as an investment adviser.

such services is solely incidental to the conduct of his business as a broker or dealer and who receives no special compensation therefore,

D) A publisher of any bona fide newspaper, news magazine, business or financial publication of general and regular circulation,

E) Any person whose advice, analyses, or reports relate to no securities other than securities which are direct obligations of or obligations guaranteed as to principal or interest by the United States, or securities issued or guaranteed by Corporations in which the United States has a direct or indirect interest which shall have been designated by the Secretary of the Treasury, pursuant to Section 3(a)(12) of the Securities Exchange Act of 1934, as exempted securities for the purposes of that Act, or

F) Such other persons not within the intent of this paragraph, as the commission may designate by rules and regulations or order.

The SEC, in Release No. IA-1092, has adopted a three-pronged test to determine whether a firm or individual person needs to be registered as an investment adviser. The release also looked at financial planning activities and how they apply to the Act. Although this Release applies to SEC RIAs, many states will use the same analysis. Persons need to be an RIA or affiliated with one if they:

◆ Provide advice, issue reports, or analyze securities
◆ Are in the business of providing such services
◆ Provide such services for compensation.

As few people reading this book are excluded from the "in the business" element, it will simplify matters to focus on three words: compensation, advice, and securities. Each of these words is construed very broadly by the SEC. **COMPENSATION** Receiving any economic benefit from any source is, according to the SEC, compensation. Contrary to popular opinion, it is not necessary for the benefit to be a separate fee directly related to the investment advice or financial plan. Nor is it necessary for this to be a commission from the sale of securities. It has been determined that the receipt of commissions from a client's insurance product or other investment is sufficient to satisfy the compensation test.[5] In short, any fees for plans, commissions from product sales, or remuneration from any source is compensation.

DILEMMA

GEORGE, A LIFE INSURANCE salesperson, holds himself out to be an estate planner. In performing his services, he reviews a client's balance sheet and makes recommendations for specific insurance products. At a meeting with Mr. and Mrs. Client, he makes the following recommendation: "Since your ABC stock has been underperforming for the last five years, I recommend selling that stock and placing the proceeds in a whole life insurance policy." George receives no fees for investment advice and no commission from the sale of the ABC stock. He will, however, receive commissions from the sale of the whole life insurance policy.

Question: Has George received compensation under the rule and is he required to be an RIA?

Answer: Yes. George gave advice regarding securities and he was compensated by an insurance commission. George has just committed a felony, could be facing five years in jail, and probably does not even know it. George could eliminate this problem completely either by registering as an investment adviser or by limiting all his recommendations to insurance and avoiding any advice about securities.

ADVICE is also interpreted broadly by the SEC. It is not unusual to find planners or consultants trying to avoid registering as an Investment Adviser by not giving specific investment advice. Instead of recommending the client buy the XYZ mutual fund, they will just recommend generic balanced mutual funds. The SEC, however, has found giving general advice about securities is sufficient to trigger the registration requirement; the advice need not be specific.[6] The giving of advice need not constitute the primary or even major activity in order to satisfy that part of the test.[7] The SEC envisioned that in order for most financial planners to do their jobs properly, they must discuss both the pros and cons of a particular investment with their clients.[8] It is difficult to imagine any financial planner doing a good job without making some comments regarding the client's savings and investment strategy. If planners fail to discuss securities with their clients, they would probably be breaching their fiduciary duty.

The following have been found to fit the requirements of advice:

1 Analyses or valuations of particular securities, or securities markets in general, even without specific buy, hold, or sell recommendations.[9]

2 Market timing recommendations concerning the time to move a percentage of assets into a category of investments such as mutual funds or foreign stocks.[10]

3 Advising clients on the choice or retention of another investment adviser (a solicitor) or serving as a person who evaluates investment advisers.[11]

4 Providing statistical or historical data about securities that incorporate the writer's judgments.[12]

DILEMMA

TOM, A CFP LICENSEE with a large brokerage firm, does not hold himself out to be a financial planner, although he does do financial planning incidental to his business as a broker. To build a client base, he has developed a seminar entitled "Financial Planning for the 21st Century." This seminar is offered to current and prospective clients for the nominal fee of $25. The fee was designed to cover the cost of renting a hotel room, refreshments, and printing a 100-page workbook. During the seminar, Tom reviews all aspects of financial planning, including how to evaluate stocks and bonds and what to look for in investment purchases. He does not give anyone individual advice regarding securities at the seminar, but he may meet with them privately later.

Question: Is Tom giving advice regarding securities for which he is compensated, and must he register as an investment adviser; or does he fit into one of the exclusions?

Answer: Tom would be required to register. Even though the modest fee for attending the class was used only to cover Tom's expenses and Tom did not make a profit, it is still considered compensation. Furthermore, Tom does not fit into the broker-dealer exclusion because the activities of giving a seminar are not considered to be incidental to his brokerage business.

SECURITIES Once again, the SEC has construed the word "security" in the widest possible sense. The legal definition of a security is quite lengthy and includes any scheme involving the investment of money in a common enterprise with profits to come solely from the efforts of others. [13] It includes all sorts of investments that most people never consider to be securities, such as certificates of deposit, notes, and mortgages. There are only two exclusions under the definition: annuities and life insurance.

Exclusions and Exemptions

THE INVESTMENT ADVISERS ACT and numerous rules, regulations, and releases have defined not only who is required to register but also who is not. Note: there is a big difference between exemptions and exclusions. Those persons or entities who are exempt from registering must still follow the laws; for example, anti-fraud provisions. This group consists of those few advisers who limit their clients to insurance companies, have fewer than 15 clients or limit their practice to one state, and do not give advice regarding nationally listed securities. However, those who are excluded from registration are not considered to be investment advisers and therefore need not follow the anti-fraud or other provisions.[14]

Three excluded categories are pertinent to this section: certain professionals, broker-dealers, and exempted advisers.

PROFESSIONALS Some professionals, including accountants, lawyers, engineers, and teachers, are excluded from the Act. At first glance, these exclusions may look promising, but when you delve more deeply into the statutes you will notice the exclusions only work if these professionals are giving securities advice *solely incidental to the practice of their profession*. Qualifying for this exclusion may be extremely difficult, because financial planning is rarely *solely incidental* to these professions. The SEC looks at three different factors when determining if a professional can be excluded:[15]

◆ Does the professional hold himself out as an investment adviser or financial planner?

◆ Is the investment advice reasonably related to the professional services rendered?

◆ Is the professional's fee for investment advisory services structured differently from the schedule for professional services?

DILEMMA

CARLA CPA HAS A regular accounting practice and also advertises that she is available for financial planning services. She makes a detailed evaluation and comparison of investment alternatives. She may recommend specific no-load funds or even direct her client to an investment adviser. She is well known for her investing expertise and clients will frequently ask her questions about trading specific securities.

Question: Should Carla register?

Answer: Yes. She is in the business of giving advice about securities, and she is receiving compensation. Furthermore, she holds herself out as a planner. Accounting firms have only recently begun to take this law seriously. Consequently, now more and more accountants are registering, realizing they can no longer rely on the *solely incidental to* exclusion.

DILEMMA

IN SOME CITIES it is becoming a common practice for local law firms to serve as trustees and provide investment advice to the trust.

Question: Are these attorneys, who are acting as trustees, providing investment advice solely incidental to their profession as attorneys?

Answer: No. Without even looking at the conflict of interest issues, there is no question that these law firms would also need to be registered investment advisers, as this activity is not incidental to the practice of law.

Another group of professionals, banks, and publishers of news articles are also excluded from the registration requirements. In order for publishers to be excluded, they must meet the following test:

◆ The publication is of a general and impersonal nature, in that the advice provided is not adapted to any specific portfolio or any client's particular needs;

◆ The publication is bona fide or genuine; and

◆ The publication is of general and regular circulation. It is not timed to specific market activity or to events affecting or having the ability to affect the securities industry. [16]

DILEMMA

CHARLIE WANTS TO give stock tips and general investment advice over the telephone using a 900 number.

Question: Does he have to register as an RIA?

Answer: If Charlie can fit his activities into the criteria listed for the publisher's exclusion, he does not have to register. However, if he is giving individual advice, he will need to be an RIA or affiliated with one.[17]

BROKER-DEALERS The Act also excludes any broker-dealer, or its registered representatives, who provide investment advice solely incidental to the conduct of their business as broker-dealers *and* who receive no special compensation for the advice. Note there are two requirements in order for registered representatives to fit the broker-dealer exclusion. Their investment advisory services must be solely incidental to their conduct as brokers and they must receive no special compensation for them. This completely eliminates the possibility of stockbrokers preparing a financial plan and charging a fee for it, unless they are RIAs.[18] In addition, the giving of investment advice must be done with the broker-dealer's approval. Consequently, registered representatives of broker-dealers who are performing their financial planning services completely independent of their broker-dealers are not allowed to claim the broker-dealer exclusion.[19]

It has been found permissible for broker-dealers and their registered representatives to distribute to customers periodic market reports or analysis containing investment advice, provided there is no special charge for the reports and rendering this advice is solely incidental to the conduct of the broker-dealer's securities business.[20] The SEC has also indicated that investment advice offered as part of an overall financial plan for the client is not considered "solely incidental" to the brokerage business, whereas investment advice on individual securities transactions is. [21]

ROGER IS A REGISTERED representative with Abundant Profits Broker-Dealer. Roger assists clients in choosing an investment adviser, and Roger monitors the adviser's performance on a continuing basis. Frequently the adviser is given discretionary authority over the client's funds and is required to funnel all securities transactions through the broker-dealer so Roger will receive a commission.

Question: Does Roger have to register as an investment adviser?

Answer: Yes. Such activity is outside the scope of normal brokerage operations. [22]

In summary, to fit into the broker-dealer exclusion, securities and insurance professionals are bound by the following rules:

◆ They cannot hold themselves out to the public as financial planners or investment advisers, or as persons providing those services. Instead they must hold themselves out as securities or financial services professionals, stockbrokers, or insurance agents.

◆ They can provide investment advice only in the capacity of registered representative of their broker-dealer, under the broker-dealer's control, knowledge, and approval.

◆ They must disclose their dual capacities of both securities and insurance product sales when dealing with any client or potential client.

◆ They are not allowed to charge nor receive any clearly definable fee other than normal and customary commissions for the provision of any investment advisory service.

◆ Finally, the brokerage and insurance commissions charged to clients who obtain brokerage and insurance services are based on the same factors as those used to determine the commissions for clients who obtain only one of the services.[23]

DILEMMA

SALLY STOCKBROKER does not hold herself out as a financial planner, nor is her broker-dealer a registered investment adviser. However, as a service to her clients, she uses the firm's computer system to do estate planning projections, retirement projections, and asset allocation models. After gathering the data from the computer, she makes written recommendations to purchase specific investment products in line with the clients' goals.

Question: Does Sally qualify under the broker-dealer exclusion and not have to be an RIA?

Answer: Sally, or her firm, should register as an investment adviser. It seems the services she is performing are beyond those incidental to a stockbroker. They have definitely moved into the financial planning area as defined by the SEC, particularly because she is providing clients with a written plan. In short, if she is doing planning, she must register.

EXEMPTED ADVISERS The following advisers are exempt from registering even if they fit the definition of investment adviser.

◆ Advisers who maintain their principal place of business in the same state as all their clients *and* who do not furnish advice regarding securities listed on any national securities exchange,

◆ Any investment adviser whose clients are only insurance companies, or

◆ Any investment adviser who, during the preceding

twelve months, had fewer than 15 clients and neither holds himself out generally to the public as an investment adviser nor acts as an investment adviser to any investment company. Incidentally, this last exemption is frequently not available on the state level.[24]

Few planners can escape the SEC definition of investment adviser.[25] Any person in the business of preparing financial plans will certainly meet the SEC's definition of investment adviser, and very few individuals will qualify for the exclusions and exemptions. Even people who are not preparing plans, but solicit business for a third party, must register. Those relatively few planners who do not have to register with the SEC or their states must still follow other provisions of the Investment Advisers Act and refrain from certain prohibited activities.[26]

In summary, although almost all financial planners will have to be investment advisers, not all investment advisers are financial planners. Some RIAs limit themselves to managing or supervising investments, but know little about other areas of financial planning. For example, a planner will be expected to address a client's need for insurance; an investment adviser will not. Investment advisers may not have any insurance expertise, and so long as they function only as advisers, they will not be legally responsible for other areas of financial planning such as insurance.

State Registration

THE INVESTMENT ADVISERS ACT of 1940 and the Uniform Securities Act have similar definitions of investment advisers. Under the latter, investment advisers must be licensed by each state that has passed this portion of the Act if the adviser is doing business in that state. Penalties for failure to comply with each state's registration requirements can be severe, subjecting the planner or adviser to civil and criminal penalties, including jail time.

However, the exceptions from the definition can vary from state to state, and each state's interpretation of the same exception may also vary. Using a "holding out" provision, Maryland defines an investment adviser as any person who ". . . indicates the person is a 'financial planner' . . ."[27] Although this definition seems pretty plain on the surface, it can encompass gray areas.

Maryland and Washington have also found persons using the ChFC designation on stationery, business cards, and other media are holding themselves out as investment advisers if they are licensed to sell securities.[28]

The California and Georgia statutes, on the other hand, declare the various exclusions from the definition of investment adviser do not apply to persons who hold themselves out to be financial planners.[29] Idaho also has this provision.[30] More simply stated, some states have found persons who hold themselves out to the public as planners must comply with state investment adviser laws.[31]

Many investment advisers will find they are required to hold dual registrations: their firms must be registered with the SEC and their investment adviser representatives, affiliates, or supervised persons must be registered in the state in which they practice. Many states allow a registrant to use the same ADV forms that are filed with the SEC. Some states require a securities test to be taken. Many states require annual registration and, of course, all require a registration fee.

Failure to Register

IF, AFTER READING ALL THIS, you are still seriously thinking of avoiding registration, *stop*. Before you take that serious step, see if you can meet all the criteria on this checklist:

1 You do not hold yourself out using the label finan-

cial planner, investment consultant, financial counselor, financial adviser, financial consultant, or any similar terms.

2 You do not provide personal financial plans as
defined by the SEC or your state. None of your data-
gathering sheets or recommendations has the words
"financial planning" on them.

3 You receive only commissions, paid by third parties;
you never receive any fees or compensation directly
from the client.

4 All your activities are supervised by your broker-
dealer, and it is aware of all your activities.

5 You always disclose that you are acting solely as an
insurance agent or stockbroker.

If you fail to meet any one of these criteria, you
should register.

State and SEC Registration

ON OCTOBER 11, 1996, President Clinton signed The
National Securities Markets Improvement Act of 1996.
Included within the new law is Title III, "The Investment Advisers Supervision Coordination Act," which
makes extensive changes in the registration requirements for all investment advisers. The Coordination
Act became effective on July 8, 1997.

The clear intent of Congress was to reallocate regulatory resources and reduce the number of SEC registered investment advisers by approximately 72 percent.
This means that most investment advisers, planners,
and consultants will only have to register on the state
level. However, those operating in Colorado, Iowa,
Ohio, and Wyoming—the four states that do not have
any investment adviser regulations—will still need to
maintain registration with the SEC.

If you know you or your firm must register, this section will help you determine if you are subject to SEC
registration, state registration, or both. Key compo-

nents and terms of the Act as far as registration is concerned are as follows.

◆ **The $30 Million Dividing Line.** All investment advisers who have more than $30 million of assets under management must be registered with the SEC. These firms will no longer be required to maintain a state registration with any state securities regulator. This eliminates the current system of dual firm regulation, which requires most investment advisers to be registered on both the federal and state levels.

Those investment advisers who have less than $25 million of assets under management, including investment advisers who do not engage in any asset management, but operate as fee-based financial planners, will no longer be required or permitted to be registered with the SEC. The smaller firms must be registered with the states.

Firms whose assets range between $25 million and $30 million may choose to be registered with either their state or the SEC.

◆ **Assets under Management.** The Act defines "assets under management" as "the securities portfolios with respect to which an investment adviser provides continuous and regular supervisory or management services." In Release IA-1633 (released May 1997), the SEC defined "assets under management" as a securities portfolio consisting of any account at least 50 percent of the total value of which is securities. Real estate, commodities, and collectibles are not considered securities and therefore not included. In addition, cash and cash equivalents are also excluded from the computation. Therefore, if an account has at least 50 percent in securities, all of its assets are counted for purposes of determining assets under management.

◆ **Continuous and Regular Supervisory and Management Services.** In order to qualify for the $30 million cutoff, the accounts must receive "continuous and regular supervisory or management services." This will exclude most firms who are not active portfolio managers. Generally the SEC will consider accounts over which RIAs have discretionary authority and for which the RIA provides ongoing management services to fall under the "continuous and regular supervisory or management services" guideline. However, Release IA-1633 makes it clear that nondiscretionary authority accounts will not automatically be considered as part of the $30 million.

It is the belief of the SEC staff that a limited number of nondiscretionary advisory arrangements will fit their definition of assets under management on a continuous and regular supervisory or management basis. To make the determination, the SEC will look upon the nature of the adviser's responsibility.

According to the SEC, the greater the amount of day-to-day responsibility an adviser has, the more likely the adviser would be providing continuous and regular supervisory or management services. If an adviser has traditional portfolio management responsibilities, but must obtain client consent before executing a trade, that adviser would still be considered to provide continuous and regular supervisory or management services. However, most financial planners who periodically review a client's portfolio or the selection of an investment adviser will not fit the definition of providing day-to-day supervisory services.

The following language from SEC Release IA-1601 (proposed rules released for public comment in December 1996) outlines the Commission's opinion that few financial planners, financial advisers, or consultants will qualify for SEC registration:

> The Commission believes that Congress intended to exclude from Commission registration most advisers that do not engage in traditional ongoing

portfolio management, including most financial planners and consultants. Under the proposed instructions, a financial planner that merely undertakes to monitor the markets and advise its clients as to the advisability of changes to their portfolios would not be providing continuous and regular management or supervisory services. A financial planner that otherwise would be regulated by the states could not "opt" to be regulated by the Commission by revising its financial planning agreements to include the statutory language or similar language unless such a revision materially changes the nature of the services being provided.

In elaborating on its opinion, the Commission states that the reason most financial planners were excluded is that if they were permitted to treat assets they monitor as assets under management and thereby remain registered with the SEC, the intent of Congress to reallocate regulatory responsibilities and decrease the number of SEC RIAs would be defeated.

◆ *De Minimis* **Rule.** Previously each state had the right to decide what its own *de minimis* registration rule would be. The *de minimis* rule allowed an out-of-state adviser to avoid registration if it had a small number of clients in the second state. This area has been particularly confusing in the past because some states, such as Virginia, Florida, Minnesota, Texas, and Wisconsin, have absolutely no *de minimis* rule, so investment adviser registration was required in each of those states before any work could be commenced with a client who resided in that state. On the other end of the spectrum, some states had liberal *de minimis* standards. In New York, an adviser needed 40 clients, and in North Carolina, 10 clients, before the adviser needed to register in those states. Under the new law, Congress created a uniform National *De Min-*

imis Standard for RIAs with five or fewer clients in a state, providing the adviser does not have a place of business in the second state.

One final distinction is important. SEC RIAs will always have at least one investment adviser representative that meets directly with clients. That person will need to be registered in the state in which the firm has a place of business. A state-registered RIA representative could still be required to register in other states even if the RIA representative did not have a place of business in those states. [32]

◆ **Place of Business.** The new legislation preserves the ability of a state to register and regulate investment adviser representatives of SEC RIAs, as long as the state's authority is limited to those investment adviser representatives who have a "place of business" within the state. The SEC defined a place of business as "an office at which the investment adviser regularly provides investment advisory services, solicits, meets with, or otherwise communicates with clients; and any other location that is held out to the general public as a location at which the investment adviser provides investment advisory services, solicits, meets with, or otherwise communicates with clients." [33]

◆ **Exemptions from Prohibitions against Registration.** Rule 203A(c) exempts four types of advisers from the prohibition against registration. They include: nationally recognized statistical organizations (NRSOs); pension consultants; certain affiliated investment advisers who use separate subsidiaries to conduct different types of advisory operations; and newly formed investment advisers with a reasonable expectation of eligibility for SEC registration. These groups are allowed to register with the SEC if prohibiting registration would be unfair or burdensome on interstate commerce.

Registration Test

Although the laws are confusing and sometimes contradictory,they may be somewhat
clearer after you take this quick test to figure
out how these regulations apply to you:

1 Are you a planner or are you compensated
for giving advice about securities?

_____ **YES**   _____ **NO**

*If yes, you must register as an RIA or affiliate with
one as an RIA representative. Go to question 2.
If no, get an opinion from your compliance
department or your attorney before opening
any bottles of champagne.*

2 Do you provide day-to-day managment services for portfolios in excess of $30 million?

_____ **YES**   _____ **NO**

*If yes, you or your firm must be registered with
the SEC and the representatives or affiliates
must be registered with your state. If no, you
or your firm must be registered with your state
as an RIA (unless your office is in a state without regulation).*

3 Does the thought of having to sort all this
out and file the necessary forms give you an
anxiety attack?

_____ **YES**   _____ **NO**

*If yes, hire a consultant to do the paperwork
and worrying for you, while you do what you are
good at: helping clients reach all their financial
goals.*

ACTION ITEM

◆ REGISTERING AS AN INVESTMENT adviser with
the SEC is relatively easy as it requires no specific
test or fee. Request Form ADV, including Parts I
and II. Sometimes applicants will prefer to hire an
attorney or consultant to help them wend their way
through the paperwork more quickly. NASD and
NASAA are developing a Central Registration
Depository (CRD) to allow RIAs to fill out one form
electronically and forward the application, along
with any state fees, to the appropriate states.[34]

*The author is grateful to Dale E. Brown and Jeffrey Kelvin
for their considerable assistance in preparing this chapter.
Kelvin, an attorney in Plymouth Meeting, Pennsylvania,
works with planners and investment advisers. He has prepared detailed information about the 1996 Coordination
Act. You may request it by contacting him at (610) 825-
9008.*

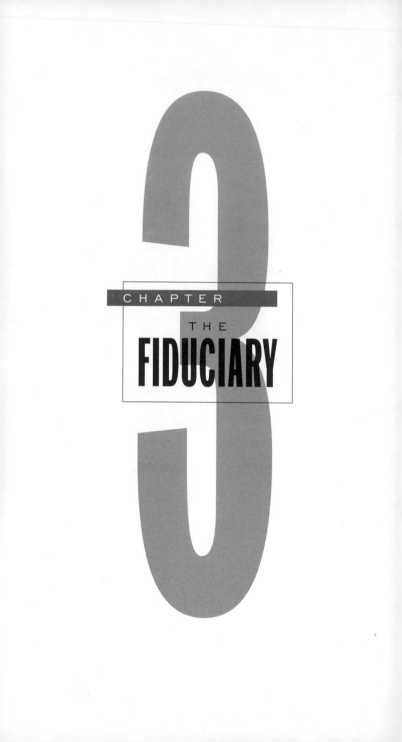

CHAPTER

THE

FIDUCIARY

AUTHOR'S NOTE: *Providing clients with what they want, honest advice free from self-interest, is good business. It is also acting as a fiduciary, whether or not the law requires it.*

As I assess my own business practices and ethics, I believe my recommendations and business judgments would not change, whether I was labeled registered representative, investment adviser, or planner. No matter what label I carry, it is always good business to put the client first. Long before Stephen Covey made the concept popular, I was taught that the golden rule was the only way to deal with people, both in business and in personal relationships.

There is a great movement in our country

today to provide quality goods and services for the client. This means figuring out what clients really want and giving them exactly what they want, instead of what we think they need. As we read consumer articles on financial services, we consistently see that consumers want an adviser who will:

◆ *Put the client's interest above his or her own*

◆ *Be trustworthy*

◆ *Be honest and straightforward with them, particularly about fees and commissions.* [1]

The same qualities consumers want in an adviser describe a good fiduciary.

Definition of Fiduciary

BLACK'S LAW DICTIONARY describes a fiduciary relationship as "one founded on trust or confidence reposed by one person in the integrity and fidelity of another." [2] The fiduciary has a duty to act primarily for the client's benefit in matters connected with the undertaking and not for the fiduciary's own personal interest. Scrupulous good faith and candor are always required. Fiduciaries must always act in complete fairness and may not ever exert any influence or pressure, take selfish advantage, or deal with the client in such a way that it benefits themselves or prejudices the client. Business shrewdness, hard bargaining, and taking advantage of the forgetfulness or negligence of the client are totally prohibited in a fiduciary.

As fiduciaries, planners, investment advisers, and trust officers must make fair and complete disclosure of all material facts and must employ reasonable care to avoid misleading their clients. The utmost good faith is required in all their dealings. [3] Simply put, fiduciaries must exhibit the highest form of trust, fidelity, and confidence, and are expected to act in the best interest of their clients at all times.

Obvious and Not-So-Obvious Fiduciaries

THERE ARE TWO WAYS individuals may find themselves draped with the mantle of a fiduciary: one is by state or federal law, the other by court decree.

Investment advisers are uniformly recognized as fiduciaries. In the case of the *SEC v. Capital Gains Bureau, Inc.,*[4] the court held, "The Investment Advisers Act of 1940 thus reflects a Congressional recognition of the delicate fiduciary nature of the investment advisory relationship." Colorado followed this trend when the Colorado Court of Appeals also held that financial planners, in addition to RIAs, have a fiduciary duty to their clients.[5]

Financial planners also have a fiduciary duty to their clients. This duty arises, as discussed in Chapter 2, because most financial planners need to be registered as an RIA or affiliated with one.

In the absence of a specific state statute, many stockbrokers, insurance agents and broker-dealers can escape the extra liability of a fiduciary. Some, however, may be surprised to find they are under a higher standard of care created by their local judges. Courts have frequently addressed the issue by creating or recognizing the fiduciary duty on a case-by-case basis. In one case, both a broker and the brokerage house were found by the Supreme Court of Colorado to have a fiduciary duty to the customer. The court identified several factors to be considered, including the degree of practical control of a customer's account by a broker and the degree of trust and confidence reposed by the customer in the broker.[6]

Reluctant Fiduciaries

SOME FIRMS HAVE MADE the conscious business decision for their representatives and agents to remain salespeople, instead of taking on the additional liability and exposure of planners. From their point of view, this is a prudent decision to decrease exposure and save money on claims. However, this decision does not reflect the character of many representatives or identify the consumer's real concerns.

One reason many financial consultants do not want to be labeled as financial planners is they do not want to assume the additional obligations of a fiduciary. In many states a registered representative's statutory obligation is limited to recommending suitable investments and processing trades accurately. However, if that registered representative takes on the additional duties of a fiduciary, the entire nature of the client relationship changes, and there is increased exposure for the registered representative-planner. No longer can registered representatives recommend just any investment so long as the trades are processed accurately; they must make sure the trade is in the best interest of the client.

Brokers and insurance agents who are in the business of financial planning or preparing plans are probably deceiving themselves if they think avoiding the label of "planner" or "investment adviser" will actually save them from liability. The SEC or your state securities administration will consider you a planner with all of a planner's duties, liabilities, and responsibilities, even if you are not registered. Failing to register as an investment adviser does not mean you can escape a fiduciary duty. It just subjects you to penalties, sanctions, and fines from the SEC or your state for failing to register.

Managers of some broker-dealers would argue that their registered representatives must know their clients (as required by NASD), make suitable recommendations, and process trades accurately. If these criteria are all met, a representative would be free to promote any product that has special incentives for the representative over a similar product that would not reward the representative as generously. As a fiduciary, a planner or investment adviser does not have this freedom. In addition to a representative's responsibilities of suitability, accuracy, and knowledge, the planner or adviser must also make sure every recommendation is good for the client, not just rewarding for the planner or adviser. This goes beyond suitability, because not all investments that would pass a suitability screen would also be in the client's best interest.

Perhaps an even tougher problem is encountered by the representative-planner who frequently does planning but sometimes handles clients who do not want to pay for the planning process and just want brokerage services. Can the planner take off one hat, become a broker for these clients, and handle the case without the additional requirements of a fiduciary? This is a more complex issue than whether to register and more fraught with danger for the planner.

The safest approach would be to act like a fiduciary to all clients, even if no planning services are provided. If you sometimes want to act like a sales representative, contact your broker-dealer for guidelines on how to distinguish these two different types of clients, and how to leave a paper trail that will protect you. Once the business lines become unclear, it may be difficult for planners to defend an action by stating they were working only as brokers in that case, not planners. Truly the worst thing for planner-representatives would be for their business activities to become so ill-defined that a brokerage client could sue for breach of fiduciary duty or not adhering to a higher standard of care.

Captive Fiduciaries

CAN YOU ACT AS A FIDUCIARY if you are a captive insurance agent? A treatise by two attorneys expressed the opinion that serving as a captive agent or broker was a violation of the planner's fiduciary duty. According to them, only independent financial planners and agents who are free to recommend any product, from any company, could maintain their true fiduciary duty. Unfortunately, these attorneys did not have a clear picture of the relevant issue.

The more relevant issue here is not captive versus independent but recommending products and services in the best interest of the client. Without a doubt, if your company is offering any product or service you do not think is good for your client, no matter whether you are captive or independent, you should not recommend it. Consequently, it makes sense to affiliate with strong companies that have a long list of top-quality investments. The key issue then becomes recommending products that are suitable and in the best interest of your client. If that is not possible with your company, then move to a company that carries products in which you have confidence.

Do not be confused by the captive versus independent argument. To paraphrase Andrew Tobias: If God were creating a captive company, He would make sure it did a thorough job in the due diligence of its products. The company would have a strong capital base, giving its agents and representatives a high level of confidence and an assurance the company would stand behind them.

Fee-Only Fiduciaries

MANY CONSUMER ADVOCATES believe that fee-only planners alone can fulfill a fiduciary duty, because fee-and-commission planners receive commissions from the advice they give. This argument is extremely short-sighted. Some writers go so far as to suggest that clients should patronize fee-only planners exclusively. This argument also seems to miss the most relevant issue: doing what is best for the client. There is nothing inherently wrong in obtaining a fee for a plan and a commission for a sale as long as the fee and the commission are equitable and carefully disclosed to the client and the planner acts as a fiduciary.

As more financial planners, insurance agents, stockbrokers, and other financial advisers put the client first, the public will grow to perceive them as trusted advisers. When this occurs, many of the concerns about fees and commissions violating the fiduciary duty will disappear.

Fiduciary Responsibilities

THE FOLLOWING REVIEWS some of the key aspects of serving as a fiduciary.

BEST INTERESTS OF THE CLIENT The distinction between a planner or investment adviser with a fiduciary interest and a salesperson is crucial. The financial planner, under common law and by some statutes, is a fiduciary and not a salesperson, a professional similar to an attorney, trustee, or accountant. The planner or investment adviser must always provide services and advice in the best interests of the client. Whereas salespeople may have their own motives and interests at heart and offer goods and services for a price, the fiduciary must serve the client, if necessary at the cost of the fiduciary's own interests.

It is generally believed fiduciaries perform their trades for reasons other than money and feel a sense of responsibility that goes beyond simply making a living. To paraphrase Supreme Court Justice Brandeis: "It is an occupation which is pursued largely for others and not merely for oneself. It is an occupation in which the amount of financial return is not the accepted measure of success." On the other hand, the accepted measure of success for the salesperson is usually the amount of financial return.

HIGHER STANDARD OF CARE According to Eli Bernzweig, "The law regards the duty of a fiduciary as a very high one, higher than the negligence standard applicable to most of the planner's other legal obligations."[7] A planner must exercise a higher standard of care when he knows that the client has relied almost exclusively upon his advice.[8]

ADDITIONAL RESPONSIBILITIES A fiduciary duty may also shift additional responsibility for investments from the client's shoulders to the planner. One court found the fiduciary relationship created such a climate of trust that facts that would ordinarily require investigation by the client may not excite suspicion. Therefore, the court found, the same degree of diligence on the part of the client is not required when dealing with a financial planner.[9]

DUTY TO DISCLOSE CONFLICTS OF INTEREST AND COMPENSATION The SEC and many states have required investment advisers and planners, as fiduciaries, to disclose any conflicts of interest in addition to compensation. This is particularly important in cases where the planner is receiving fees for advice plus commissions on sales. One court held, "The planner who charges a fee for his planning services and also receives commissions on investments and insurance products he has recommended to the client is extremely vulnerable to a claim of breach of fiduciary duty *if he fails to inform the client of the potential conflicts of interest*" (emphasis added).[10]

DILEMMA

DOUG IS THE VICE PRESIDENT of a small family business and also a financial planner. The board of directors of Doug's company wants to buy insurance and investments through Doug, a family member. There are a number of conflicts of interest here. Doug, as an officer and director of the company, has a fiduciary duty to the company to do only what is in the company's best interests. As a financial planner, Doug also has a fiduciary duty to the company to provide the best services. The situation is further complicated by Doug's commissions on the investments he recommends to the corporation.

Question: What can Doug and the company do to protect two different sets of interests?

Answer: A statement to the corporation should be drafted defining the conflicts of interest, and asking the board of directors to waive them in writing. This letter should be put into Doug's file at his financial planning firm. In addition, the corporation needs a resolution to put in their minutes stating the directors have carefully reviewed the conflicts of interest, are aware of them, and have waived any problems because they have confidence in Doug. It should further state that the directors have knowledge that Doug would be receiving commissions on his recommendations. The best defense here is a paper trail for both Doug and the company.

LIABILITY FOR DAMAGES Almost uniformly, a breach of fiduciary duty can make the financial planner or investment adviser personally liable to the client for damages and costs caused by the breach. This can make the planner or investment adviser a guarantor of an investment's success if he violates his responsibilities as a fiduciary. In extreme cases, violation of the fiduciary duty could also subject the adviser to criminal liability.

DUTY OF CONFIDENTIALITY Planners and advisers also have a duty of confidentiality, requiring them not to disclose personal information about their clients without the clients' consent. This is another area frequently violated in an innocent manner, for example, when a planner discloses information about a client's financial affairs to another family member or a professional such as an attorney or CPA.

DILEMMA

STANLEY CLIENT, AGE 60, is one of your investment advisory clients. He is single and in excellent health. Susan, his oldest child, has been helping him with his business affairs. You have never met Susan, she is not a client of yours, and Stanley has never said anything to you about disclosing personal information to Susan. Susan calls and asks for an exact balance on two of Stanley's funds.

Question: Should you give her this information?

Answer: Not without Stanley's consent, noted in the file.

Question: Would your answer change if Susan were not Stanley's daughter, but his attorney or CPA?

Answer: No. It still would not be appropriate without Stanley's consent.

Question: Would your answer be different if Susan were an SEC auditor asking to take Stanley's entire file back to the office to review?

Answer: This is a difficult call. If at all possible, you have a responsibility for protecting confidential client information. You cannot refuse to disclose the information to the SEC, but you may have to take steps under the Freedom of Information Act to keep it private.

Question: Would your answer be different if Susan were Stanley's wife, but still a person you had never met and who did not appear on any of your forms or engagement letters as a client?

Answer: This becomes an extremely touchy situation, as you navigate between a duty of confidentiality and not making your client's spouse angry. To be on the safe side, you must get Stanley's approval before disclosing this information, because in this situation his wife is not a joint client.

STAFF TRAINING Discuss the concept of fiduciary responsibility with your staff. Make sure they understand all its ramifications and responsibilities and the necessity to put the client's interests first, always. As shown in the following example, be sure your staff knows what they must do and, more important, what they cannot do.

DILEMMA

BETTY PLANNER HAS employed Mike Assistant as an able and self-starting secretary. Mike has no licenses of any kind. When clients call they frequently ask for Mike. It is not unusual to hear Mike say over the phone, "I know Betty would not want you to sell that investment, because it is just perfect for you. You know, her own mother owns that stock. Don't do anything until you can talk with her."

Question: If the investment goes bad, could Betty be liable?

Answer: Yes. Betty may have civil liability for her assistant's actions. Mike not only violated the duty of confidentiality, he violated securities statutes by giving advice without being registered. Mike has probably violated a number of criminal statutes also. As Betty is the fiduciary and the person who is registered, she will ultimately be personally responsible for all of Mike's actions.

ACTION ITEM

◆ WORK WITH YOUR MARKETING and public relations departments to develop a corporate image
and mission statement that lets the consumer
know you are on their side, with advice they can
trust, because their interests come first. You are
not afraid to act as a fiduciary because consumers
want that level of service. Flaunt your desire to
make the client number one and watch the world
beat a path to your door.

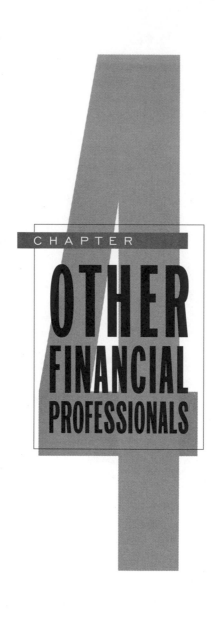

OTHER
FINANCIAL
PROFESSIONALS

FEDERAL AND STATE RULES and regulations have a wide reach among financial services professionals. The first three chapters covered the obvious targets of these laws: financial planners, investment advisers, and fiduciaries. This chapter describes other members of the financial services industry, many of whom may be surprised to learn that some of their activities are strictly regulated and that they are subject to both fines and lawsuits for not complying with these rules. If you find your job description listed below or you supervise some of these people, much of the information in this book will be key to protecting and building your business.

Wire Houses, Broker-Dealers, and Brokers

THE UNIFORM SECURITIES ACT defines a **broker-dealer** as "a person engaged in the business of effecting transactions in securities for the accounts of others or the person's own account."[1] As described in greater detail in Chapter 7, broker-dealers are subject to numerous regulations by NASD, individual state governments, and the federal government. Frequently sales representatives, issuers, and certain financial institutions are excepted from this definition, as are people who have no place of business in the regulating state.

A **stockbroker** or a **sales representative** for a broker-dealer is defined by the Act as "a person other than a dealer who represents the dealer or the issuer in a securities transaction." As broker-dealers are generally required to have their employees registered, sales representatives are widely referred to, and are described in this book, as **registered representatives** or **brokers**.

As wire houses and brokers expand their services, many firms are moving beyond providing traditional brokerage services and moving into the areas of financial planning. This has created opportunity but also risk. Later chapters explain how to reduce this risk.

Insurance Personnel

THE DEFINITION OF AN **insurance analyst** or **consultant** can vary, but a typical one provides a consultant or analyst is "a person who, for a fee or compensation of any kind, paid or derived from any person or source other than an insurer, advises, . . . any person insured under, named a beneficiary of, or having any interest in a life or disability insurance contract . . ."[2] Attorneys and accountants are excluded from this definition in some states.

Most states do not require separate registration for

insurance consultants or analysts. However, the definition of insurance broker in those states might be so
broad as to require financial planners to register as
insurance brokers even though they would normally
be considered insurance consultants.

An **insurance broker** is defined by *Black's Law Dictionary* as a middleman between a company and an
individual who "solicits insurance from public under
no employment from any special company."[3] The
insurance broker "researches policies for a client and
sells him the one which best suits his needs."[4] Those
last three words, as discussed in Chapter 1, often determine whether or not the insurance broker is legally
held to be engaged in financial planning or has a fiduciary duty.

An **insurance agent** is defined by *Black's Law Dictionary* as an insurer's authorized representative "in
dealing with third parties in matters related to insurance."[5] As noted in Chapters 1 and 3, when the form
of insurance has to do with building an estate or preserving an estate, it makes sense that those selling it are
engaged in estate planning. This would include life,
disability, and long-term care health insurance policies. Although on the surface, the role of the insurance
agent appears to be more narrow than that of the
insurance consultant or analyst, many agents will find
that their job duties come under state regulations with
regard to financial planning. In Minnesota, for example, almost all life insurance agents are classified as
financial planners by a broad statuary definition that
includes estate planners.

Financial planners or others who render advice
regarding life insurance contracts must be licensed by
the department of insurance in some states. This registration may be required even if the planner or adviser
is not a life insurance agent and does not sell life insurance policies but only renders advice about insurance.

Accountants

ACCOUNTING FIRMS ARE MOVING into the financial planning area at a rapid rate. People who engage in this business fall into one of three categories: accountants, Certified Public Accountants, and Personal Financial Specialists.

An **accountant**'s duties "range from preparing tax returns and financial statements to auditing financial records and developing financial plans."[6] An accountant may also focus on one of these areas. Whereas bookkeepers record transactions, an accountant analyzes the financial effects these transactions have on a company or an individual. An accountant is often a financial planner without any special training beyond his license. Many accountants may not realize the extent of their liability in their unlicensed, unregistered role as financial planners.

A **Certified Public Accountant** completes corporate and personal tax returns in addition to usual accounts and auditing work. In order to become a CPA, a person must pass the Uniform Certified Accountants Examination that is administered by AICPA. In addition, the experience requirements of the home state must be completed. The CPA designation is regulated by state boards of accountancy, with each state's requirements varying. New York, for example, has a minimum qualification of two years' experience. As discussed in Chapter 1, the tax expertise of many CPAs often leads them into the field of financial planning.

As described in Chapter 5, CPAs who wish to concentrate on financial planning can earn the **Personal Financial Specialist** designation through a prescribed program of study. This book provides much valuable information for all accountants and particularly for those earning the PFS designation.

Tax Specialists, Estate Planners, and Others

ALTHOUGH THE PROFESSIONAL titles used by many people in this group do not reflect their financial planning activities, their duties and responsibilities may qualify them as financial planners.

One title that skirts the definition of financial planner is that of **planned giving development officer**. This position is among the growth industries in higher education and nonprofit institutions. Individuals who hold this title confer with alumni and potential donors on establishing different kinds of trusts in which the institution is the ultimate beneficiary. As these trusts all have tax implications, the planned giving development officers are in the business of estate planning and would qualify as financial planners in some states.

The **enrolled agent** title is another example. Individuals who hold this designation are "licensed by the federal government . . . to appear in place of the taxpayer at the Internal Revenue Service."[7] According to the National Association of Enrolled Agents, some enrolled agents engage in financial planning.

Generally, **tax lawyers** review all forms of tax reduction strategies including income and estate tax. In many states, this constitutes financial planning. Depending on the definitions of financial and estate planner and the state's exemptions, a tax lawyer could be viewed as both. Attorneys also become involved in financial planning when serving as trustees or executors of estates. Sometimes these activities can subject even attorneys to securities and investment adviser regulations.

Currently the banking industry has devised no formal standards for the titles of **personal banker** or **trust officer**. Though no specific training is required for either position, individuals holding these titles are subject to myriad regulations because the primary purpose of their jobs is to provide financial guidance. The American Bankers Association is currently offering a program, through its Institute of Certified Bankers, for personal trust officers to earn the Certified Trust and Financial Advisor designation.

Investment Advisers and Financial Analysts

AS DISCUSSED IN CHAPTER 2, not all **investment advisers** are financial planners. Those who, for compensation, engage in the business of advising others as to the advisability of investing in, purchasing, or selling securities must register with the SEC or the states as an RIA. However, an investment adviser can also be a person such as a writer or publisher who, for compensation and as part of a regular business, issues or promulgates analyses or reports concerning securities. These individuals may be excluded from having to register as an investment adviser in certain circumstances.

Technically, all who examine financial data can call themselves **financial analysts**. However, the Association for Investment Management and Research in Charlottesville, Virginia, awards a special designation, known as Chartered Financial Analyst. Only those who have completed a rigorous three-year program on investment analysis earn this designation. A financial analyst is not necessarily but may be a financial planner.

ACTION ITEM

◆ IF YOU HAVE ANY QUESTION as to whether or not your activities fall under financial planning definitions, carefully read Chapter 1.

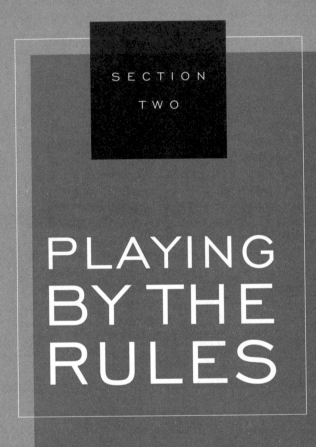

SECTION
TWO

PLAYING
BY THE
RULES

ONE OF THE MANY confusing aspects of the financial services industry is that rules and regulations frequently overlap or are applied simultaneously. Not only that, but you may find yourself subject to rules of which you are unaware, or trying to meet requirements that have just changed. The client wants an investment decision, but you may be wondering whether you need a legal opinion.

This section addresses rules that apply to all financial advisers and rules specifically for insurance agents, broker-dealers, and investment advisers. It covers regulations that govern your face-to-face, written, and electronic communications.

CHAPTER

5

THE

COMPETENCY
FACTOR

THE ABILITY TO DOCUMENT your competency is absolutely crucial to the protection
of your practice.

Hard to believe? Take note of what one
of the industry's most knowledgeable
experts has to say: "Most complaints are a
result of the planner's ignorance or lack of
attention, not willful misconduct or overt
action."[1] This observation was made by
Malcolm Makin, a Westerly, Rhode Island,
planner who served as Chairman of the
Board of Ethics and Professional Review of
the IBCFP, now the CFP Board of Standards. The following demonstrates Makin's
observation.

MR. AND MRS. RETIREE went to their financial planner and applied for a life insurance policy on Mr. Retiree. In the process, the life application was amended to an annuity application and the insurance company returned an annuity, not a life insurance contract, to the planner. The planner delivered the annuity. Attached to the top of the annuity was the life application and, underneath, the amended application for an annuity.

Sometime later, Mrs. Retiree contacted her financial planner and asked if she should keep her life insurance policy in force. The planner, just glancing at the top of the file, noticed the old life application and, not reviewing all the documents to see that an annuity had actually been delivered, said, "You should absolutely keep your life policy, because your husband is in poor health." Mrs. Retiree kept the policy on her husband who died a short time later. When she applied to the insurance company for the death benefit proceeds under the life insurance policy, the insurance company, advising her it was really an annuity, offered to refund her premiums. She sued for death benefits under the life contract.

Question: Should Mrs. Retiree get the proceeds of the life insurance policy or the rather meager refund of premiums under the annuity contract?

Answer: She should receive death benefits under the life insurance contract. In a similar case, the court found incompetence on the part of the agent was no excuse. The agent, through sloppy work habits, failed to review the documents carefully and erroneously advised Mrs. Retiree she had a life insurance policy when it was really an annuity. Neither the agent nor the insurance company could benefit from the agent's incompetence. The local insurance agency was held responsible for paying the death benefits to Mrs. Retiree.

Although we would like the public to view financial consultants as highly trained experts, in fact, 41 percent of the public believe the industry lacks internal controls to prevent irresponsible or wrongful actions.[2] To some extent, the public may be right. Unlike attorneys and accountants, planners and other financial consultants have no universally accepted minimum standards for education and expertise.

The lack of formal educational and professional requirements has been identified by some experts as a major source of potential abuse among all types of financial advisers. In addition, the relatively low level of inspection by the SEC and state agencies creates an environment where incompetence can go undetected until it is too late.[3]

National Standards Update

FOR THE LAST FEW YEARS, NASAA has been reviewing the options on setting competency and licensing requirements for financial planners and investment advisers. Currently more than half the states require investment advisers to pass either the Uniform Investment Advisers State Law Exam, known in the industry as the Series 65, or the Uniform Combined State Law Exam, known as the Series 66.[4] The Series 66 is a combination of the Series 65 and the Series 63, the Uniform Securities Agent State Law Exam. They are administered at the state level and test the applicant's knowledge of state and federal regulatory practices and disclosure rules. They also incorporate questions on ethical practices. However, none of these exams tests how well or competently financial planners or investment advisers perform their job.[5]

"Financial planners should be tested for their competency under applicable state investment adviser laws," said CFP Board of Standards President Robert Goss when he testified before a NASAA panel.[6] As there are no state or federal competency examinations for investment advisers or financial planners, Goss suggested NASAA use the private credentialing process already in place "instead of reinventing the wheel."[7] Goss offered the CFP exam for use by individual states as a uniform exam or suggested state commissioners could make use of the CFP Board's expertise in developing a new uniform exam for state-registered investment advisers.[8]

Establishment of Competency

IN THE ABSENCE OF UNIFORM national standards, there are several actions you can take not only to demonstrate your competency but also to protect yourself should you ever be sued over a recommendation. These include earning a professional designation from a nationally recognized organization, recognizing your limitations, and using outside consultants when necessary.

EDUCATIONAL AND PROFESSIONAL DESIGNATIONS There are numerous educational and professional designations associated with the industry. Each of these designations has its own educational requirements and code of ethics. The following is a brief review of those common to planners and advisers.

◆ **CFP.** The *CFP* and *Certified Financial Planner* professional designations are two federally registered service marks, which are for the use of individuals who have completed the requirements established by the CFP Board. The marks are licensed for use by the CFP Board, which sets the standards for these credentials including education, examination, work experience, and ethics.

The CFP Board identifies the body of knowledge in

the field of personal financial planning, sets the core curriculum, and registers educational institutions that provide the model curriculum. Presently 85 college and university programs across the country have been registered with the CFP Board, including the College for Financial Planning in Denver, Colorado. The CFP Board also established a Code of Ethics and Professional Responsibility, to which all CFP licensees are obliged to subscribe, and administers disciplinary action up to and including revocation against those licensees violating its Code. The CFP Board administers its certification program in keeping with nationally accepted licensure and certification program requirements.

Educational course work covers 175 topics in six core areas: fundamentals of financial planning, insurance planning, investment planning, income tax planning, retirement planning and employee benefits, and estate planning. After the candidates have completed the education requirement, they sit for a two-day comprehensive examination covering the whole body of knowledge, similar to the CPA or bar examination. Candidates must also show three years of work experience in a financial planning-related job, and a BA degree. In addition, CFP licensees must complete 30 hours of continuing education every two years and make an annual ethics disclosure to the CFP Board.[9]

◆ **ChFC and CLU.** *ChFC* stands for *Chartered Financial Consultant,* and *CLU* stands for *Chartered Life Underwriter.* Both the CLU and ChFC educational designations are granted by The American College, Bryn Mawr, Pennsylvania. The American College was founded to serve the life insurance industry, but has expanded its offerings and now grants a Master's degree in both Financial Services and Management. The American Society of CLU and ChFC is a national association for life insurance and financial services professionals also headquartered in Bryn Mawr. Most members of the American Society of CLU and ChFC hold the CLU designation, and about half have also been awarded the ChFC designation.

In order to be awarded the CLU or ChFC designation, an applicant must successfully complete a 10-course study program offered by The American College, a fully accredited, nontraditional educational institution. Both the CLU and ChFC programs consist of six required courses and four electives, and the curriculum usually takes four to five years to complete. In addition, students must pass a two-hour multiple choice exam at the end of each course. Three years of qualifying professional experience and commitment to the high ethical standards established by the college are also required before the CLU or ChFC designation may be granted. [10]

◆ **RFC.** *RFC* stands for *Registered Financial Consultant,* a designation awarded by IARFC. It is limited only to those who meet high qualification standards, including four years of full-time experience in the financial planning area, and satisfying licensing requirements for securities and life and health insurance. All IARFC members must have earned an undergraduate or graduate degree related to financial services or have one of the several professional designations. They must also agree to satisfy continuing education requirements and adhere to the IARFC code of ethics. [11]

◆ **NAPFA.** Although NAPFA has not yet created an educational designation, it does have requirements for membership. Applicants must have three years of work experience in the financial planning area, plus an undergraduate degree related to the field, or a professional designation such as CFP, ChFC, or CPA. They must also present a financial plan for peer review, verify that they are fee-only (i.e., they do not accept compensation based on commissions, rebates, bonuses, finder's fees, or other types of compensation based on financial planning recommendations), and have a clean record.[12]

In 1997, however, NAPFA trademarked the adjective "fee-only" and created a fee-only certification mark. Faced with stinging rebukes from other industry groups, NAPFA defended its action by stating it was the association's intent to protect the public by making sure consumers were not confused over the term "fee-only."[13]

Although no one knows exactly how many advisers use the term "fee-only," there are certainly thousands of individuals who have been using it for many years before NAPFA took this action.

NAPFA has taken the stand that only financial advisers who practice at all times as fee-only will qualify for the new certification mark. According to a May 1997 NAPFA press release, financial advisers who charge fees some but not all of the time will not qualify for the mark. NAPFA has developed a system that allows fee-only planners who are not NAPFA members to use the certification mark.

Unable to reach a consensus with NAPFA about the use of the term "fee-only," IARFC, AICPA, and the CFP Board of Standards filed petitions with the U.S. Patent and Trademark Office to have the mark withdrawn. It is important to note that the NAPFA fee-only certification mark is not a sign of competence but merely a designation of how an adviser is compensated.

◆ **PFS.** *PFS* stands for *Personal Financial Specialist.* AICPA created this special designation for CPAs who want to specialize in financial planning. In order to earn a PFS designation, a CPA must pass a comprehensive exam given by the AICPA, have at least three years of financial planning experience, perform a minimum of 750 hours of personal financial planning services, and complete 72 hours of continuing education every three years. [14]

RECOGNITION OF LIMITATIONS The leading professional organizations have taken a strong stand against incompetence. The CFP Board requires competence as a minimum requirement for its licensees and directs in its code of ethics that it is improper to give advice outside one's area of expertise. Incompetent advice can subject a CFP licensee to discipline by the CFP Board of Ethics and Professional Review.

The IAFP's Code of Professional Ethics addresses competence with three different canons, reprinted in Appendix A. Canon 2 requires members to "seek continually to maintain and improve their professional knowledge, skills, and competence." Canon 3 requires members to "obey all laws and regulations and avoid any conduct or activity which would cause unjust harm to those who rely upon the professional judgment and skill of the members." Canon 4 requires members to "be diligent in the performance of their occupational duties."

Principle 3 of the CFP Board's Code of Ethics and Professional Responsibility and Disciplinary Rules and Procedures covers competence by stating: "A CFP designee shall provide services to clients competently and maintain the necessary knowledge and skill to continue to do so in those areas in which the designee is engaged."

Clearly, if financial planners or advisers are asked to perform duties beyond their level of expertise, they are required either to decline or associate with another professional who is competent in the area. In certain circumstances, it may be necessary to obtain additional education in order to manage a particular client. It can be particularly tempting for new advisers who are hungry for income to take cases beyond their level of competence. Resisting the temptation is good business.

Inevitably these seem to be the very cases that go bad and create lawsuits later.

Take the all too frequent example of financial advisers holding themselves out as estate planning experts. This is an extremely complex field, not only for attorneys who specialize in estate planning, but also for advisers who need a broad base of knowledge in many areas. The subject is so complicated, financial advisers can be giving false advice and not even know they are in trouble.

For instance, it is not unusual to hear well-meaning advisers tell a client there are no tax consequences to owning a life insurance policy. While it is true there is usually no income tax due on death benefit proceeds, many financial advisers do not realize there can be sizable estate tax consequences to even term life insurance. Consequently, a financial adviser can unwittingly create an estate tax liability for the unsuspecting client who trusts the professional's expertise.

USE OF OUTSIDE CONSULTANTS Because of the complexity of the industry, even experienced professionals can face situations beyond their level of expertise. In particular, a planner or an investment adviser, with greater responsibilities as a fiduciary, must be especially cautious when advising a client and may find it is sometimes necessary to use an outside consultant.

Some financial services professionals hesitate to use a consultant because of the cost. However, the few dollars you pay to have an attorney, accountant, or tax expert review your recommendations are dollars well spent. Not only does it show you are taking the extra step to make sure your client is well served; in the event of a lawsuit later, you will have an extra layer of protection because you relied on a consultant.

You need to be particularly cautious when dealing with property and casualty (P&C) insurance. When clients come to planners, they expect to get comprehensive financial planning services, covering every aspect of their lives. Although that may be their expectation, it is rare for financial plans to deal with this type of insurance. Yet this is an area of exposure for most clients: the amount of money they could lose as a result of a car accident or someone's slipping and falling on their front doorstep could completely wipe them out. It is important to explain clearly to clients that you will not be addressing this issue in your plan, unless you are experienced in this area.

Include a statement in your engagement letters saying you will not be reviewing the clients' property and casualty insurance and it is important for them to seek out a specialist in this area. This not only protects you, it is good for the clients to realize this is an area of exposure that needs to be addressed. You may want to refrain from referring clients to a particular P&C specialist because, in many states, the person who makes the referral can be as liable as the specialist if the specialist makes an error in dealing with your client.

ACTION ITEMS

◆ IT IS IMPORTANT for you to clarify if you may legally use the term "fee-only" to describe your method of compensation or your business practices. CFP licensees should contact the CFP Board of Standards for an opinion. The IAFP also has information on this subject for its members. You can contact NAPFA directly at (800) 366-2732.

◆ ALL FINANCIAL PROFESSIONALS, including those who are highly experienced, should occasionally have their recommendations reviewed for accuracy. Consider working with another professional on a peer review basis, offering to review each other's plans and recommendations periodically. Attending classes and professional meetings is another way to keep sharp and up to date.

◆ BEFORE USING CONSULTANTS, be sure to ask them some tough questions. Ask them how long they have been in the business, how many cases they have handled of this kind, and whether they have malpractice insurance. This is important for you in case you ever have to make a malpractice claim because of their bad advice.

CHAPTER

INSURANCE
REGULATIONS

UNTIL RECENTLY, the life insurance industry was considered a sleepy part of our economy that was rarely subject to any lawsuits or bad press. As our society has become more litigious, however, even insurance agents have become the target of civil suits or media assaults. These can be quite costly—as one company discovered when it had fines levied against it for more than $20 million, because of abuses in marketing its "private pension plan."[1] This does not even include the billions of dollars in restitution costs to injured customers.

State insurance commissioners, the sole regulators of insurance activity, are taking a new look at their responsibilities and, as a result, are cracking down on the industry. The New York State Insurance Commissioner said: "It is clear that the conduct of the life insurance industry with regard to its sales and marketing practices has been inexcusable. Too many life insurance executives have ignored their own internal control warnings and condoned the questionable, unethical and illegal activities of some of these top sales people."[2]

Long before the adverse publicity, the states created NAIC to coordinate efforts and maintain consistent standards, to study issues related to insurance regulations, and to recommend appropriate legislation, called "model regulations." Although states are not obligated to enact these regulations, most look carefully to NAIC for guidance. NAIC's Model Insurance Act was adopted by most states before financial planning became an active profession; nevertheless, it covers the activities of planners and advisers with respect to life insurance.

The following guidelines will help you safely navigate your practice through this heightened litigious and regulatory atmosphere. They first describe practices and language prohibited throughout the insurance industry and then review the crucial role of disclosure in not only protecting but also enriching your practice.

Prohibited Practices

THE FOLLOWING REVIEWS insurance practices that have legal consequences.

◆ **Planning fees.** The Model Insurance Act prohibits insurance agents from charging fees other than commissions for financial planning, unless the fees are based upon a written agreement signed by the client in advance. The agreement must describe the service for which the fee is charged and the amount of the fee.

The agreement must also specifically state the client is under no obligation to purchase any insurance product through the agent. Finally, the insurance agent must retain a copy of the agreement for at least three years after completing the services. [3]

◆ **Rebating.** The direct or indirect refunding of premiums to the client is illegal in most states. Rebating laws also prohibit offering anything of value as an inducement to buy insurance. Sales inducements can range from actual cash kickbacks to conditional agreements.

New York's law is a good example of how rebating is frequently defined: "No person shall knowingly receive any rebate, allowance, or deduction from any premium, or any valuable things, special favor or advantage whatever, not specified in the policy, as an inducement to take any policy of life insurance." [4] California may be one of the few states that allow rebating, because voters repealed the prohibition against direct or indirect rebating when they approved Proposition 103. [5]

Rebating laws can be violated in the most innocent ways. Sometimes planners will use commissions received from insurance and securities sales to offset financial planning fees. Although most states allow the rebating of securities commissions, this practice is usually illegal in states that have outlawed rebating of insurance premiums. [6]

DILEMMA

ANDY AGENT AGREES to purchase all of his tires from Jake's Tire Store, or to make a contribution to Jake's favorite charity, if Jake buys an insurance policy from Andy.

Question: What should Andy do?

Answer: Avoid either of these arrangements altogether. They would be considered rebating in the states that prohibit it.

DILEMMA

ANDY AGENT IS ALSO an RIA. He explains his fees to Jake by giving him a choice: "I can charge you 2 percent of your earned annual income and recommend no-load insurance products, or I can charge you 1 percent of your income and use full-commission insurance. Which would you prefer, Jake?" Jake decides to pay 2 percent.

Question: Is this arrangement legal?

Answer: This would probably pass muster in states with rebating laws.

Using insurance commissions to offset financial planning fees is illegal in most states. If you are in doubt about this practice, get an opinion from your state insurance department.

◆ **Twisting.** It is not illegal to replace an existing life insurance product with a better performing one. However, twisting—the unethical practice of convincing a client to replace an insurance policy unnecessarily—is illegal in most jurisdictions.

If you are considering replacing a client's existing insurance policy, carefully document your file. List all the information you have on the old policy along with comparisons to the new one and note why you thought the new policy was significantly better. If it is a gray area—one where your new policy is probably as good as, but not significantly better than, the old—it is probably better to leave the existing policy in place. As much of this information is difficult or impossible to obtain years after the fact, your best defense in a charge of twisting is to have a carefully documented file.

◆ **Suitability.** Although most broker-dealers are careful about educating their representatives on suitability requirements for securities, it appears that many general agents do not explain to new agents that it is illegal in most states to recommend unsuitable insurance products.

The requirement to recommend only suitable insurance policies seems to give insurance agents great cause for alarm. Typically, planners and agents who have a bias toward whole life insurance products are concerned that their permanent insurance recommendations are going to be found to be unsuitable by a state regulator who prefers a term product. However, the best protection an agent can have is to document the file carefully, noting why a permanent policy was a good choice for the client, given the client's age, health, marital status, net worth, investment temperament, and existing policies.

◆ **Insurance comparisons.** Life insurance agents are prohibited by some state statutes from referring to insurance as an investment. It is also illegal in certain states to compare insurance to a security product unless the agent is a registered investment adviser. A few states prohibit insurance products with a securities component from being compared to a traditional insurance product unless the agent is also a registered investment adviser.

◆ **Misrepresenting insurance.** If a life insurance policy is being presented, state regulations require that it must be clear and obvious to the customer that it is indeed a life insurance policy. It is not only bad business, but it is illegal to try to disguise life insurance by referring to it as something else.[7]

The following terms should not be used in place of the word "insurance:" [8]

— accumulation plan/program/strategy
— college funding alternative
— funding plan/program/strategy
— guaranteed retirement plan
— income plan/program/strategy
— interest plan/program
— pension maximization plan

— private pension plan/strategy
— savings plan/program/strategy
— business plan/program/strategy
— educational plan
— estate plan/program
— future gifting plan/program/strategy
— insured retirement savings plan
— pension predicament
— personal retirement plan
— retirement plan/program/strategy.

The word "plan" can also get agents into trouble if used incorrectly. It is permissible to refer to something as a plan when the customer receives something beyond the actual contract policy, such as a split-dollar plan, deferred compensation plan, or estate plan that includes trust agreements.[9]

There are certain terms that should only be used by RIAs according to Dennis M. Groner and Mary B. Petersen:[10]

— asset management plan/program/process
— asset plan/program/strategy
— asset correlation plan
— financial planning program/strategy
— investment plan/program/strategy
— money planning program/strategy.

Required Disclosures

THE FOLLOWING REVIEWS current areas that must be disclosed to all clients and discusses items that may have to be disclosed in the near future.

◆ **Professional status.** Almost uniformly throughout the country, life insurance agents and planners who are agents must disclose the fact to each client. The name of the insurance company or companies must also be disclosed before a presentation can be made.

◆ **Commission disclosure.** The Model Insurance Act requires that, prior to soliciting a sale, an insurance agent must tell the client that a commission from the sale of the insurance product will be received in addition to a fee for financial planning, if that is the case.[11]

One area that will be receiving a lot of attention in the future is disclosing not only the fact of but also the amount of commissions agents receive from the sale of policies. Utah Insurance Commissioner Robert Wilcox, who chaired NAIC's life disclosure working group, said: "I think we're not too far away from the time the support will be there for disclosure of agent's compensation. Once we get to that point, it will automatically turn in favor of a levelized commission structure. Then all the incentive for the inappropriate twisting of business goes away. We also attract a different kind of agent as a result of it."[12]

Some investment advisers have handled this issue by including a range of commissions in their Form ADV, required by the SEC. Others have offered clients a different fee structure, with a higher advisory fee when no-load insurance products are offered and a lower one when fully-loaded insurance is recommended.

There is no doubt that disclosing the amount of commissions will change the industry considerably. If this is indeed the future wave, it makes sense to get involved now while you have some say in how the disclosures will be defined. This can be a good chance to be seen by the public as on the leading edge and concerned about the clients' best interests. Waiting for your state insurance commissioner's office to make rules could prove to be risky.

◆ **Policy disclosure.** The most recent efforts of NAIC have been focused on improving the quality of life insurance illustrations. Until 1996, there was no formal standard for life insurance product illustrations. This led to a proliferation of illustration formats and assumptions ranging from extremely conservative to

extremely aggressive. In order to eliminate misleading comparisons and to reduce confusion regarding
illustrated and guaranteed values, NAIC designed regulations that disallow assumptions not supported by
current results. The new model regulation also
requires a clear presentation of results based on less
attractive, or midpoint, assumptions, as well as guarantees only. In addition, the new model regulation
also requires a policyholder signature on a compliance illustration and annual updated illustrations
from the insurance company.

Some states have already enacted the model regulations. By the beginning of 1998, most insurance companies will have updated their illustration software to
comply with the new model regulations.

Until your state changes its regulations, make sure
you keep a copy of all illustrations used in insurance
proposals. Clearly advise clients that interest rate
assumptions are just that, assumptions, and they are
not guaranteed, unless that is the case. It is also helpful
to give clients a worst-case scenario, particularly when
considering a policy such as Universal Life. Use conservative assumptions whenever possible.

To help hone your policy disclosure skills, consider
using the Life Insurance Illustration Questionnaire
(IQ). This voluntary educational tool was developed
by the American Society of CLU and ChFC to help
educate insurance agents on the methodology used by
companies to generate sales illustrations and insurance
proposals. As all such illustrations are merely estimates,
it is highly unlikely actual interest rate and expense
cost performance will ever match projected figures.
Using the IQ will help you obtain the information you
need to clearly understand and evaluate how the different elements of a life insurance policy can affect
future performance.[13]

The Life Insurance Design Questionnaire

LAWRENCE J. RYBKA, a national authority on large life insurance purchases, says "selling the lowest premium rate doesn't work and it's bad for the client." Many agents illustrate and sell low premiums, he said, and the policy runs the risk of blowing up in a client's face without the agent having understood or disclosed to the client what a low interest rate could mean. Some carriers illustrate premiums at dangerously low levels, using tight assumptions for interest crediting, mortality, and lapse rates. Agents should be skeptical about ledgers because they are based on undisclosed price assumptions. Selling a hot illustration is a good way to get burned.

To help clients understand how to buy life insurance, Rybka designed the Life Insurance Design Questionnaire. This questionnaire addresses the critical link in the chain: getting across to the client how insurance products work, so that the client can, with the agent's help, make more informed insurance purchase decisions. The six-item questionnaire is designed for an agent or planner and a client to fill out and sign together. The questions are created to help the client understand concepts such as solvency ratings, mortality, interest rates, and death benefits.

With this information, clients can:

◆ Create a range of companies that have an acceptable rating and financial strength;

◆ Narrow the choice, types, and design of acceptable policies;

◆ Set the mortality and interest rate assumptions needed to determine the premium; and

◆ Select how the premium will be paid.

Rybka recommends that the agent should also send an engagement letter, which confirms both the companies used to construct the policy illustrations and the client's selection of nonguaranteed criteria. For more information on how to use the Life Insurance Design Questionnaire, contact Lawrence Rybka at (800) 765-5201. The following illustrates how key information from the Life Insurance Design Questionnaire is then incorporated into a follow-up letter.

RYBKA LIFE INSURANCE PLAN LETTER

Date

Dear:

Thank you very much for allowing me to help you with the design of your life insurance plan.

To keep you updated on the progress we are making, I wanted to confirm how we will prepare the illustrations for $_____
of life insurance on the life (lives) of _____
_____.

In our last meeting, we discussed that your parameters will govern how my staff will prepare all proposals/estimates. I have enclosed a copy of the specifications you selected and have summarized them below.

◆ **Financial Strength** - You indicated we should limit our consideration only to companies having _____ ratings from the major agencies. This criterion will limit our selection to _____ companies. I have enclosed that list as Attachment A.

◆ **Death Benefit Need** - Because the insurance is needed for _____**TYPE**_____, you indicated you would require a death benefit of $ _____.

Therefore, we will be providing you with ____**TYPE**____ life insurance proposals and recommend _____**TYPE**_____ life insurance.

◆ **Method of Payment** - Your preference is to pay the premium mode over the next _____ years. This payment preference will be based on assumptions you supplied in Questions 4-6. We discussed how the pricing elements will change over the time you own your policy. Actual product performance will determine:

◆ The number of years you pay premium.

◆ Whether the current premium will remain level.

◆ **Interest Rate** - You indicated you would like me to evaluate several products using a _____% interest rate. This type of rate would require _____ _____.

Remember, actual credited rates will depend on what happens over the remaining _____ years you own the policy. Should the actual rate be higher, you may recognize savings by paying fewer years. If the actual rate is lower, you will pay more.

◆ **Mortality Assumptions** - Just as the interest rate component of the product may change, so, too, may mortality. All ledgers will be prepared using _____ mortality charges. Actual mortality charges may vary.

◆ **Other Factors** - While projected interest and projected mortality are two of the most important factors impacting the projections of what you will pay for your life insurance, other factors must also be considered. I have enclosed a brochure prepared by one of the companies I represent which explains these factors.

◆ **Maximum Premium** - Because you indicated you do not wish to look only to the guarantees of the life insurance contract in designing your plan, we will be relying on some nonguaranteed elements. For example, if actual interest earned was _____% rather than the _____% you indicated, you would have to pay more for your insurance. However, you indicated all products considered would:

SELECT ONE:

A. Have a death benefit that was guaranteed and a premium that could not be increased. Thus, only the number of years would be dependent on non-guaranteed elements.

B. Have a death benefit that is guaranteed with a premium that could never be increased by more than _____%.

C. Have a guarantee to your life expectancy of age _____ at the initial premium.

D. Have a death benefit that is guaranteed for _____ years at the initial premium.

E. Not consider guarantees. You would rely exclusively on projected nonguaranteed elements for both your death benefit and future premium payment.

I look forward to reviewing this proposed insurance coverage with you on _____. If you have any questions, please do not hesitate to call.

Sincerely,

Securities offered through a Registered Representative of_____
Sales Corporation.

ACTION ITEM

◆ COPIES OF THE LIFE Insurance Illustration Questionnaire should be available at your home office.
Call and ask for this helpful educational tool.

*The author is grateful for the assistance of Lawrence J.
Rybka, President of Executive Insurance, in preparing this
chapter. For more information on his Life Insurance
Design Questionnaire, call him at (800) 765-5201.*

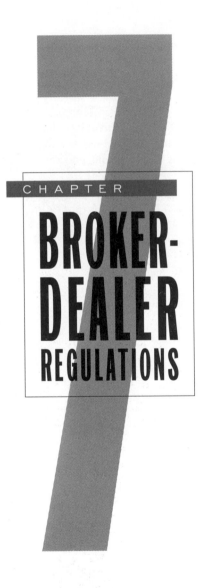

BROKER-DEALER REGULATIONS

THE VAST MAJORITY OF financial advisers who sell securities are regulated by federal and state securities laws in addition to NASD regulations. Generally, a dealer or issuer cannot employ an agent or sales representative who is unregistered, or they will be prevented from transacting business. For practical purposes, most financial planners and advisers will have to register as a representative of their broker-dealer unless they want to limit their compensation to fees for advice.

Clearly, broker-dealers must deal with a myriad of regulations as they come under the jurisdiction of many different levels of government. You should be aware some large financial firms do not track state laws for the benefit of their planners or representatives. These companies prefer to wait until an investor files a claim. At that time, they will review the statute in question and advise the other planners or representatives in that state if action needs to be taken. Until recently, it was not unusual for firms to have no designated person charged with tracking insurance compliance issues. However, this will be changing in light of the huge judgments against a few large insurance companies.

This chapter addresses some of the major issues affecting broker-dealers and their registered representatives.

Selling Away

NASD HAS IDENTIFIED "selling away" as one of the biggest problem areas in the securities marketplace. This violation occurs when registered representatives recommend investment opportunities not on their broker-dealers' approved product lists. NASD rules could make broker-dealers liable for all their representatives' securities transactions, whether they originated with the broker-dealer or not.[1] Under common law vicarious liability, a broker-dealer as principal may also be deemed responsible for the representative-agent's actions.

Unfortunately, selling away can happen in the most innocent of ways. Occasionally, well-meaning clients with limited financial resources will approach financial advisers or representatives for assistance. Perhaps all they can invest is $25 or $50 per month. The adviser may not have any investment products that take amounts that small, or they may not want to bother with the paperwork for such minute commissions. Frequently the adviser or representative will recommend the prospective client use a no-load mutual fund which does not have any minimum investments. Although this may be good advice for the client who can start an investment on limited resources without paying a load, it may violate the rule, as no-load products are sometimes excluded from the broker-dealer's approved list.

Selling away also occurs because many financial advisers do not realize how broadly the SEC defines a security. For example, solar panels and windmills may fit into the definition of a security when the investors also pay for a maintenance contract and the seller continues to handle the sale of electricity to local power companies. Even cattle embryos have been found to be securities under certain circumstances. Consequently, unsuspecting but very creative planners and financial advisers may be putting their clients into investments that are not only unregistered when they need to be, but also that are not on the broker-dealer's approved list.

DILEMMA

ROGER REGISTERED REP is asked to solicit business for the Very Good Venture Capital Deal. Roger is told Very Good's deal is not a security. Very Good turns out to be very bad, and investors sue for relief. Very Good is later determined by the court to be a security.

Question: Is Roger in trouble?

Answer: Yes. Once the court ruled Very Good was a security, it was determined Roger had not only sold away from the broker-dealer, but also sold an unregistered security.

Notice to Members 94-44

IN MAY 1994, NASD ISSUED Notice to Members 94-44 to clarify the requirements of broker-dealer oversight of "selling away" activities by affiliated RRs. This notice is an elaboration of Article III, Section 40 of the NASD

Rules of Fair Practice, which requires an RR who participates in a "private securities transaction" to notify the broker-dealer in writing prior to participating in the transaction. The notification must describe the RR's role and whether the RR is receiving a selling commission in connection with the transaction.[2] If the RR has received or may receive selling compensation, the broker-dealer must approve and record the transaction. In addition, the broker-dealer must supervise the RR's participation in the transaction.

Section 40 defines "private securities transaction" as any securities transaction outside the regular course or scope of the RRs' employment with the broker-dealer. "Selling compensation" has been broadly construed to include the receipt of any item of value, received or to be received, directly or indirectly, from the execution of any such securities transaction.[3]

When RRs are required to report a private securities transaction to their broker-dealer, the broker-dealer must then notify the RR as to whether it approves or disapproves of the representative's participation in the transaction. The transaction must be recorded on the broker-dealer's books and supervised by the broker-dealer if it is approved. On the other hand, if the broker-dealer disapproves of the transaction, the RR may not directly or even indirectly participate in the transaction.[4]

The issue of "selling away" arises frequently with RRs who are also RIAs, often referred to as RR/RIAs. In the typical scenario, planners would issue a financial plan pursuant to their RIA license. Instead of recommending a loaded mutual fund through their broker-dealer, they may recommend a no-load fund with a discount brokerage firm. In the past, these activities have escaped the scrutiny of the broker-dealer because the no-load mutual fund would not be listed on the broker-dealer's approved list. This area is changing as more broker-dealers include no-load funds on their approved lists and representatives use the broker-dealer's advisory services to monitor no-load funds.

It was clearly the intention of the NASD to cover any participation of RR/RIAs in the execution of transactions that go beyond mere recommendations. When RR/RIAs enter an order on behalf of the customer for a particular securities transaction, either with a brokerage firm other than their own broker-dealer or directly with a mutual fund or adviser, and receive any compensation for the overall advisory services, they will be covered under NTM 94-44.

DILEMMA

RUTH RR/RIA REVIEWS her clients' 401(k) fund and recommends that they move their assets from the Aggressive Growth Fund to the Growth and Income Fund. The clients are responsible for contacting the plan manager and executing this transaction.

Question: Does this transaction have to be reported to and approved by Ruth's broker-dealer?

Answer: No. Although a fee for giving this advice would be covered under "selling compensation," Ruth did not participate in executing the transaction.

DILEMMA

RAY RR/RIA DID a financial plan for his parents and did not charge them a fee. He recommended a no-load mutual fund group, and he personally executed the transaction on their behalf.

Question: Does Ray have to report this activity to his broker-dealer?

Answer: No, because transactions executed on the customer's behalf without any form of compensation are excluded from the reporting requirement.

RITA RR/RIA HAS AN arrangement with a third-party money manager to handle her client's accounts. Rita made the initial investment recommendations for the client based on alternatives provided by the money manager. Rita received a percentage of the money manager's fees for performing the initial recommendations and the introduction to the manager. Rita does not execute any trades.

Question: Does this activity have to be reported to and approved by Rita's broker-dealer?

Answer: Yes, this activity would be covered by NTM 94-44.

The introduction of NTM 94-44 created a clamor in the financial services industry. Many brokers were worried about intrusion into their separate RIA affairs, and others were concerned that broker-dealers would increase their fees for providing the extra supervisory services and acceptance of vicarious liability. Some industry pundits suggested that in the future there would be increasing NASD jurisdiction that would eventually include supervising authority for all RIA activities.[5] These fears have largely been unfounded.

In May 1996, NASD issued Notice to Members 96-33 to clarify the record keeping responsibilities of member firms and to respond to frequently asked questions raised under NTM 94-44. The notice makes it clear that member firms must supervise and approve these securities transactions, not just accept reports from RRs. Members are allowed a great deal of record keeping flexibility.

NTM 96-33 differentiates between RR/RIAs who provide investment advisory services for an asset-based or performance-based fee and those who receive transaction-based compensation. The former must give prior notice of the advisory services, rather than prior notice of each trade effected for a particular client. However, if the RR/RIA receives transaction-based compensation, the broker-dealer must approve each trade in advance.

Supervision

IN 1989, NASD AMENDED the supervisory obligations of broker-dealers. In Notice to Members 88-84, which amended Article III, Section 27 of the Rules of Fair Practice, each firm is required to establish and maintain written supervisory and review procedures. Among other things, they are also required to assign a supervisor to each registered representative in the field force. The broker-dealer must schedule audit examinations of each branch office. The broker-dealer is also required to review the transactions of each office, usually accomplished by statistically sampling the trade tickets.[6] Finally, a compliance seminar and continuing education must be presented to every broker annually.

Failure to provide adequate supervision can make the broker-dealer vulnerable to lawsuits, as clients rarely sue only their planners or representatives. They usually join in the suit the broker-dealer, managing executive, RIA, product sponsor, and any other deep pockets they can find. Savvy attorneys know representatives may have committed an error, but they are frequently judgment-proof and not likely to have the funds to reimburse the investor. Consequently, plaintiffs will follow the money. A large number of complaints filed against broker-dealers charge them with failure to supervise their registered representatives.

The additional claim of failure to supervise can cause problems for the broker. On the surface, it appears as if the broker and broker-dealer are on one side of the table and the unhappy investor is on the other. The dynamics completely change, however, when the broker-dealer must defend a failure to supervise claim. Now the broker-dealer will commonly assert superior supervision. Its counsel will produce compliance manuals, audit notes, and even testimony from the managing principal to prove that the broker is the rogue and that the broker-dealer is not liable for the broker's acts.

The unfortunate broker is now looking at accusing fingers from two parties and finds himself in the difficult position of having to defend his actions on two fronts: in the suit with the investor and against the broker-dealer's allegations that he did not follow all the rules. The situation worsens because, under the E&O coverage provided by the broker-dealer, the two have usually started out sharing the same attorney. That attorney is probably privy to confidential information that could be used against the broker in the suit.

DILEMMA

PETER PLANNER WORKS for ABC, a large financial services corporation known for its thorough and conservative due diligence. Charlie Client approaches Peter, with whom he has a long-standing relationship, requesting information on the commodities market. Peter says he is not involved in commodities trading and certainly thinks it would be far too risky for Charlie. Charlie pushes; Peter resists. Charlie pushes again. Finally, Peter says, "Well, I attended a seminar last week by the D&E firm, but I don't know anything about them, so I can't say if they're good or not." Charlie does business with D&E, loses a boatload of money, and sues Peter and ABC Broker-Dealer for failure to supervise.

Question: What should Peter do?

Answer: Peter should be aware that ABC will use their thorough compliance manuals, notes from annual compliance meetings, and supervisory personnel to prove that it always conveys to its sales force that representatives should never, under any circumstances, make referrals to other firms. ABC will take the position that it not only supervises better than any firm on the planet but can also prove it.

Before he has any conversations with ABC's compliance department or legal staff, Peter should confirm how ABC is planning to defend its portion of the case. Will ABC be with him or against him? It is absolutely critical for Peter to do this before he discloses any information that could be used against him later by ABC. In fact, Peter should take the extra precaution of retaining his own lawyer to make sure his interests are fully protected.

RIA Affiliation

BOTH LARGE BROKER-DEALERS and small ones need to address the registered investment adviser issue head-on by making a conscious business decision on the subject. The first step is to ascertain the true business activities of the representatives. If they are performing planning as defined by the SEC and state statutes, then some form of registration, at either the broker-dealer level or the representative level, must occur. Broker-dealers should take an active role in making sure their representatives are in compliance. Because the broker-dealer is responsible for many of the representative's planning activities anyway, it is good protection for the broker-dealer and the representative-planner to assure compliance.

On the other hand, the representatives may be performing thorough suitability evaluations or financial planning-related functions on all their clients, but not actually planning as defined by the SEC or states. In such cases it is important for the compliance department to help the representatives set up their business to fit into the *incidental to* exclusion discussed in Chapter 2.

Other Issues

TWO OTHER ISSUES THAT require the attention of broker-dealers are product due diligence and general requirements.

DUE DILIGENCE Most broker-dealers are aware of the importance of doing due diligence for *all* of the investments approved for sale by their registered representatives. However, some broker-dealers do not take the time to train their brokers on how to review investments or how to legally explain them to clients. This is an extremely important part of the business. Not only do planners and representatives need to be able to say they have carefully reviewed every investment, but they need the home office to demonstrate that due diligence has been done.

MAJOR REQUIREMENTS If you are thinking of starting your own broker-dealer, consider some of the major requirements.

◆ A broker-dealer must have a formal written supervisory procedure and a formal system for handling complaints.

◆ A broker-dealer has a duty to exercise diligent supervision over the activities of all of its selling representatives.

◆ A supervisor must be appointed for each member of the sales force and must ensure all client investments are suitable.

◆ A broker-dealer cannot allow unlicensed people to solicit business on its behalf. This includes staff people supporting the sales force.

◆ A representative who solicits an application for the

purchase of a security has to have reasonably documented beliefs that the purchase is suitable for the applicant.

◆ A representative is prohibited from misrepresenting a material fact or failing to state a material fact in connection with a sale of securities or insurance.

◆ Generally all ads, sales literature, prospecting letters, seminar invitations, seminar material, and seminars have to be approved by the broker-dealer's compliance office and filed with NASD and various states. In all cases this material must be maintained in files available for inspection.

ACTION ITEMS

◆ BE AWARE THAT THE SEC was considering extensive and controversial changes in its broker-dealer books and records rules as this book was going to press.[7]

◆ IF BOTH YOU AND YOUR broker-dealer are sued, consider retaining separate legal counsel before you make any incriminating admissions to the compliance department or legal staff.

◆ IF YOU ARE CONSIDERING any investment that is outside the norm, contact your broker-dealer's compliance department to verify it is on the approved list. This is also good protection for you, because it provides an extra layer of due diligence given that the broker-dealer must investigate the product before approving it. Check with your firm to see what their requirements are for selling securities off of an approved list. Ask how no-load mutual funds are treated.

INVESTMENT ADVISER REGULATIONS

MANY CONSUMERS believe RIAs are more trustworthy than other financial services providers. Whether you are an individual RIA or are part of your broker-dealer's RIA, you are certainly subject to many more rules and regulations. The higher standard of care required of RIAs is discussed in Chapter 3. Inspections by the SEC and your state securities commission are discussed in Chapter 20.

This chapter reviews other key regulations for SEC RIAs and covers advertising rules, disclosure requirements, and record keeping. It concludes with a review of how the 1996 Coordination Act will significantly affect your business activities. Although SEC RIA rules are primarily covered here, they are a good starting point for how your state may address the same issues.

Advertising Rules

THE SEC HAS CREATED rules governing advertising by advisers that apply to all planners who are RIAs.[1] Because the SEC has determined that a registered investment adviser has the higher duty of a fiduciary, SEC staff have taken the position that the standard of conduct for adviser advertisements should be more strict than that for other vendors of products or services.[2] This tight control of adviser advertisements was accomplished in a number of ways. One was to make extensive limitations on acceptable advertising. Another was to define advertising in such a way that many activities not normally considered advertising are covered under the rule.[3]

An advertisement, according to the SEC, includes any written communication addressed to more than one person and any notice or announcement in any publication. It also includes information disseminated on radio and television.[4] This definition covers all form letters and the standardized written material in booklets used by investment advisers for presentations to prospective clients. The investment adviser's brochure can also be an advertisement under these rules.[5]

The rules generally prevent any investment adviser from using false or misleading advertisements. In addition, graphs, charts, formulas, and devices cannot be represented as making an investment determination unless limitations with these techniques are also disclosed. The rules also disallow testimonials and most statements regarding past profitable recommendations. Although the SEC will not review an ad in advance, the ad can be subject to an SEC audit.[6]

PERFORMANCE ADS Because of the complexity of the performance rules, you are strongly encouraged to avoid performance advertising altogether or to have your legal counsel review any ads in advance of circulation. In general, advertising regarding past recommendations is not permitted except under certain strict guidelines. For instance, it is permissible to offer to furnish a list of all recommendations the adviser made within the immediately preceding period of not less than one year. However, the list must show the price of the recommended investment at the recommended buy, sell, or hold date and the price of the security as of the most recent date practicable.[7] The following disclaimer must also be included: "It should not be assumed that recommendations made in the future will be profitable or will equal the performance of the securities in this list."[8]

TESTIMONIALS Testimonials have been another troublesome area. SEC staff does not permit an investment adviser to circulate or distribute advertisements that refer directly or indirectly to a testimonial of any kind. A testimonial includes any statement by a former or present client that endorses the adviser or refers to the client's favorable investment experience with the adviser.[9]

DILEMMA

GETTING YOUR MONEY'S WORTH magazine does an annual review of the 10 hottest financial planners this country has ever seen. Geraldine Planner is on the list. She copies the article and sends it to prospective clients.

Question: Has she violated the rules?

Answer: Although this looks like a testimonial, the SEC has held that this kind of promotion could be used, even if the adviser had paid the third party to verify its performance.[10] However, attorney Jeffrey

Kelvin of Plymouth Meeting, Pennsylvania, recommends avoiding this practice because he has seen it create problems during SEC audits.[11]

DILEMMA

RIGHTEOUS ROGER, a financial planner and an RIA, wants to prepare an advertising brochure that includes the following statement from his minister: "This is one of the finest Christian men I have ever met. I would trust him completely with all my investments."

Question: Does this violate the testimonial rule?

Answer: The SEC found that it did in the case of *Dan Gallagher, of Gallagher and Associates.*[12] Gallagher requested permission to use endorsements in the following areas: religious affiliation or general moral character, community service, trustworthiness and ethical character, diligence and attention to details, ability to listen and be sensitive to client concerns, knowledge of investing, insurance and tax strategies, prudence, and judgment. He specifically stated he would decline to include any reference to returns on investments and made an argument that these testimonials should be allowed under the First Amendment right of free speech. The SEC found none of his arguments persuasive. Staff said, "Testimonials are prohibited because they are likely to give rise to a fraudulent or deceptive implication or mistaken inference that the experience of the person giving the testimonial is typical of the experience of the adviser's clients."

DILEMMA

THE FANTASTIC GROUP of Mutual Funds wants to develop name recognition for the group and, at the same time, build a reputation for doing endruns around the competition. They decide to hire Dickie Dakota, the NFL's player of the year, to do an institutional ad. Dickie gets in front of the television cameras and states Fantastic has helped him manage his spectacular fortune and can help all of us armchair quarterbacks achieve financial success. Dickie is careful to avoid three things: he does not refer to any specific fund, or his own particular investments, nor does he give any figures for returns.

Question: Is this legal?

Answer: No. This is a violation of the testimonial rule.

DILEMMA

ARTIE BUPKUS, FINANCIAL planner and RIA, is completely enchanted with a prominent marketing firm. At considerable expense, Artie orders 1,000 copies of his own personalized audiocassette that advertises Artie's financial planning services, and records actual comments from satisfied clients in their own voices. After the purchase, Artie begins to wonder if the tapes violate the testimonial rule and requests a no-action letter from the SEC allowing him to continue using the cassettes.

Question: If you were the SEC staff, would you allow Artie to continue using the tapes because he has many thousands of dollars tied up in them?

Answer: In a similar case, the SEC found this was a violation of the testimonial rules and refused to grant the adviser a no-action letter.[13] Artie is stuck with a lot of expensive tapes he cannot use.

Advertising rules for registered representatives and other financial professionals are discussed in Chapter 9.

Disclosure Requirements

INVESTMENT ADVISERS ARE subject to numerous disclosure requirements. The following are among the most important.

◆ **Brochure Rule.** SEC RIAs are required to give their clients Part II of the Form ADV at least two days prior to entering into an agreement with a client. As an alternative, they may give the Form ADV II at the time of the agreement, providing the client has at least five days to cancel without a penalty. Advisers may also opt to substitute a specially drafted brochure that contains all the information in Form ADV II.[14] At least once annually thereafter, they must offer, in writing, to give the client a copy of the brochure.[15] This can be accomplished by making a written offer to deliver the brochure at the bottom of the client's statement.

One study indicated that only 27 percent of all registered investment advisers actually comply with the brochure rule. Of those who did comply, a majority failed to disclose that part of their earnings were composed of commissions.[16]

The information required by Part II of Form ADV calls for the adviser to describe the services provided, particularly if they are "financial planning," an explanation of the fees charged and how they are computed, and the adviser's affiliations with other securities professionals, including broker-dealer and insurance company affiliation, if any. Also to be included is information about the adviser's education, experience, and background; how securities are analyzed; and whether the adviser affects securities transactions for advisory clients. Advisers must also state if they have brokerage or investment discretion for clients.

Although the 1996 Coordination Act still requires SEC RIAs to fulfill the brochure rule, this rule is not an SEC requirement of state RIAs. However, if your firm is a state RIA, it is likely your state regulations will still require you to give your ADV Part II or its state equivalent to clients. Check with your state securities administrator for rulings.

◆ **Disciplinary Actions.** SEC RIAs are required to disclose to clients and prospective clients any disciplinary action taken against them during the preceding 10 years that may reflect on their integrity or ability to meet their contractual commitments to clients. Certain judicial and administrative actions are presumed to be material, including false statements or being the subject of an action involving an investment-related business fraud. Also included would be actions based on the allegations of wrongful taking of property, bribery, forgery, counterfeiting, or extortion. Advisers who have been sanctioned by being significantly limited in their investment-related activities must also disclose this information.[17] All of these disclosures are usually done on the Form ADV, Part I, Section 11.

◆ **Financial.** Investment advisers who have custody or control of client assets, or who receive advance payments in excess of $500 for services to be provided over periods greater than six months, are required to provide an audited balance sheet as a part of Form ADV, Part II.[18] Most advisers skirt this requirement by billing semi-annually. Advisers must also promptly disclose to clients any materially adverse change in financial condition or event that is reasonably likely to impair the adviser's ability to meet contractual obligations to clients.[19]

◆ **Right to Shop.** Registered investment advisers who are also registered representatives are required to inform clients they have the right to use a different broker-dealer.[20] Insurance agents need to make similar disclosures on the right to use different insurance companies.

◆ **Wrap Fees.** Wrap fees, an arrangement whereby the client pays one fee for both investment advisory services and execution, are subject to special disclosure rules.[21] A separate brochure describing the arrangement, or Schedule H of Form ADV, must be given to clients. The brochure must disclose how the wrap fee is calculated, the services to be provided for the fee, whether the fee is negotiable, and any additional fees a client might incur. In addition, it must state the wrap fee might be higher than the cost of paying separately for advisory and brokerage services. It must also describe the factors that affect whether the wrap fee would be more expensive for the client.

The portion of the fee paid to portfolio managers, as well as compensation paid to the person recommending the program, must also be disclosed. The methods by which portfolio managers are selected and restrictions on clients' contact with managers are some of the other items that must also be included.[22]

Required Record Keeping

UNDER RULE 204-2, an SEC RIA must keep the books and records listed below. It is possible to store many of these on computer, diskette or tape, subject to certain conditions that ensure their access and safekeeping.[23]

◆ A cash receipts journal, disbursement journal, and journals of original entry that form the basis of entry into any ledger;

◆ A general ledger and auxiliary ledgers showing assets, liabilities, reserves, capital, income, and expenses;

◆ Memoranda of security purchases and sale orders given by the adviser and instructions regarding such purchases and sales received from clients;

◆ Banking records, including checkbooks, bank statements, canceled checks, and cash reconciliations;

◆ Financial statements and working papers related to the business of the investment adviser;

◆ Bills or statements relating to the advisory business;

◆ All bills and statements, paid or unpaid;

◆ All trial balances, financial statements, and internal audit working papers;

◆ Powers of attorney and other grants of discretionary authority;

◆ Written contracts and agreements;

◆ Every notice, circular, advertisement, article, investment letter, or other communication circulated to 10 or more persons (not counting internal circulation);

◆ Written statements given to clients and prospective clients in compliance with the brochure rule (Rule 204-3);

◆ All documents necessary to support any calculation of performance or rate of return, or recommendations made in communications circulated to 10 or more persons. Investment advisers must maintain all communications to clients that contain performance data. If the communication recommends a specific security, but no reason for such recommendation is given, a memo to the file must be maintained by the adviser documenting the reason for the recommendation. Additionally, all internal working papers, including software programs used to calculate performance, must be maintained.

In addition, Rule 204-2 requires advisers to retain originals of all written communications received and copies of all communications sent relating to:

◆ A list of all accounts over which the adviser has any discretionary power;

◆ Any recommendation or advice;

◆ Receipt of funds or securities; and

◆ Trade orders.

If you find yourself subject only to state supervision under the 1996 Coordination Act, contact your state department of securities and request a copy of the records you will be required to keep. Smaller advisers will find a benefit from this new law in that they will only need to comply with the books and records requirements of the state in which their principal place of business is located. If they register in another state and have no place of business in the second state, that state must recognize their home state's record keeping rules.

Advisory Contract

EVERY ADVISORY OR financial planning agreement should be made pursuant to a written contract. It is not possible to enforce an oral contract. The Investment Advisers Act regulates advisory contracts with the following prohibitions:[24]

◆ Assignments of the contract cannot be made without the client's consent.

◆ No provision can attempt to waive compliance with the Act or limit the adviser's fiduciary obligations.

◆ Provisions that attempt to have the client waive any available right of action against the investment adviser (Hedge Clauses) are disallowed. It is not possible to limit the adviser's liability for losses, and it is not permitted to require a client to submit controversies to arbitration.[25]

Take time to review the contract carefully with clients. It may be tempting to skip to the last page and just have the client sign on the dotted line. However, it is better to review the main points and have the clients initial the paragraphs as you go along. This is a great defensive tactic if you are ever sued. Clients may allege you did not tell them they were free to implement their investments with another broker-dealer. You can turn to the contract where it clearly states that is the case and note they have their initials in the margins, signifying they have read and understood the paragraph. This documentation is usually the end of any lawsuit.

Other Regulations

OTHER IMPORTANT RULES and regulations with which you should be familiar are covered below.

◆ **Custody of Securities.** RIAs who have custody or possession of client securities or funds are subject to extensive additional regulation and a far higher level of scrutiny by the SEC. This scrutiny includes more frequent audits because the SEC has determined that most of the fraud and deceit involving clients was committed in these situations.[26] If you do have custody or possession of client securities or funds, every year you will be required to hire a CPA to do a surprise audit and file an additional form with the SEC.

Do not make arrangements that allow you access to client funds. Clandestine borrowing from clients can also lead to trouble. Typically the RIA thinks to himself, "I will pay the money back with a high rate of interest." What started out as a borrowing arrangement becomes theft. Keep your hands out of clients' money and save yourself a lot of trouble.

◆ **Solicitor Rules and Finder's Fees.** Registered investment advisers are prohibited from making cash payments for finder's fees or referrals, unless the client has been informed of the terms of the referral fee and is also notified of the extent the referral fee will affect advisory fees.[27] The person making the referral, known as the solicitor, must have a written agreement with the adviser and must not be subject to court or administrative sanction.[28] This requirement prevents advisers who have been disciplined from being compensated for referring former clients to another adviser.[29] The solicitor is required to present a separate brochure outlining the referral arrangement, including the exact nature of the compensation and whether the client will be charged for the solicitor's service in addition to any advisory fee paid.[30] The prospect must sign and date a brochure delivery receipt, and the adviser is responsible for ensuring the solicitor meets all legal requirements.[31] Registered representatives should check with their broker-dealer compliance department to determine if commissions can be shared with solicitors who do not have securities licenses with the same broker-dealer. Also, solicitors should review the nature and extent of their activities in light of the distinction the SEC makes between impersonal and personal advisory activities.

DILEMMA

PRISCILLA PLANNER HAS a great relationship with Carla CPA. Carla calls Priscilla and offers to refer a big financial planning case to Priscilla. Carla also requests a portion of Priscilla's fee as a finder's fee. This is the first time Carla has done this.

Question: Should Priscilla agree to this arrangement?

Answer: Probably not. It would require amending Priscilla's ADV, obtaining a separate brochure for Carla, and advising the client of the referral fee. This may not be illegal, if done properly, but it certainly looks bad. The best suggestion: If Carla is helping to prepare any accounting documents needed for the plan, she should charge the client separately for these accounting services.

DILEMMA

JOHANNA PLANNER WANTS to perform services for the client whereby she will receive 25 percent of the increase in the client's assets between January 1 and December 31. If the client's assets decline in value, Johanna will receive nothing.

Question: Is this permissible?

Answer: It is absolutely prohibited under the Act, unless the amount exceeds $500,000 or the client's net worth exceeds $1,000,000.[32]

JOHANNA PLANNER proposes to charge her client 2 percent of his entire portfolio, which she will manage, as of December 31.

Question: Is this legal?

Answer: Yes. If the client's portfolio increases, Johanna's fees will increase. Likewise, if the client's assets decline, the percentage will also affect Johanna's fees.

◆ **Use Of Terms.** It is unlawful to use the term "investment counsel" unless the RIA's principal business consists of acting as an investment adviser. A substantial portion of the business must consist of providing investment supervisory services and continuous investment advice based on the individual needs of each client.[33]

The SEC staff believes it may be misleading for advisers to use the initials RIA or R.I.A. after their names because it may suggest an adviser has achieved a degree or licensed professional position requiring certain qualifications.[34] However, it is permissible to spell out the terms "Registered Investment Adviser" on business cards and letterheads, as long as the title is attached to the registered name—whether it is a corporation or sole proprietor. Consequently, Jane Doe, CFP, CLU, RIA, would be in violation. However, if she is registered as a sole proprietor, it would be permissible to state: Jane Doe, CFP, CLU, Registered Investment Adviser. If Jane is registered as Doe Financial Advisory, she could not use the phrase "Registered Investment Adviser" after her own name. It would be acceptable to list Doe Financial Advisory, Registered Investment Adviser.

◆ **Compliance Manual.** Many RIAs may not be aware that they are required to have a dedicated compliance manual for the RIA. It will not suffice to rely on the one provided by your broker-dealer, as not all the issues and requirements are the same. In effect, when you become your own RIA, you must also assume the duties of being your own compliance officer. Many people may not want to take on these responsibilities and, for that reason, they will affiliate with another RIA or with one provided through their broker-dealer.

New Regulations

THE 1996 COORDINATION ACT, first discussed in Chapter 2, not only affects the registration of investment advisers but also the operation of their businesses. In the long run it appears that all investment advisers will be subject to much more stringent and aggressive compliance supervision. Even for those investment advisers who only need to be registered with the SEC, the states will still maintain jurisdiction over them in the areas of fraud, criminality, major abuses, notice filings, and fees.

One very positive attribute of the new law is that it eliminates confusion over books, record keeping, and bond requirements. Under the new law, no additional state may impose more strenuous book or record keeping requirements or have higher bond requirements than those already required by the adviser's home state's laws and regulations. If advisers are domiciled in a state with easier record keeping rules or bonding requirements and they want to practice in a state with stricter rules, the stricter rules cannot be applied to them unless they have a place of business in the second state.

One negative attribute for many investment advisers is that those who are not SEC registered may not be able to have any ERISA qualified plans as advisory clients after October 1998. ERISA currently states it is unlawful for anyone to provide investment advice to a qualified plan unless the practitioner is registered as an investment adviser with the SEC "or under the laws of any state." The state provision was written to expire in 1998 in order to give the congressional committees with jurisdiction over ERISA issues time to review its impact under the 1996 Coordination Act.

As attorney and RIA expert Jeffrey Kelvin observed, the law does distinguish between the "big boys" and the "little guys." The "little guys" will lose the prestige of being able to state they are an SEC investment adviser, and if the ERISA laws are not changed in 1998, only "the big boys" will be able to play in the ERISA market. This is a marketing and psychological advantage for the bigger firms.

While not disputing this position, Dale E. Brown of IAFP asserts the many benefits of the 1996 Coordination Act outweigh the concerns. Brown notes the national *de minimis* standard and the simplifying of bookkeeping, bonding, and record keeping requirements between states will greatly reduce confusing and duplicative paperwork for all RIAs. This is especially helpful for smaller firms.

ACTION ITEMS

◆ AS FAILURE TO PROVIDE clients with a brochure is one of the major problems uncovered by an SEC inspection,[35] use a brochure receipt or checklist to note in your file that proper delivery of the brochure was made. Annually you can create a memo to the file that details all clients to whom you made the offer and who requested the brochure. This can be done by attaching a form letter to your list of clients and highlighting those who responded to the request.[36]

◆ CONTACT THE FOLLOWING for more information on how the 1996 Coordination Act will affect your practice:
—IAFP members may contact their association at

(800) 945-4237 or on the Web at www.iafp.org. Members may also obtain a copy of the final six-page Bill by calling (888) IAFP-FAX and requesting document #3043. For a three-page section-by-section analysis of the Bill, request document #3044. For a three-page summary of the final rules implementing the Act, request document #3055.

—CFP licensees may contact the CFP Board of Standards at (800) 433-4292.

—The SEC's Web site (www.sec.gov) has a great deal of information on all aspects of investment adviser rules.

—Jeffrey Kelvin has put together a detailed and comprehensive manual to answer questions about the new law and help RIAs remain in compliance. You can contact him directly at Financial Planners Assistance, Plymouth Meeting, Pennsylvania (610-825-9008) for more information.

The author is grateful to Jeffrey Kelvin and Dale E. Brown for their considerable assistance in preparing this chapter.

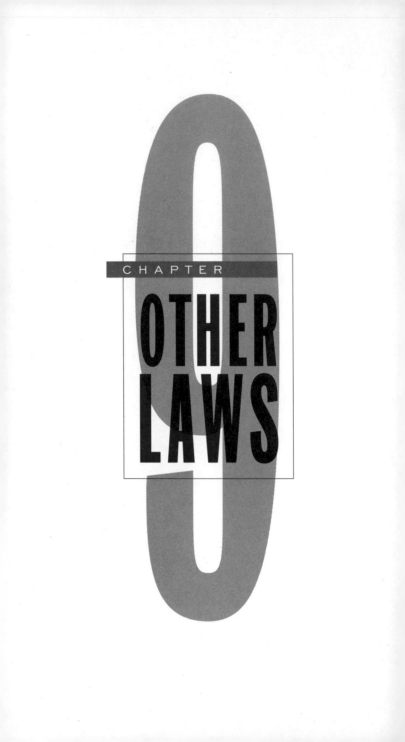

CHAPTER

OTHER LAWS

THERE IS NO END to the ways financial advisers can get into trouble or to the rules and regulations they must follow. This chapter reviews print and electronic advertising rules, the evolving field of Internet communications, the complexity of living trust regulations, important aspects of the Uniform Prudent Investor Act, and telemarketing violations and sales incentives.

Advertising Rules

WHETHER YOU REALIZE it or not, every day you are using some form of advertising to promote yourself and your services and products. Most of us think of advertising as the process of making any public announcement that is intended to directly or indirectly aid in the promotion of our services or products. In an industry as heavily regulated as financial services, it is not surprising to note NASD, SEC, and most states have enacted definitions about advertising that affect your practice by expanding on the traditional definition.

NAIC's definition of "advertisement" includes everything that is said and done before, during, and after the sale of insurance. It even includes material used to create public interest in life insurance and annuities and can include the training material used to teach agents.[1]

Advertising should always be presented in a fair and nonmisleading way. NASD's advertising rules for its members and registered representatives were constructed to ensure that all communications are based on principles of fair dealing and good faith. The NASD definition of advertising[2] is expansively construed to include letters, business cards, and many items most people would not consider to be advertising.

Many new representatives may not realize that every piece of advertising must be filed with NASD in advance, a chore usually performed by the home office compliance department. The compliance department will then require representatives to use only materials that have successfully passed their screens. Although NASD does not technically approve materials submitted to it for review, they will return them to the broker-dealer or product sponsor with suggestions for changes. They also identify statements they feel are inappropriate.[3] Needless to say, all firms follow the suggestions. NASD requires sales material to be kept for three years.[4]

If you are a registered representative, that information, along with the address of your broker-dealer, must be included on your letterhead and business cards. Your company affiliation must also be communicated to the public in all your advertising pieces, such as brochures, videos, or tapes. If you use different stationery for different aspects of your business, make sure your office procedures and compliance manual describe when each letterhead is to be used.

The advertising rules violated most frequently, and whose violation is hardest to prove, involve showing clients literature that has not been approved. Many financial advisers and stockbrokers are familiar with statements across the bottom of certain investment information such as "for broker-dealer use only, not to be distributed to clients." Even though it is strictly prohibited, it is not unusual for managing executives to train new representatives to show this information to the clients but not leave them copies.

Sometimes an overzealous stockbroker or adviser will try to sell a new fund by handing a client a newspaper article describing a particular mutual fund's ranking or touting its manager. This sales practice is strictly prohibited under NASD rules, unless the materials have been routed through the mutual fund company's legal department, approved by NASD, and approved by the broker-dealer's compliance department. In that case, the material should be clearly labeled as approved for client distribution.

DILEMMA

RITA REGISTERED REP is recommending a new fund to Sally, a very savvy investor. Sally requests copies of magazine articles before making a decision. Rita copies the appropriate pages and gives them to Sally.

Question: Has Rita violated any rules?

Answer: As this literature was not filed with NASD or approved by her broker-dealer, it is a technical violation. Incidentally, the mutual fund could have asked to have the information approved. It is entirely possible that it would have passed muster and then been appropriate for distribution. How can you tell? On the bottom of pieces, look for information stating they are supplied by the product sponsor; this allows you to distribute them to clients.

Many states have developed their own advertising rules covering both securities and insurance. Some state laws also require advertisements for securities or insurance be approved prior to public dissemination. Advertising rules for RIAs were discussed in the previous chapter.

Internet Communications

USING THE INTERNET to take your business into the 21st century can activate a number of different regulations on both the federal and state levels. The issues are complex and evolving as the paper-full financial industry tries to catch up with the paperless high-tech society.

Perhaps the mind-set of most regulators about the Internet and electronic communications is summed up by Melanie Lubin, Maryland Assistant Attorney General, who stated: "I'm not all that concerned with the methods through which the information is transmitted. Our concerns are: Are the people meeting the definition of an investment adviser, and are they doing what they are supposed to do under the statutes?" Her office is actively monitoring the Internet for compliance. If the Attorney General's office identifies people who are providing services, they investigate them in the same manner as someone advertising in the newspaper or yellow pages.[5]

Three main Internet issues are reviewed here: advertising, advice/registration, and electronic mail. Because of the evolving nature of the electronic industry, NASD is continuing to review these areas and the current regulations governing them.

ADVERTISING In 1995, NASD amended the definitions of advertisement and sales literature to include electronic messages provided by member firms and their registered representatives. The definition and rules are not meant to apply to communications by the general public.[6] Advertising on the Internet may take a number of different forms: a home page that expands upon a traditional business card, a bulletin board listing, or more elaborate advertisements for securities and personal financial services.

Many firms have not clearly thought through the issues of advertising on the Internet. For instance, a boilerplate column on portfolio diversification or the advantages of investing in mutual funds may be easy to place on a Web page. However, if it lists a name to contact for more information, it could be construed as advertising, triggering numerous regulatory violations. Unwitting financial advisers could find they have not only violated the advertising rules of their own state with their home pages or informational columns, but also the rules of 49 other states, NASD, SEC, and even some foreign countries.

To clarify this rapidly changing area, NASD reminded broker-dealers they have the same obligations communicating on the Internet, or with other electronic means such as audio- and videotapes, as they do using traditional paper letters, brochures, and prospectuses. This is especially true regarding advertising and sales literature, which is already subject to extensive regulation.

Without question, the NASD Rules of Fair Practice, SEC regulations, and state rules all apply to the burgeoning domain known as cyberspace.[7] As this area is not yet clearly defined but has a large potential for problems, some firms have advised their brokers not to do any soliciting on the Internet until all the legal and regulatory issues have been resolved.[8]

The following is a brief review of how various advertising rules can come into play on the Internet.

◆ **Bulletin boards.** NASD has stated that communications posted by members or their representatives on electronic bulletin boards are considered to be advertisements because the material can be viewed by anyone with access to the service. Consequently, a registered principal must review and approve all Internet advertisements before they are posted. Depending on the content, electronic bulletin board messages may be subject to filing with NASD under existing advertising rules.[9]

◆ **World Wide Web (WWW) sites.** A registered representative or broker-dealer who establishes a Web site is subject to the existing standards for communications with the public currently listed in Article III, Section 35 of the NASD Rules of Fair Practice, in addition to relevant SEC rules. As a result, any advertising on the Internet is subject to existing approval, record keeping, and filing requirements. Currently there are no separate guidelines on preparing sales material for the Internet.[10]

DILEMMA

PHYLLIS IS ONLY REGISTERED as an RIA in her home state and with the SEC. She puts a home page on the WWW which discusses the pros and cons of using variable annuities and invites people who have questions to call her office. She is careful to state her page is only directed at people in her home state and she is not licensed to do business outside the state.

Question: Is she safe?

Answer: Probably not. It is possible that another state regulator could construe this as an advertisement for rendering services in another state and cite her for failing to register. Disclaimers may not be effective when the obvious intent is to solicit business.

◆ **Chat rooms.** NASD does not generally consider exchanging information in chat rooms to be advertising or sales literature. Nevertheless, registered representatives must remember they are accountable under the Rules of Fair Practice as well as state and federal securities laws for what they say regarding securities products or services while participating in chat rooms. This means misleading or fraudulent statements are strictly prohibited. [11]

DILEMMA

PHYLLIS PLANNER is an RR/RIA and likes to spend her evenings in chat rooms. She goes by the name Wall Street Whiz Kid and is frequently asked for advice on hot new stock issues, market timing, and general trends.

Question: Has she violated any laws?

Answer: Assuming none of these people become her clients, she receives no compensation for this advice, and does not make any false and misleading comments, she has probably not violated any laws.

DILEMMA

PHYLLIS IS AN investment adviser to Better Profits, Inc., which she knows is about to land a $2 billion deal with Microsoft. She tells everyone in the chat room they should go long on Better Profits. They do and they make a bundle.

Question: Has she violated any rules?

Answer: This looks likes a violation of the insider trading rules.

◆ **Content on the Internet.** NASD may require members to repeat material disclosure and disclaimers, such as risk disclosures, in different sections of a Web site in order to ensure this information is available to all potential users. This is especially important because an Internet user can navigate the WWW by skipping from section to section.[12]

Material that is listed for broker-dealer use only cannot be used on the Internet unless the broker-dealer can control access so that only registered persons may receive it. Broker-dealers or representatives who provide their own Web pages could find themselves responsible for the content of sites that are linked to theirs even if created by an outside third party. NASD warned members not to link to sites when the member knows the site contains misleading information. In short, members and representatives must exercise the same care in choosing links to Internet sites as they would in referring customers to any outside source of information. NASD will also want to review the information from the linked site.[13]

Your broker-dealer can be your best advocate. A Florida-based broker-dealer recently received approval from New Jersey, North Dakota, and South Dakota for a Web site featuring its registered representatives and investment advisers. The three states based their approval contingent on a series of checkpoints that allow site visitors access to the information only if the registered representatives and investment advisers are properly registered to do business in their states, the pages have the necessary disclaimers, and the site also receives prior approval as required for other types of advertising.[14] This kind of negotiation may be easier for broker-dealers who have the staff and resources available to meet individual state requirements.

ADVICE/REGISTRATION The second major issue involves giving advice over the Internet and whether this will necessitate registering as an investment adviser. This may be free advice through discussion groups and chat rooms, or, in certain cases, an online service may be compensating the adviser for providing free counsel to other users.

Counselors and advisers who are providing advice and who are compensated either by the online service or by future business from those they meet on the Internet will be subject to current regulatory requirements for registering as an investment adviser and registered representative. These seemingly innocent activities can have widespread consequences for planners and advisers who suddenly find they must be complying with the laws of all 50 states and the SEC.

NASAA has cautioned broker-dealers and investment advisers to apply the current rules on business activities to business conducted through electronic means. The borderless nature of the Internet may require securing additional registrations before conducting any business. [15]

ELECTRONIC MAIL The final issue, communicating by e-mail, is treated differently by NASD, depending on whether the messages are broadcast or sent to a single individual.

◆ **Broadcasted.** Identical electronic messages sent to multiple individuals, or broadcast e-mail, may include form letters, brochures, research reports, and market commentary. They are considered sales literature, and consequently must have advance written approval by a registered principal. Based on the content, the information in a broadcast e-mail may also have to be filed with NASD. [16]

◆ **Individualized.** Although it is permissible to use e-mail in lieu of written correspondence, when these letters pertain to the solicitation or the execution of securities transactions, existing rules require they must be reviewed and endorsed by a registered principal.

Unlike advertising and sales literature, principals may review this correspondence after it has been sent. Although NASD sales literature filing requirements do not apply to individual e-mail communications, e-mail messages must comply with the content standards included in Article III, Section 35 of the Rules of Fair Practice, as well as any other applicable rules, including those on misleading or fraudulent statements.[17] State regulators are beginning to regulate this area, too. The state of Arizona addressed e-mail by declaring that the definition of advertising would no longer include electronically transmitted communications designated by RIAs for access by only one person.[18]

A recent SEC release explained it is the staff's belief that the Internet, online services, electronic mail, and documents stored on disk are all acceptable means of communicating information required under the Securities Exchange Act of 1933 and the Investment Advisers Act of 1940. However, certain conditions must be met. One major issue is proof of delivery. When a paper copy is sent to an individual, a financial adviser has reasonable assurance that the document will arrive and the recipient will view it. When using electronic means, the following areas need to be considered: delivery method agreements, ensuring confidentiality, and proof that a possible supplemental notification of document delivery exists.[19] The SEC expects a paper version of any electronic document to be available upon request.[20]

Living Trust Regulations

LIVING TRUSTS HAVE BEEN hot items among retirees for the last few years. In some states, such as Florida, having one has become a status symbol.

Although they may go under a number of different names, including loving trusts, a living trust is merely a legal device consisting of a grantor who transfers assets to a trust to be managed by a trustee for the benefit of a beneficiary. *Living* means the trust came into existence during the grantor's lifetime. Trusts that come about at death are called testamentary trusts.

All too frequently, these trusts are sold in a slick manner during seminars that instill fear in the prospects. The unscrupulous tend to prey upon older clients who are concerned about high attorney fees, long delays in probate, and high estate taxes. Of course, not all people who promote living trusts are unscrupulous. A number of companies furnish professional slides and scripts for planners and agents to assist them in presentations for living trusts.

In 1990, one state simultaneously censured and publicly reprimanded 33 insurance agents/financial planners for selling living trusts to senior citizens. The state department of commerce found they had misrepresented the probate and the trust's tax advantages. After noting that the department had received an unusually large number of complaints about living trusts, the Commissioner said, "I am certain this is the tip of the iceberg."[21]

A letter by the Wisconsin Department of Insurance to all of its insurance agents warned that the Commissioner's office had received many complaints from consumers about living trusts. The department went on to state that illegal and improper practices may be the basis for action to revoke or suspend an agent's license. It found the complaints usually fell into these categories: misrepresentation by the agent during the solicitation; high pressure sales tactics; excessive prices; failure of the trust to comply with Wisconsin laws; and preparation of legal documents without an attorney.

Without going into all the pros and cons of living trusts, there are certain occasions when living trusts are very appropriate. They can be particularly useful when the trust holds individual stocks and bonds. This enables the trustee to immediately trade these securities on the death of the grantor. Regrettably, an executor of a will may have to watch the market fall while waiting for authority from the probate court to sell. However, living trusts can be oversold, many times to the client's detriment.

Key living trust problem areas to be avoided by planners and other financial advisers are described below.

◆ **Practicing law without a license.** Financial advisers who are providing clients with boilerplate documents or books on the subject may find themselves actually practicing law. This is almost always a criminal violation and can subject the violator to jail time and fines.

DILEMMA

ALICIA ADVISER IS meeting with her new client, Big George, who owns Big George's Barbeque. George has many estate planning issues: creditors hounding him, problems with firing a longtime employee, and limited resources to pay for advice.

Alicia tells George: "I can help you with most of these issues, and because I am being compensated by commissions on the investments you are putting into your pension plan, you will not owe me any fees. You need a living trust with spend-thrift provisions. That will solve your estate planning concerns and protect your assets from creditors. I will help you draft the documents using a form book that has worked well with my other clients. Also, I will draft you a letter firing your employee. One of my friends had an attorney create one for her. We can just retype it for you and it will avoid any discrimination lawsuits."

Question: Is this legal?

Answer: Alicia is definitely over the line for a number of reasons. Not collecting a special fee for this advice will not save her. Alicia helped draft legal documents, the trust and the letter, without a license to practice law. George could have created these documents himself. Otherwise, generally only licensed attorneys can perform this function. Alicia also gave legal advice about avoiding creditors and creating an estate plan. Another area to avoid.

If Alicia had been George's neighbor, this kind of situation might go unnoticed. After all, why would George ever complain? However, Alicia has a much higher duty and more exposure as a financial adviser. If the investments lose money, all of Alicia's advice will be scrutinized and these improprieties will come to the surface. They can form additional grounds to sue.

◆ **Referral commissions.** A small percentage of insurance agents focus their entire business on selling living trusts. Frequently, they work with an attorney who does a seminar presentation. The agent closes the sale and receives commissions on each trust sold. Perhaps the agents are unaware this arrangement is illegal from every perspective. The attorney is not allowed by the canon of ethics to share legal fees with anyone other than another attorney and, in most states, only with an attorney within the same firm. The insurance agent, on the other hand, could be construed as practicing law without a license, as the agent was being compensated for legal advice. The entire situation is one big malpractice suit and criminal action just waiting to happen.

◆ **Erroneous advice.** Like many areas in the practice of financial planning, estate planning is extremely complicated. Because of the large number of claims, attorneys who practice in the area have one of the highest charges for malpractice insurance. Consequently, even the most astute financial adviser or estate planner may have trouble understanding living trusts thoroughly. This raises the risk of the financial adviser giving the client erroneous advice. One of the worst things a planner or adviser can do is state to the client, "You must have a living trust."

◆ **Complicating the estate.** When a living trust is done properly, it can frequently be a great advantage to a client. When done improperly, it can greatly complicate, rather than simplify, the estate, creating a quagmire of expensive problems. Regrettably, clients will need an attorney to straighten out the mess, increasing the very costs they were trying to reduce.

◆ **Using inappropriate forms.** Ads for generic living trust forms stating they are "legal in every state" are becoming increasingly common. Unsuspecting consumers do not realize the forms can be out of date in short order, with state legislatures in session almost daily and laws changing minute by minute. Newly reported cases can also change the impact of the law or the wording on the forms. Even if the forms are up to date, because of the technical nature of this business, it is not unusual to see cases where the wrong form was selected for use. Properly drafted documents will save clients money and frustration in the long run.

◆ **Leaving assets outside the estate.** Another common situation is a properly drawn living trust in which the clients, who may have drafted the document themselves, fail to transfer all the assets to the trust. As the assets are outside the trust, they will pass through probate and be subject to all the problems the client was trying to avoid.

The Uniform Prudent Investor Act

OVER THE LAST 30 YEARS the investment practices of trustees have changed dramatically. Formerly limited to legal lists, most trustees were charged with the responsibility of preserving capital and producing modest income. The advent of modern portfolio theory has changed the playing field. One trustee, a business owner who had sponsored a qualified plan, was recently held accountable for being too conservative. Most of the plan assets were held in treasuries earning a safe 7 percent annual return. However, when the bull market gained 13 percent per year, the trustee was held personally responsible for the shortfall.[22]

UPIA sought to update trust investment law and trustees' responsibilities in recognition of the many changes that have occurred in modern investment practice. This Act, also known as the Restatement (Third) of Trusts: Prudent Investor Rule (1992), has been adopted and modified by many states to cover the activities of trustees.

UPIA makes five fundamental changes in the former criteria for defining prudent investing for trustees:[23]

1 Whether or not an investment meets the proper standard of prudence will be determined by looking at the entire portfolio rather than specific or individual investments. The term "portfolio" in the Act includes all the trust's assets.

2 The fiduciary's central consideration is balancing investment return with risk.

3 There are no longer categorical restrictions on types of investments. Consequently, a trustee can invest in anything that might appropriately achieve the objectives of the trust and meet other requirements of prudent investing.

4 Now integrated into the definition of prudent investing is the familiar requirement that fiduciaries diversify their investments.

5 The previous rule of trust law forbidding a trustee to delegate investment and management functions has been reversed. Delegation is now not only permitted, subject to certain safeguards, but may be required for an inexperienced trustee.

Although UPIA was primarily concerned with the

investment responsibilities arising under the private gratuitous trust, the common vehicle for transferring wealth within a family, its rules also apply to charitable and pension trusts, among others.[24] The provisions in the Act also apply to ERISA trustees and can easily be extended to other fiduciaries such as executors, conservators, and guardians.[25] Although the Act does not specifically address the fiduciary responsibilities of financial planners or RIAs when they are not acting on behalf of a trust, it is possible that in the future this Act will be used to determine a standard of care for those activities.

Finally, UPIA does not create remedies or methods for computing damages in trust matters. The drafters of the Act felt that remedies and damages were already the subject of other laws.[26]

The practice of a financial planner or adviser is affected in a number of ways by this Act. First, it provides a higher and more complicated standard of care.[27] Second, planners and advisers who advise trustees must emphasize total returns as it is now necessary to preserve purchasing power as well as preserve capital. Third, trustees are now able to avoid hindsight micromanagement of individual investments because they are not penalized for a single underperforming investment but rather for an inappropriate overall investment mix.

Although there are certain duties a fiduciary will not be able to delegate, such as timing and the amount of distributions to beneficiaries, fiduciaries will be able to delegate investment responsibility and avoid their own personal liability. For inexperienced trustees it will become an obligation to select a professional for assistance with investment advice. Trustees will probably be able to escape liability if they conscientiously choose competent and reputable advisers and monitor them carefully.

Telemarketing Law Violations

AS OF JUNE 9, 1995, ALL brokerage firms are required to establish policies and procedures to protect investors from unsolicited phone calls. This rule was part of a proposal by NASD to the SEC requiring brokerage firms to set up procedures for central do-not-call lists. The list includes investors whom the firm has already approached and who asked not to be called again. [28]

The Telephone Consumer Protection Act of 1991 already limited telemarketing activities for many firms. The Act prohibits interstate telephone calls to deliver a recorded commercial message without the prior consent of the party called. The Act also requires telemarketers to maintain a do-not-call list.

Sales Incentives

AN AREA THAT IS just starting to get media attention is the longtime industry practice of offering sales incentives to brokers as a way of motivating them to recommend particular products. These incentives can be trips, prizes, cash bonuses, or increased commissions for selling proprietary products. "[A particular insurance company] showed us how sales contests and paying higher commissions for in-house products led brokers to sell customers unsuitable products," says Idaho State Securities Commissioner Wayne Klein. "These sales techniques . . . put the integrity of the industry at risk." [29]

There are at least two issues here for the professional financial adviser: one is disclosure, and the other is the client's reaction to the practice.

First, SEC disclosure requirements for investment advisers, and the laws of many states, require that all forms of compensation must be disclosed to clients. This is also a requirement for CFP licensees who prepare financial plans. In practice, this information is rarely, if ever, disclosed. Failure to disclose could lead to sanctions by regulators or provide ammunition for an unhappy client to sue you.

Second, and equally important, is the mind-set of the client. According to *Business Week*, one public opinion poll found only politicians and lawyers ranked lower than brokers. [30] What does the practice of accepting sales incentives do to your personal reputation and to the reputation of the industry? Ask yourself this question: What would my client think of me if she knew I would be getting a trip to Disneyland for recommending this investment? Most of us must honestly report that clients do not like it. They feel deceived and believe they are not getting unbiased advice.

Although disclosure resolves some of these issues, it does not get to the essence of the practice itself: selling products that otherwise would not be sold. "I know my proprietary sales went down when we removed the differentials," says a [large wire house] executive. "That tells you there was a bias." [31] Although many firms would like to abandon the practice, they have found that pressure from the competition forces them to keep offering incentives.

ACTION ITEMS

◆ FOR YOUR OWN PROTECTION, make it a practice never to give clients any items that have not been cleared by your compliance department. Make a note in your file listing the advertising items given to the client and keep copies of the advertisements on file for easy reference. If you are using third party materials or software, make sure they have been passed by NASD. Get a response from the supplier in writing and keep it in the event of an audit. Check with your broker-dealer, insurance home office, or RIA to see if in-house rules on advertising are available.

◆ HAVE YOUR REGISTERED principal approve all your advertisements. Save these documents and their approval dates.

◆ HAVE ANY MATERIAL THAT could possibly be construed as advertising, including all Internet sites, columns, and even data transmitted by computer diskette, CD-ROM, or tape, approved by your compliance department or an experienced law firm.

◆ WHEN IT COMES TO Web sites designed to promote your brokerage or insurance business, let your home office negotiate with state regulators and NASD for approval.

◆ GET A WRITTEN POLICY statement from your compliance department about using e-mail and transmitting confidential client data electronically by diskette, CD-ROM, or other means.

◆ IF, AFTER DUE CONSIDERATION, you believe a living trust might be appropriate for your client, be careful how you present this recommendation. The best course of action is to say: "Mrs. Client, you may be a candidate for a living trust. Let's talk to an attorney who specializes in estate planning to see if it makes sense for you." This kind of recommendation takes the burden off your shoulders and puts it on the attorney to make a recommendation in the best interest of the client. Naturally, if you are making a personal recommendation as to which attorney to choose in this situation, check the attorney out carefully first. Make sure the attorney you recommend will give very balanced advice about living trusts and is not one of the few who believe these trusts are the answer to all of life's problems.

◆ FINANCIAL PLANNERS and advisers should approach serving as a trustee with extreme caution. The increased responsibilities of a trustee may demand that financial consultants limit their role to acting as an adviser only. If they do serve as a trustee, planners would be advised to retain as a co-trustee a substantial financial institution with deep pockets and liability insurance. [32]

◆ PLANNERS AND ADVISERS should advise clients who are fiduciaries of the importance of careful, ongoing documentation of their investment activities and rationale in order to comply with the requirements to invest prudently.

◆ IF YOU ARE NOT CURRENTLY disclosing sales incentive information to your clients, there is a good chance you are required to do so. Check with the appropriate regulators and adjust your disclosure statements accordingly. Better still, bite the bullet and decline the sales incentives; you will sleep better tonight.

◆ CONTACT YOUR BROKER-DEALER and your major insurance carriers to ask them what telemarketing activities are appropriate and legal.

SECTION

THREE

GOING ON THE OFFENSE

WITH ANY UNDERTAKING, an early and decisive offense can make the difference between victory and defeat. This section reviews a two-pronged approach to avoiding litigation:

1 Keep clients happy. You do this by identifying—and sometimes managing—their expectations and then meeting or exceeding them. Constant two-way communication is the prime method for ensuring that you understand your clients and that they are aware of what you are doing to satisfy their needs.

2 Construct a well-documented paper trail. This means establishing a written communication system and having your files and documents in good order.

CHAPTER

PRODUCT
AND
SERVICE
PROVIDERS

10

A WORLD-CLASS FINANCIAL adviser not only provides top-quality service but also outstanding products. Your clients trust you to pick the best: the best broker-dealer, the best insurance companies, the best asset managers, and the best investments. Sometimes, this means you are a middleman. Even the most ethical, educated, and communicative advisers can still fail to serve clients properly if they have chosen inferior product or service providers. The first step in going on the offensive is to make sure your "shop is clean" before you open the door. To protect your clients and yourself, this chapter provides guidelines on how to choose the best.

Back Office Checklist

BROKER-DEALERS AND insurance companies can vary greatly in their corporate philosophies. Some firms believe in standing squarely behind their representatives and agents. If a client files a complaint, these companies will support the representative or agent and even provide free legal counsel. On the other hand, some firms step far away from any conflict and require the representative or agent to hire counsel. Know the kind of firm with which you are affiliated—it could save you or cost you at a later date.

Careful agents and representatives will spend far more time researching their broker-dealers and insurance companies than these companies spend trying to recruit and hire them. This business is so complex and fraught with danger, it makes sense to reduce the risk whenever possible. One way to do that is to affiliate only with top-ranked insurance companies and broker-dealers. There is no point in taking a risk on a lower-rated firm, particularly when even top-ranked firms have gone into receivership.

After the recent demise of several large insurance companies, it is important to be careful when choosing insurance companies and products. The days are past when agents can simply rely on an *A.M. Best* top rating. Financial advisers should also be looking at *Weiss, Standard & Poor's, Duff and Phelps, Moody's,* and other firms ranking the financial strengths of insurance companies.

When investigating a broker-dealer or insurance company, be sure to cover these areas:

◆ **Financial soundness.** Clearly it is important to have broker-dealers and insurance companies who are going to be there today, tomorrow, next year, and thirty years from now, when your clients will still need them.

◆ **The due diligence department.** How carefully are

they reviewing the deals and products they approve to sell? Check to determine how many of their deals have gone bad. If it is a large percentage, there may be something wrong with their internal checks and due diligence.

◆ **Compliance.** Is there a home office support person who can assist representatives with compliance questions? Most advisers need answers that are a phone call away; they will not drive across town and try to do their own legal research. Does the firm make a point of tracking laws on a state-by-state basis and advising planners and representatives in that state how to protect themselves?

◆ **Support.** What kind of support can they give you? What is their legal department like? Are they available for phone calls if you have questions? Do they have attorneys, tax experts, and other consultants available?

◆ **Training.** What kind of training do they offer? How often and where? It may not be helpful if all the training sessions are thousands of miles away. Is it just sales training, or do they focus on the compliance issues that can save you time and lawsuits?

◆ **Claims.** How many lawsuits and claims have been filed against them by agents, registered representatives, or clients? What were the outcomes? What is their philosophy in handling claims? Do they support the representatives and agents, or do they expect them to hire an attorney on their own?

◆ **NASD.** Check with NASD and your state securities and insurance commissioners to see if the company has had many claims filed for compliance irregularities.

◆ **Payout.** What is their commission payout? If they are paying far in excess of what is standard in the industry, there may be something wrong. There are no free lunches in this business, and high payouts can mean they are skimping in other areas.

◆ **References.** Ask to speak with a planner, broker, or agent who has been with them for five years or more.

Find out what these people like and, more important, what they do not like about the firm. Be sure to ask if they know of any brokers or agents who have been sued. What was the response of the home office? Is the firm supportive if a client makes a complaint, or do they stand back and force you to pay for all the legal work yourself?

◆ **Wholesalers.** Are wholesalers screened to present what can go wrong as well as right with an investment?

Supervisor Checklist

SOMETIMES YOU MAY START with selecting a particular managing executive or supervising principal before selecting a broker-dealer or insurance company. Once you have found the person that fits your needs, you will automatically be working with their broker-dealer. On the other hand, you may first choose a broker-dealer or insurance company, and then you may have the opportunity to select a particular person to supervise your brokerage, insurance, or RIA activities.

Early on, you will be meeting with this supervisor in person. It is important to keep the dynamics of this interview in perspective. Most new registered representatives or insurance agents will be thinking this is a job interview and they will be trying to impress the principal or general agent in order to be "hired." In fact, these people are frequently sales managers and will probably be looking for a top sales performer. Whether you are new to the industry or a seasoned veteran, always remember these professionals receive a percentage of all business you bring to the firm. They should be trying to impress you with their integrity, service, products, and expertise.

Take the time to interview prospective supervisors carefully. While they are looking for a good salesperson, you need to be screening for an ethical mentor, an experienced professional who can assist you in making your business profitable, steer you past regulatory potholes, and help you avoid lawsuits. You will never have more power than right now: the meeting before you sign on with a firm.

Arnie Abens of Abens Financial Services, Inc. in Edina, Minnesota, is just the kind of supervisor sought by brokers and planners. He epitomizes the phrase "running a clean shop." Use the guiding principles developed by Abens to start your search for someone of his caliber and philosophy.

◆ **Keep clients happy.** The best way to avoid a lawsuit is to keep clients happy by providing good service.

◆ **Read all prospectuses.** At first, Abens found it was time-consuming and tedious to read even one prospectus. Now he has become such an expert at it, review time is minimal. Today's prospectuses are better written and more "reader-friendly", and have become a tremendous sales tool for him.

◆ **Track NASD violations.** Abens follows the reports from NASD to see what areas NASD is focusing on to reprimand planners and advisers. Abens then develops ways to protect himself from violations in these areas.

◆ **Act in clients' best interests.** In all his dealings, Abens makes sure he is working for the client and not for himself.

◆ **Separate commissions from fees.** Abens makes it clear to clients he is paid a commission in order to put them into an investment product. This is entirely different from financial planning or asset management services, which are done for a flat fee or a fee related to the percentage of assets under management. He carefully explains the difference between these functions and roles.

◆ **Document every client interaction.** The Abens office is highly computer automated. He keeps notes on his computer of every conversation he has throughout the day. The computer file then creates a daily work list with deadlines so nothing falls through the cracks.

◆ **Review subordinates' recommendations.** As a manager, he reviews the recommendations of every planner in his network. Abens keeps track of their clients' goals and objectives, cross-checking them with a sales blotter to make sure his planners are recommending only suitable investments.

◆ **Document reasons for recommendations.** For every recommendation Abens makes, he carefully notes the reasons in the file. He says even if it turns out in retrospect his reasons were incorrect, courts will look at his thought process at the time of the recommendation to evaluate his level of due diligence.

◆ **Keep clients informed of their investments.** So clients have a clear picture of their portfolio performance, make sure they are receiving readable quarterly statements and reports from their RIA and broker (if permitted by the broker-dealer).

◆ **Pass the "Nightline" test.** Abens checks every client recommendation by the "Nightline" test. He never makes a proposal unless he feels he can justify it to Ted Koppel on national television.

◆ **Use a written risk tolerance questionnaire.** A questionnaire is used to carefully assess each client's tolerance for risk. The Abens questionnaire appears in Appendix B. In conclusion, Abens said, "If you do these things and always keep your clients' interests ahead of your own, clients should not sue you."[1]

RIA Affiliation

YOU MAY FIND YOU WANT to affiliate with an RIA rather than register on your own. If that is the case, the same kinds of suggestions made about broker-dealers, insurance companies, and supervisors also apply to your RIA selection.

◆ **Are you required to use their planning service,** or can you use your own? What is their policy on Section 40 business? Do they allow certain business away from the firm, such as no-load mutual fund business?

◆ **Have they ever been cited for any investment violations** through the SEC or their state securities department?

◆ **What are the credentials of the person** who reviews or develops the plans?

◆ **Finally, to be on the safe side, you may want to submit a dummy plan with some problems in it,** to see what kind of recommendations they would make. If their recommendations are always geared for the broker-dealer's products with the highest commission rates, this is probably not the firm for you.

Product Due Diligence

WHEN IT COMES TO DUE DILIGENCE, too often brokers and planners rely entirely on their broker-dealers to perform this service. Indeed, a selling point for many broker-dealers is their due diligence departments. Cautious representatives and planners want to make sure every investment is thoroughly inspected and reviewed by a competent group of attorneys, accountants, and due diligence experts. This may not always be the case, however, as many representatives and clients have discovered in recent years when some of these deals collapsed.

Lawsuits are not decided strictly on an investment's return at the time of the suit. Just because an investment goes bad does not mean a broker did something wrong and will be responsible to the client for damages. It is important for you to demonstrate the depth of your due diligence at the time you recommended the investment. Keep all your notes on your personal review, who you talked with, and how the numbers looked. You may want to attach these notes to the one copy of each prospectus you keep in your file for back-up. Good due diligence departments at your broker-dealer should be keeping the same kind of records.

Although planners are held to a higher ongoing standard of care than sales representatives, planners will not automatically lose a case just because an investment went down. The courts look at the facts you knew when you made the recommendation. Whether you are a planner or a broker, the courts want to know how carefully you investigated an investment before you recommended it to a client.

CHAPTER

THE

FIRST CLIENT MEETING

11

THE FIRST CLIENT MEETING is essential for establishing the framework you need to become a world-class adviser to your clients. This is where you begin building trust, ensuring client satisfaction, and creating a lifetime relationship.

As you go into the meeting, your overriding objective should be to identify expectations. This is critical. It lets clients know not only that you understand them and their concerns but also that you are serious about meeting their expectations. This all adds up to creating trust and demonstrating good ethical behavior—the key issue with most clients.

This chapter first focuses on ascertaining client expectations. Once you have identified these expectations, it reviews how you can start to use the information with a meeting agenda and disclosure statement. Finally, this chapter provides techniques for identifying ideal clients and avoiding difficult ones; this will not only protect your practice but also build your production.

Client Expectations

WHAT MOST FINANCIAL ADVISERS think clients want and what clients *really* want can be entirely different. Most brokers, planners, and advisers would probably list "returns" or "good advice" as the most important way to keep clients happy. However, a 1993 IAFP survey of consumers came to strikingly different conclusions. Of 1,000 adults, 53 percent said trust and ethical behavior were the most important elements in their relationship with a financial adviser. Only 24 percent listed "good advice" or "makes me money" as key factors. "Expertise" was most important to 18 percent, while only 9 percent considered "record of performance," or returns, as the critical factor.[1]

The first step in keeping clients happy is ascertaining their expectations. Clients have two types of expectations: spoken and unspoken. Most advisers do a good job of identifying the spoken expectations: rates of return, retirement income, or tax reduction strategies. It is the unspoken expectations that get most planners and advisers into trouble.

Unspoken expectations can be almost anything. In a straightforward case, the clients may have a deep need to trust their adviser and expect their adviser will take the initiative to explain why investments are going down. Others may be reluctant to admit it, but they are really looking for someone to arbitrate serious financial disputes between warring spouses. If they are busy professionals, they may expect you always to come to their offices on Saturday mornings. Explore what clients really want from your relationship. Do they want you to be an informal employee? A gofer? An extended-family member?

Your first meeting is a good time to explain how you work and the types of services you are able to provide. Be sure to ask them, "Will this meet your expectations?" Now is the time to find out.

Identifying all expectations, both spoken and unspoken, is the first step in building trust. If clients refuse to tell you what their spoken or obvious expectations are, it is unlikely that the relationship will be successful, no matter how conscientious your efforts. These clients are moving targets and will be impossible to satisfy, because you can never establish the criteria they need to feel comfortable and successful.

Questions to identify spoken or obvious expectations are probably already in your fact-finding materials. A few of these will include:

◆ What is your expected rate of return? Over what period of time?

◆ What level of risk is comfortable for you?

◆ Are you prepared to lose any money in order to meet your financial goals?

◆ What exactly are your goals?

◆ What is the best and worst investment you have ever made, and why?

◆ How often do you want to meet and where?

◆ How often do you want to hear from me?

◆ What should I do in an emergency if I cannot reach you?

◆ What concerns do you have about your finances, your future, and the future of your loved ones?

Getting at unspoken expectations is much harder. Clients may not have thought about these and may find them difficult to articulate. Use the following questions as a starting point to determine what really motivates your client to work with you.

◆ What do you expect of me as your adviser?

◆ A year from now, what will make you happy?

◆ What needs to happen in order for you to feel our relationship has been successful?

◆ What can I do to make this relationship more comfortable and satisfying for you?

◆ Have you had any previous financial advisers? How many? Why did you terminate the relationship?

◆ What did you like about the previous relationships? What would you have wanted to change?

◆ Have you ever been involved in litigation or arbitration? With a financial adviser? Tell me more. How many times? Be sure to ask about each case.

◆ If there is one thing I might do that would cause you to terminate our relationship, what would it be?

You will notice that some of these questions are the same, just rephrased. This is to help jog the client's mind to get at the deepest concerns. Make sure you write down each of these expectations, so you will always know the rules of the game. The more you ask, the better you will be able to identify expectations and the better you will know your client.

Meeting Agenda

AS EXPLAINED IN GREATER detail in the next two chapters, Ed Morrow has developed a software program called *Text Library System* that prints out forms for every phase of client contact. The form below is sent to prospective clients before the first meeting so they have seen the agenda for the day even before stepping into the office. Morrow has generously allowed this form to be printed in the sample letter below.

Date

Dear Mr. and Mrs. Client,

I look forward to meeting with you next Tuesday at 2 P.M. To help our meeting run smoothly and to ensure we cover all your areas of concern, I have listed an agenda below. Be sure to bring any documents you want me to review.

FIRST MEETING AGENDA

I. Overview
    A. Brief Review of the Financial Planning Process
    B. Participation of Spouse and Other Family Members
    C. Discuss Confidentiality of Information
    D. Review the Interview Notetaking Procedure

II. Review Data Gathering Forms and Documents
    A. Review Personal Information Booklet
    B. Discuss Employee Benefits and Career Path
    C. Investment Attitudes and Risk Tolerance
    D. Current Will and Estate Arrangements
    E. Attitude on Gifts to Children/Grandchildren
    F. Current Attitude towards Charitable Bequests
    G. Review any Documents and Information Still Needed
    H. Authorization Form Signed
    I. Social Security Audit Card Signed (if desired)

III. Review of Notes and Personal Objectives
    A. Anticipated Retirement Date, Location and Philosophy
    B. Estate Liquidity and Survivor Income Objectives
    C. Prioritize the Personal Objectives
    D. Education Goals for Self/Children/Grandchildren
    E. Review Other Personal Goals

IV. Our Next Steps and Your Next Steps
    A. Confirmation of Interview Notes

B. Confirmation of Planning Assumptions and Objectives

C. Confirmation of the Initial Data (By Interview or Phone)

D. Expected Timetable

Please call me right away if I have left anything out.

With warmest personal regards,

Ed Morrow

In addition, Morrow's *Text Library System* software prints a second form for the financial adviser. It contains reminders of points to be made at each step of the meeting and becomes a template for creating meeting notes.

For example, under I.A, Brief Review of the Financial Planning Process, there are the following notations: Insert materials or references you plan to make at this point. Ask if there are any concerns. Under III.B, Estate Liquidity and Income Objectives, he adds these notes to jog the adviser's memory: Special bequests. Charitable bequests. Survivial income needed for family and/or spouse. Would house be sold? Would other assets be sold? Special liabilities that must be paid at death?

Once the agenda and questions are established, it is easy to use the same format to create meeting notes. These notes can be given to the clients at the end of the meeting or mailed in a follow-up letter. For more information on sample documents, contact Morrow at (800) 666-1656.

Data Gathering

IN ADDITION TO DETERMINING client expectations, a large portion of the first meeting is devoted to data gathering and reviewing documents. Arnie Abens of Abens Financial Services, Inc. in Edina, Minnesota, has created a questionnaire to determine client risk levels and investment objectives and has generously allowed this questionnaire to be printed in Appendix B. With the information obtained from the replies, you will be able to confirm the client's investment temperament and develop the IPS, which is discussed in the next chapter.

There are numerous reasons to gather client data carefully. A well-documented and organized file is one of the best defenses against a suit by an unhappy client. Furthermore, NASD requires representatives to *know your clients,* and of course the best way to prove this is by making copious notes and memos in the file. It is also the evidence you need to prove that your invest-ment recommendations are suitable and that you have done a good job for your clients.

A good data-gathering sheet is the first step in acquiring client information and at the very least should provide these minimal details:

◆ The name, address, telephone number, and social security number of the client;

◆ Employment salary;

◆ Current investments and insurance;

◆ Assets and liabilities, in a balance sheet format;

◆ Monthly cash flow statement;

◆ The level of the client's education, as an aid in deter-mining level of sophistication;

◆ Investment goals and objectives;

◆ Risk tolerance levels;

◆ Short- and long-term goals; and

◆ Years of investment experience.

One way to prove you do know your client is to have the client sign the New Account Form and verify all the data. Although many New Account Forms do not require the client's signature, you should always ask the client to sign it. This can be a good way to prove you did ask these questions and you did not fabricate any answers. A well-prepared New Account Form is one of the best ways to defend a suitability claim.

CLIENT COMFORT ZONE Although NASD requires brokers to know their customers, there has been little discussion on what that actually means. It does mean more than just filling out a New Account Form. It also means knowing your clients' comfort zone. Do they like a lot of paperwork and numbers? Do they prefer the quick-and-dirty approach? If they are extremely analytical, a yellow pad plan is not going to satisfy them. They will want to see reams and reams of computer printouts before they are going to feel comfortable. Clients who thrive on the stress associated with high risk are usually not satisfied with safe but lower-performing investments. Conservative investments are outside their comfort zone. They need higher risk, higher-performing investments in order to feel comfortable.

In short, providing good-quality service first means figuring out who the clients are, what they really want, and then providing them with exactly what they want. This may be entirely different from what you think they need. Once clients are outside their comfort zone, they are much more likely to mistrust your recommendations and be unhappy with investment results. Keep clients comfortable by asking them questions like, "How does this feel to you? Does this make you feel comfortable?" Then probe for reasons why they feel that way.

Disclosure Forms

THE MORE YOU DISCLOSE to clients about your background, philosophy, and compensation, the happier they will be. A Gallup survey for the IAFP determined that 95 percent of the public wanted to know how their planners were being compensated and felt they should be informed in writing before any work was done. Also, 90 percent said advisers should be required to tell clients about their education, expertise, and training.[2] Although there is currently no requirement to disclose how much you are paid from insurance sales, it is important to let clients know if you do receive commissions from insurance or investments.

While clients may not ask you outright, they all want you to cover the following areas at your first meeting. Disclosing this information up front is a powerful way to start satisfying unspoken expectations:

◆ Your education, experience, and any designations you may have
◆ Your licenses
◆ The kind of products you generally recommend
◆ Your professional affiliations
◆ Any conflicts of interest
◆ How you are compensated. Are you fee-only, commission, or fee and commission?

In July 1992, after three years of extensive debate and industry input, the CFP Board of Standards adopted a new *Code of Ethics and Professional Responsibility* for CFP licensees. One of the Code's most significant sections calls for comprehensive written disclosure to clients prior to the engagement. The Code also requires disclosure of the method and source of compensation and information on the CFP licensee's educational background, experience, conflicts of interest, and practice philosophy.

The following form is a sample disclosure document to be given to clients before beginning the engagement or at the initial meeting. Note, all key issues of importance to clients are included, along with the strong statement, "I only recommend products in my clients' best interests."

Financial Adviser Disclosure Form

Name _____

Title _____

Company _____

Address _____

City _____ State and Zip _____

Broker/Dealer Affiliation _____

Services Provided

1 I provide the following services:

☐ Cash management, budgeting

☐ Tax planning

☐ Investment implementation

☐ Investment review and planning

☐ Estate planning

☐ Comprehensive written financial plans & strategies _____

☐ Other _____

☐ Insurance needs in these areas:

    ☐ Life   ☐ Disability   ☐ Health

    ☐ Long-term care   ☐ Property/Casualty

☐ Retirement planning

☐ Education planning

2 My financial planning services ☐ **DO** ☐ **DO NOT** include recommendations for specific investment products.

☐ Not applicable

3 I ☐ **DO** ☐ **DO NOT** offer assistance with insurance and investment implementation.

4 I ☐ **DO** ☐ **DO NOT** offer continuous, ongoing financial planning services.

5 I ☐ **DO** ☐ **DO NOT** take either full or limited discretionary authority over the management of assets.

My Background and Experience

1 My Licenses and Certifications

INSURANCE:

☐ Life/Health Insurance

☐ Disability Insurance

☐ Property/Casualty

☐ Fixed Annuities

INVESTMENT ADVISER:

☐ Registered Investment Adviser or Representative (SEC)

☐ Registered Investment Adviser or Representative, state of _____

SECURITIES:

☐ General Securities

☐ Mutual Funds

☐ Limited Partnerships

☐ Variable Annuities

OTHER:

☐ Certified Financial Planner (CFP)

☐ Chartered Financial Consultant (ChFC)

☐ Chartered Life Underwriter (CLU)

☐ Other _____

2 My Professional Affiliations

☐ International Association for Financial Planning (IAFP)

☐ Institute of Certified Financial Planners (ICFP)

☐ National Association of Personal Financial Advisers (NAPFA)

☐ Other _____

_____

(continued on following page)

3 My Education

DEGREE	AREA OF STUDY	SCHOOL	YEAR
☐ Bachelor	_____	_____	____
☐ Master	_____	_____	____
☐ Other	_____	_____	____
	_____	_____	____
	_____	_____	____

4 I have been offering financial advisory services for _____ years.

5 I have completed _____ hours of financial planning continuing education units (CEUs) in the last full calendar year.

6 I will provide you with references, if requested.

7 I ☐ **HAVE** ☐ **HAVE NOT EVER** been cited by a professional or regulatory governing body for disciplinary reasons. Explanation: _____
_____

8 To my knowledge I have the following conflict of interest: _____
_____
_____

My Method of Compensation

1 I will be compensated on the basis of:

    ☐ Fees   ☐ Commissions

    ☐ Fees & commissions ☐ Other_____

    Explanation: _____
    _____
    _____

If you are a CFP licensee, you should review the requirements contained in the Code. In general, you will find you will need to add information on your basic philosophy in working with clients, on the principle of financial planning you will use, on your areas of competence, your employment history, contin-

2 Sources of compensation _____

_____

_____

_____

3 I ☐ **DO** ☐ **DO NOT** receive any compensation from any person or firm to whom you may be referred.

4 I ☐ **DO** ☐ **DO NOT** pay referral fees.

Explanation: _____

_____

_____

_____

5 My clients' interests come first. I only recommend products in my clients' best interests.

6 An affiliate of my firm, or a member of my firm ☐ **DOES** ☐ **DOES NOT** act as a general partner, participate in, or receive compensation as a general partner, from investments that I may recommend to you.

_____
Client Signature

_____
Date

_____
Client Signature

_____
Date

gency aspects to the payment arrangement, relationships with third parties, and a description of information you feel is relevant to the client relationship. If this additional information is contained in your ADV, it may not be necessary to duplicate it on the disclosure form.

The Difficult Client

UNFORTUNATELY, THERE ARE a few clients you do not want to keep for a lifetime. The data-gathering process at your first meeting presents an excellent opportunity for you to identify these people and screen them out. The following five rules will prove helpful.

1 Understand the 80/20 guide. Understanding how the 80/20 guide applies to your practice can reduce your frustrations and increase your profitability. First application: About 80 percent of your income comes from 20 percent of your clients. Second application: About 80 percent of your frustrations come from another 20 percent of your clients. Your goal should be to focus on the 20 percent of your clientele who are making your business truly profitable and eliminate the 20 percent who are creating all your stress and frustration.

2 Do not take problems on in the first place. Speaker and business development authority Steve Moeller, in an article for the *Dow Jones Investment Advisor*[3] tells the story of his father, who had practiced as an orthodontist for more than 20 years. Toward the end of Dad's career, his practice was doing so well he was making five times more money than when he started. Knowing he was only working three or four days a week, Steve asked him if he had learned to work quicker over the years. "No," he said, "I was pretty fast when I left dental school and I'm not any faster now."

Then Steve suggested he must be charging a lot more. "No," he replied. "There are so many new orthodontists that I've had to cut my fees."

Finally, Steve asked if the technology had made him more efficient. "No," his father replied, "Teeth straightening hasn't changed much over the past 20 years." Steve confessed he was perplexed. How could his father be working less, charging less, not working faster or with the benefits of improved technology, and still increase his income five times over the previous 20 years?

His father finally explained his secret: "I've simply gotten a lot more selective about the people with whom I do business."

Dad went on to explain that a small fraction of his patients generated almost all of his profitable business because they kept their appointments, were easy to work with, and always paid on time. The obvious solution was to maximize his income by working with as many of those clients as possible while at the same time eliminating others.

He accomplished this by creating a profile of the ideal patient. He even described it in detail to his referral sources, including other dentists. When he first met a potential patient who fit the profile, he poured on the charm. At the same time, he developed a profile of his worst patients and did everything he could to screen out problem patients before they became patients.

3 Develop profiles of the ideal client and the difficult client. Moeller suggests a system for developing client profiles. Some of his thoughts were used as a starting point for developing the following scorecard.[4]

DIFFICULT CLIENT PROFILE

Give each characteristic a score: 1 point if you strongly disagree, 5 points if you are not sure, and 10 points if you strongly agree. Then use the score to calculate your results.

SCORE

◆ They have little money or just enough to entice you to work with them. _____

◆ Short on capital, they are consistently pushing to earn above-market returns. _____

◆ They are so young they know your job better than you do. Or, they are so old they cannot make decisions.

SCORE

◆ They are not good referral sources because they have few social or business contacts they could pass your way. _____

◆ They are past their peak earning years and do not expect to make additional contributions to their investments. _____

◆ They miss a lot of appointments. _____

◆ They do not pay you on time. _____

◆ They have had a lot of financial advisers and have even sued a few of them. _____

◆ They are performance, not relationship, oriented. _____

◆ They do not understand investments or the markets and do not want to understand them. _____

◆ They consistently focus on short-term results. _____

◆ They demand a high level of service and seem to enjoy the attention. _____

◆ They have so much time on their hands, they do not mind wasting yours. _____

◆ They are overly analytical. _____

◆ They worry about their money and need constant reinforcement. _____

◆ They get confused easily and call you constantly for help reading statements and confirmations. _____

◆ They want information rather than advice. _____

◆ They are extremely frugal and whine about your fees. _____

◆ They are constantly complaining about something: either it is your service or their returns. _____
They are never satisfied. _____

◆ They lie to you. _____

◆ They do not want to take responsibility for their own decisions. _____

◆ They have unrealistic expectations about the market or your service. _____

TOTAL SCORE _____

DIVIDE THE TOTAL score by 22. This is your final troublesome client score:

If the final score is:

9—10: Avoid this client at all costs.

7—8: Take on at your own risk.

4—6: Might work—set ground rules early.

1—3: Hug these to your breast and do not let go!

IDEAL CLIENT PROFILE

Give each characteristic a score: 10 points if you strongly disagree, 5 points if you are not sure, and 1 point if you strongly agree (note that these scores are the opposite of those used for the difficult client). Then use the score to calculate your results.

SCORE

◆ They are extremely busy with their careers or businesses and do not have the time to manage their money themselves. _____

◆ They are young enough to accept your advice and old enough to really benefit from it (40 to 70 years old). _____

◆ They have bright financial futures and will be making ongoing contributions to their accounts with you. _____

◆ They have $50,000 or more to invest each year. _____

◆ They have many social and business contacts they are willing to refer to you. _____

◆ They are likely to inherit a substantial sum. _____

◆ They understand investment markets and are highly motivated to work with a professional. _____

◆ They are oriented toward capital preservation. _____

◆ They take a long-term view of performance. _____

◆ They are in a field that interests you. _____

◆ They were referred to you by a happy client. _____

SCORE

◆ They trust you and consider you an expert in your field. _____

◆ They are open-minded and willing to learn new things. _____

◆ They are completely honest with you and fully disclose their assets, values, goals, and concerns. _____

◆ They are decisive. _____

◆ They value your service, advice, and professional relationship and are willing to compensate you for it. _____

◆ They are responsive and return your calls promptly. _____

◆ They want advice, not just information. _____

TOTAL SCORE _____

DIVIDE THE TOTAL score by 18. This is your final ideal client score:

If the final score is:

1—4:   Clone these—they are definitely in the top 20 percent.

5—7:   Might work—set your ground rules early.

8—10: Pass on to a new planner or adviser in your office.

4 Use the profiles to avoid problem clients and to identify ideal ones. Keep the profile with you as you interview new clients. If prospects do not score high enough on your score card, pass them on to someone else. As tempting as they may seem to you now, in the long run they will not be worth your time and energy. Moeller has found that 80 percent of a typical financial adviser's day is wasted talking to poorly qualified prospects. As he points out, this is not only frustrating but also not profitable.[5]

Soon you will be able to spot difficult clients before

they become problems. Once you discover you are their fifth adviser, and they have been involved in numerous lawsuits, you know you are likely to be the next one. If they appear secretive and do not fully disclose their financial affairs, you can be fairly sure this kind of client is not going to get any easier. Pass these clients on gently with, "You know, I don't think I will be able to meet your expectations as an adviser. I think you would be better suited to someone who can meet your needs. Would you like me to make a referral for you?"

5 Set your ground rules at the beginning of the relationship. Although it is important to learn how to meet your client's expectations, it is equally important for your clients to know that you, too, have expectations. Meeting expectations is a two-way street. In order for you to be efficient and effective with your own business, it is important that your clients know what you expect of them.

Think for a minute about the issues you have had with clients that drive you to distraction, frustrate you, or make it hard for you to manage your business prosperously. Perhaps it is clients who lie to you or drop in unannounced. Perhaps it is clients who cannot make a decision or who do not return your phone calls. Remember, you will never have more power than at the beginning of your relationship. That is the best time to establish your expectations and set the ground rules.

At the appropriate time during a new client interview, use this script: "Now, we have reviewed in detail your expectations of me. I should tell you that I have expectations of my clients, too. One, I can only deal with clients who are completely honest with me, because I cannot do the best job for you when I do not know all the facts. Number two, you need to return my phone calls within 24 hours." Then, list the other issues that are hot buttons for you. Lay out up front what you expect of clients; for example, they need to make meetings on time. "My time is valuable and so is yours. If you stand me up on a regular basis, I cannot continue to do business with you." In certain circumstances, you may want to add this information to your engagement letters.

The entire issue of declining the difficult client and focusing on the ideal client goes beyond avoiding lawsuits. It can be a powerful tool for helping you operate your practice in a way that is not only safer but also more prosperous and less time-consuming. It can literally put the fun back into your practice. Remember the lesson from Moeller's father: Choose your clients carefully and you could work less and increase your income fivefold.

ACTION ITEM

◆ DOCUMENT, DOCUMENT, DOCUMENT. If the three rules of real estate are location, location, location, then the three rules of protecting your practice are document, document, and document some more. Carefully documented files not only prove to regulators you have followed all the rules, they can be the single most powerful tool you have in winning a lawsuit. When in doubt, put it in the file.

The author is grateful for the assistance of Steve Moeller, President of American Business Visions. For more information on how Moeller works with top advisers to increase their business and productivity, call his fax-on-demand service at (703) 716-7280.

SUBSEQUENT CLIENT MEETINGS

MAKE THIS YOUR mission statement: "Our goal is to exceed your expectations 100 percent of the time." When clients are treated with this kind of consideration, they are deeply pleased with their advisers and will not leave. Satisfying client expectations is the second step in keeping them happy and married to you for life.

The first client meeting, however, does not lead to a "marriage." It leads to an engagement letter. With that signed, you and the client have established a legal relationship and the basis for subsequent meetings. The next step is to work together in designing a financial plan and creating an investment policy statement. These two documents clarify and put in writing the client's expectations. Checklists, the last major topic covered in this chapter, act as file managers, reminding you to keep all files complete and current.

Engagement Letter

THE PHRASE "ENGAGEMENT LETTER" is much less threatening than its synonym "contract", which clients fear. Nevertheless, an engagement letter is indeed a contract.

One important reason to use an engagement letter is to put clients on notice. It allows you to explain your understanding of the clients' situation and goals. If you have misunderstood anything, the clients are obligated to call and let you know; otherwise you will take their silence for assent. The most important language in the letter should state: "If this letter accurately reflects your understanding of our relationship, please sign below and return the original to me. The copy is for your files. If I have misunderstood something, please call me immediately."

The letter also has another important purpose: it puts all client expectations in writing. This is how clients will gauge your success. For example, your engagement letter may contain this kind of language: "You mentioned that it is extremely important for you to hear from me during down markets. I will make every effort to contact you frequently to address the current market trends. If for some reason you need additional information, please contact me immediately. I want to make sure I am meeting all of your expectations." Engagement letters are one of the many steps that help build trust. Get in the habit of always sending out engagement letters, even to clients to whom you do not charge fees.

For most planners, representatives, and agents, a

boilerplate of this letter should be prepared by an attorney. The following sample includes the points to be covered by a financial planner. It is important to realize that in this form the letter is intended to supplement an advisory agreement, not replace it. Consequently, your attorney will want to make sure nothing in your engagement letter will conflict with the advisory contract.

If you are in control of your own RIA, consider using this format to rewrite your advisory contract into a more readable and understandable document. Note that using boldface type for the paragraph headings makes the letter easier to read.

FINANCIAL PLANNERS

Dear Mr. and Mrs. Anderson:

It was a pleasure to meet with you last Monday. You have already done the most difficult part of the financial planning process—gathering the necessary data and making the commitment to improve your financial future. Congratulations! I am looking forward to helping you reach all of your financial goals.

Let me take a few minutes to summarize our relationship and to make sure I clearly understand what you want to achieve.

Goals and Objectives: You indicated that you wanted to retire in eight years on the equivalent of $10,000 of pre-tax income per month, in today's dollars. You have also indicated the desire to reduce your estate tax liabilities and to make provisions for charitable contributions to your church. Finally, you would like to set up two accounts to be used for your grandchildren's college funds.

Investment Temperament: Based on our conversations and your investment temperament questionnaire, I determined you are fairly conservative investors. Since you are looking at retiring in eight years, you are anxious to preserve as much principal as possible. However, with at least 25 percent of your portfolio, you are willing to put your principal at risk in order to improve your returns.

Capital Available: In addition to the balance sheet of your current assets, you have indicated you are able to invest $3,200 per month this year toward reaching all of your goals. You also anticipate you should be able to increase that amount by 6 percent per year between now and retirement.

Financial Plan: We have agreed a comprehensive written financial plan would be appropriate to address these issues. I will prepare an estate tax calculation to determine how much, if any, estate tax would be assessable. If there is an estate tax issue, I will recommend different alternatives for reducing the tax. I will also do retirement calculations to compute how much money you need to save between now and retirement to provide the lifestyle you desire. I will review your current investments and the new monies you have earmarked for investing to consider a college fund for your two grandchildren. Finally, we will review the options for charitable gifts.

What I Will Not Do: As I mentioned to you in our interview, I will not be giving you legal or tax advice. If we determine legal advice would be appropriate, we will meet with your personal attorney. Furthermore, I will not review any of your property or casualty policies including your homeowner and automobile policies. However, these are important areas and I strongly recommend you review them with your property and casualty insurance agent to make sure you have adequate coverage.

Fees: As we discussed, I will be charging you a flat fee for the first year of (_____ amount). At the end of the year, we will be setting up an annual retainer agreement which I will review with you then. Annual retainers are usually 40 percent to 60 percent of the initial fee, depending on how much work you want me to do.

Married Clients: I will be considering both of you as one client. That means that any information I receive from one of you, I will be free to share with the other. Also, if one of you gives me a trading authorization, it will be for both of you.

Next Meeting: Our next meeting is scheduled for Tuesday the 23rd at 1:00 P.M. I will be presenting your financial plan then. The meeting should take approximately two hours. I will need to see copies of your life insurance policies before then.

No Guarantees: Although none of our investments will have any guarantees as to performance, there is one guarantee I can make to you: something that we do will lose money! That is a natural part of investing; at any point in time, market fluctuations can make your investments worth more or less than the original purchase price.

Misunderstandings: As we discussed, open communication is the key to a successful planning relationship. If at any time you feel I am not meeting your expectations, or worse, have done something that is upsetting to you, you agreed to contact me first, so I will have a chance to make it right. This is extremely important to me, because I want to make sure you are satisfied.

Expectations: We reviewed a number of expectations that you had of our relationship. Briefly, you wanted me to return your calls within 24 hours and to keep in close contact during down markets. You also indicated that you would like me to call you at least four times a year, just to let you know how your portfolio is progressing. I am happy to accommodate you. If you do not feel I am giving you the information you need to feel comfortable, please call me at any time.

Action: If this letter accurately reflects your understanding of our relationship, please sign below and return the original to me. The copy is for your files. If I have misunderstood something, please call me immediately.

Once again, I know I am going to enjoy working with you and getting to know you better.

Warmest personal regards,
Ima Good Planner

Berda Anderson   Date

Edward Anderson   Date

REGISTERED REPRESENTATIVES AND INSURANCE AGENTS

Agents and brokers who do not do financial planning and are not RIAs will need to delete the paragraphs on "Financial Plan," "What I Will Not Do," and "Fees" that appear in the above letter. In addition, they should add the following language.

My Role in Insurance and Security Sales: As your financial adviser, I am involved in the sale of securities and insurance products on a commission basis. In order to determine which insurance products and securities are appropriate and suitable for you, I may perform certain services incidental to my role as a salesperson. These services usually involve advising you regarding the management of your financial resources based on an analysis of your goals and needs. I may review your present and anticipated assets and liabilities, including insurance, savings, and investments, as well as your anticipated retirement or other employee benefits and compensation. All recommendations made for the purchase of insurance and securities products would then be made in my capacity as a salesperson for your account. There would be no additional fees and compensation received on my part. The only compensation I would then receive would be commissions on the products I recommend. I do not charge any other fees.

What I Will Not Do: As I mentioned to you in our interview, I will not be giving you legal or tax advice. If we determine legal advice would be appropriate, we will meet with your personal attorney. Furthermore, I will not review any of your property or casualty policies including your homeowner and automobile policies. However, these are important areas and I strongly recommend you review them with your property and casualty insurance agent to make sure you have adequate coverage. I will not be serving as your financial planner or preparing a written financial plan.

Compensation/Fees: As we discussed, I will not be charging you any fees. Rather, I will be receiving commissions on the products you purchase.

Investment Policy Statement

USING THE MATERIAL gathered in the information session and from the risk tolerance questionnaire, plus any necessary further conversations with the client, you can construct a written, individualized IPS. This has become standard practice for sophisticated investors. The discipline of clearly and concisely communicating in writing builds trust by concretely demonstrating that you not only understand your clients' investment philosophy and financial goals, but that you are committed to work diligently to meet their expectations.

Although every investor needs a personal IPS, they are legally required to be written for certain clients. According to Linda Lubitz and Norman M. Boone, co-authors of *The Investment Policy Guidebook*, "In general, having an investment policy is required any time a person or group of people are making investment decisions for the benefit of others, whether or not the decision-makers also may have a direct personal interest in the assets."[1] They list the following as examples of investments and fiduciaries who must have a written IPS: ERISA; Taft Hartley Plan; trusts; foundations and endowments; estates; and fiduciaries making investment decisions, particularly in states that have passed the Uniform Prudent Investor Act.

Lubitz and Boone believe that in addition to enhancing your chances for fully helping clients attain their goals, an IPS can help reduce a fiduciary's legal liability. In their opinion, trustees who have been sued for poor investment performance were exonerated when they could demonstrate they systematically followed an established and reasonable process for investment decisions. "Generally, as long as the decision-making process was appropriate, the actual investment results—good or bad—were of virtually no concern to the courts."[2]

Although a well-drafted IPS can save your career, a poorly drafted one can damage your practice. An adviser from Pennsylvania learned this lesson the hard way when an attorney who reviewed his statement noticed a section that stated the adviser would be liable for investments about which clients gave him no information. The adviser might have been better off with no IPS rather than one that significantly increased his liability.[3]

Lubitz and Boone suggest there are four basic purposes for the IPS:[4] First, to establish clear and definable expectations, risk and return objectives, and guidelines for the investment of the assets; second, to set forth a structure and identify the investment asset classes used to achieve a diversified portfolio, as well as to determine how those assets are to be allocated toward achieving the investor's objectives; third, to provide a guide for selecting, monitoring, and evaluating the performance of those charged with managing and investing the assets and making changes as appropriate; and fourth, to provide a concise method of communicating the process and objectives among all parties involved with the investments and to assign responsibility for implementation.

IPS documents need to be taken seriously. It is possible for them to be construed as contracts or, at the very least, a standard of care by which your actions as a planner or financial adviser will be judged. A standard of care cuts two ways: if in a later dispute you can prove you followed the IPS to the letter, you will have provided significant evidence in your favor. If, on the other hand, you have an IPS that you do not follow carefully, you have given your unhappy investor a road map to the courthouse.

To avoid creating a liability document, consider the following when drafting an IPS.

◆ **Specific target language can cause problems.** Some authorities think it is a mistake to discuss objectives in terms of numbers, because it is too easy to miss them. [5] Others suggest using a range of acceptable returns such as between 150 and 250 percent of the rate of inflation. If inflation is 4 percent, then returns of 6 to 10 percent would be in the acceptable range.

◆ **Creating conflicting contracts** is all too common. Planners and advisers who have an advisory contract should be careful not to cover the same topics in two different documents. It is all too easy to have one form of compensation listed in your advisory agreement and another one in the IPS. It needs to be included only in the advisory agreement. Leave this information out of the IPS, because conflicting provisions are sure to raise a red flag at an SEC audit or create problems in a lawsuit.

◆ **Drafting the document yourself** may sound like a good way to reduce your costs, but it will pay to use an attorney who is experienced in this area to make sure your IPS complies with both state and federal laws. As an example, attorney Jeff Kelvin points out that it is permissible to include a statement that the account is subject to market risk and none of the returns are guaranteed. However, it is dangerous to go beyond this and try limiting your liability. Hedge clauses, where planners or investment advisers try to absolve themselves of liability, are illegal under SEC guidelines. That is why it is important to use an attorney who knows investment adviser rules in addition to state law.[6]

◆ **Copying the IPS used by a colleague in a different state** is another common drafting problem. Although it may be a good form in other states, it may not pass muster in yours. Also, there is no guarantee that the form was any good in the first place. It is best not to blindly use an IPS from another jurisdiction without checking with your attorney first.

NOW THAT YOU ARE aware of the actions, language, and terms not to use in your IPS, consider the following eight steps suggested by John J. Bowen, Jr. for developing an IPS:[7]

STEP 1. Set long-term goals and objectives clearly and concisely. One common long-term goal, retirement in a comfortable lifestyle, means different things to different people. Stating only the goal of a comfortable retirement is too broad. However, it can also be inappropriate to state a retirement goal of $5,000 income per month in inflation-adjusted dollars. The best strategy is to set a range of acceptable numbers that will take into consideration the client's changing circumstances and market volatility. For example, "Clients want a comfortable lifestyle, similar to their current standard of living of $5,000 income per month, in retirement. We estimate this will necessitate a lump sum investment by the age of 65 of between $575,000 and $950,000 to account for fluctuating market and inflation rates."

STEP 2. Define the level of risk clients are willing to accept. As Bowen points out, clients focus a great deal of attention on return, but tend to ignore the other half of that equation: risk. He suggests determining the absolute loss clients are willing to accept in any one year without terminating the investment program. He does this by showing clients the figures from 1973 and 1974, the worst financial recession since World War II. He reminds clients that there is a 5 percent probability that in the next 20 years our economy will experience a similar downturn. Ask your clients if they would have closed their accounts with you if they had experienced a 1973–74 downturn in their investments. If they say yes, you need to make more conservative recommendations.

STEP 3. Establish the expected time horizon for client investments. It is not unusual to hear a client define long term as 12 months. What is long term to you and the industry might be entirely different to your client. Clearly define what these words mean and make sure clients understand that equities need a minimum of five years to recover most market fluctuations. Any time frame less than five years should focus on fixed-return investments.

STEP 4. Determine the rate of return objective. Once again, relate the rate of return to risk. Bowen notes some attorneys avoid using a rate of return in an IPS. Bowen, however, uses expected rates of return and makes it clear that these are historical returns and are in no way indicative of future returns.

STEP 5. Select the asset classes to be utilized to build your portfolio. All the different classes of assets that could be included in the portfolio should be listed. If any are to be excluded, you may want to list those, too.

STEP 6. Document the investment methodology to be utilized in managing the portfolio. Bowen notes there are three basic investment methodologies: security selection, market timing, and asset-class investing. He suggests you provide your clients with the rationale for the methodology you recommended.

STEP 7. Establish a strategic implementation plan. Bowen first shows clients how different portfolios would have performed during 1973–74. He then presents them with simulated model returns for each year from 1972 to 1994. This helps clients understand how expected returns are based on the level of risk they are willing to accept. Clients can then choose the portfolios with which they would have been the most comfortable.

STEP 8. Establish the means for making periodic adjustments to the portfolio as needed. Your IPS creates a benchmark to measure how well your clients are moving toward their goals. If you have clearly defined their goals and objectives, it is much easier to determine how the portfolio is performing relative to these goals and objectives. As Bowen says, "[m]eeting with your clients quarterly to review their accounts and the IPS will give you clients for life."

Checklists

IN A COMPLICATED AND paper-intensive business, many things can fall through the cracks. Checklists help to keep this from happening. They are essential to a long, happy client relationship because they ensure the client is not neglected and that you are constantly working to meet expectations. Checklists also help keep your work legal and organized. Many lawsuits will completely evaporate once the plaintiffs discover you have a carefully documented file that proves you did everything legally and correctly. If you are audited, a checklist clearly demonstrates you have followed all the proper procedures.

SAMPLE DOCUMENT SOFTWARE Ed Morrow's *Text Library System* consists of a complete list of sample forms that you can use for your checklists. Easily printed out from a computer, these lists cover subject areas such as:

◆ **Master compliance.** This is a one-page form (CP.03) developed to review compliance issues, documents, and files on behalf of your firm. Should you ever be audited by the SEC, this document would be excellent evidence of your conscientious effort to be in compliance. Morrow says that the Master Compliance review should be carried out at a minimum of once each year.

◆ **Individual compliance.** This is a one-page form (CP.04) designed to review compliance issues, documents, and files for a single client. It is important to keep all back copies of this form and the master checklist, as clients can file complaints years after a relationship is terminated.

For further information on how you can obtain copies of these forms and other sample documents, contact Morrow at (800) 666-1656.

FINANCIAL PLANNER CHECKLIST Fred Haiker, a financial planner with Swenson Anderson Associates in Minneapolis has developed a checklist to make sure all legally required items have been carefully reviewed with the client and posted in their file. A copy of his checklist, adapted for financial planners, follows.

CLIENT CHECKLIST
Client Name _____

1st Interview (date) _____
☐ File notes   ☐ Letter   ☐ Entry in client log
☐ Next appointment scheduled for _____
    at _____ o'clock
☐ Other _____

Fact Finder (date) _____
☐ File notes   ☐ Letter   ☐ Entry in client log
☐ Prep time blocked out
☐ Next appointment scheduled for _____
    at _____ o'clock
☐ Other _____

Confirmation of Engagement (date) _____
☐ File notes   ☐ Letter   ☐ Fee amount
☐ RIA forms signed   ☐ RIA forms to RIA
☐ Prep time blocked out   ☐ Entry in client log
☐ RIA Credential Disclosure Form
☐ ADV Brochure given
☐ Other _____

Plan Presentation (date) _____
☐ File notes   ☐ Letter   ☐ Entry in client log
☐ Request for 2nd half of fee
☐ Prep time blocked out
☐ Next appointment scheduled for _____
    at _____ o'clock
☐ Other _____

Product Recommendations (date) _____
☐ File notes   ☐ Letter
☐ Insurance applied for:
    ☐ Apps completed
    ☐ Exams ordered   ☐ Exams completed
    ☐ APR requested   ☐ APR returned

    ☐ Other requirements

☐ Delivery details _____

☐ Next appointment scheduled for _____

   at _____ o'clock

    ☐ Entry in client log

    ☐ Retainer fee amount _____

☐ Insurance penalties, risks, worst case explained/Date _____

☐ Insurance company ratings explained/Date ___

_____

☐ Other _____

Delivery and Implementation (date) _____

☐ File notes   ☐ Letter

☐ Broker-Dealer New Account Form

☐ Investment Apps taken

☐ Investment Apps completed

☐ Retainer signed   ☐ Retainer to RIA

☐ Referrals requested   ☐ 1st Review scheduled

☐ Investment risk and fees explained/Date _____

☐ Other_____

Required Documents; Models; Letters; Contracts; etc.

☐ RIA Letter of Understanding

☐ Disclosure Form

☐ Fee Continuation Form RIA

☐ Financial Profile

☐ Personal Information

☐ Net Worth

☐ Cash Flow

☐ Education Projections

☐ Conflicts of Interest Waiver

   (if appropriate)

☐ Engagement Letter

☐ _____

☐ _____

☐ Retirement Projections
☐ Graphs
☐ _____
☐ _____

Recommendation Pages:

☐ _____
☐ _____
☐ _____
☐ _____

Individuals to Contact: **Reason:**

☐ _____   _____
☐ _____   _____
☐ _____   _____

Case Recommendations: _____
_____
_____
_____
_____
_____
_____

Case Strategy: _____
_____
_____
_____
_____
_____

Products, Materials, and Prospectuses
Provided/Date:

_____   _____
_____   _____
_____   _____
_____   _____

ACTION ITEMS

◆ FREQUENTLY THE CONTRACTS drafted by attorneys for RIAs are long and confusing for clients. It may be a good practice to augment the required contract with an engagement letter to explain the contract, define clients' expectations, and explain what the firm will and will not do for them. If you control your own RIA, consider rewriting your advisory agreement in a more client-friendly style.

◆ IT IS PARTICULARLY important when you are defending yourself against a legal action to prove that you spent an adequate amount of time reviewing all pertinent information. Client logs provide this proof. Haiker suggests constructing a log for each client. For every transaction, the following information should be recorded: date, action taken, date response expected, date response received, and time spent. This log is helpful in tracking how much time you spend on a case and how profitable each case really is.

◆ KEEP A RECEPTIONIST'S log, which shows when clients check in for each meeting. If you are ever sued and need to prove you spent adequate time with the client, this log can bolster your case.

◆ REVIEW ALL CHECKLISTS with your assistants and secretaries. Make sure they know the importance of each item and are committed to documenting the components in client files.

The author wishes to thank Linda Lubitz for her help with the IPS material in this chapter. For information regarding The Investment Policy Guidebook, *contact: Linda Lubitz (305-670-0545), Norman M. Boone (415-788-1952), or Ibbotson Associates (800-758-3557).*

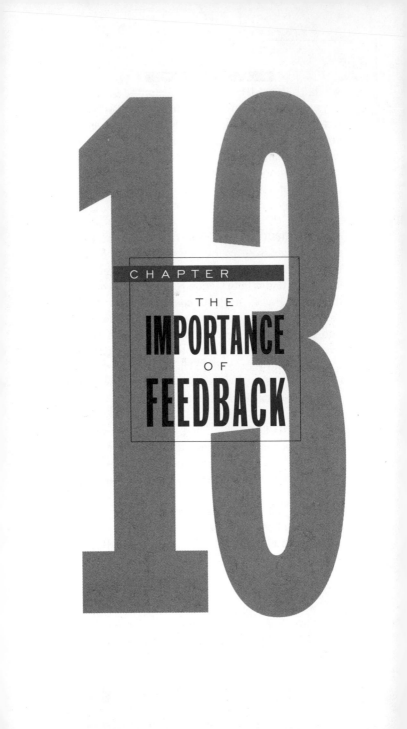

THE
IMPORTANCE
OF
FEEDBACK

13

HONEST, FREE-FLOWING communication is a key component of all successful relationships. As a financial services professional, it is your responsibility to initiate communication and solicit feedback from clients. NASD, for example, has estimated that 20 to 30 percent of all complaints filed with them are based on the failure of a broker or brokcr-dealer to communicate with the investor.[1] One state bar reported the top three complaints against lawyers involved their failure to communicate with clients.[2]

The previous chapter reviewed important communications from you to the investor so that you can fulfill the first two steps in keeping a client happy: identifying expectations and then meeting or exceeding them. This chapter emphasizes feedback, the third step in keeping a client happy. Feedback should be solicited for both spoken and unspoken expectations. Getting an investor to talk early about any frustration with you, your service, or their investments is crucial to keeping them satisfied.

There are two different factors in obtaining client feedback. One covers spoken expectations, such as goals, and the other unspoken expectations, such as feelings and attitudes.

When addressing spoken expectations, you might say, "When we first met, you told me you expected to get a 10 percent return over the next five years, in order to set aside enough money for your daughter's college education fund. We have been working together for two years and averaged a 9.5 percent return. Are you satisfied with this, given our current economic conditions?" Once you ask this kind of question, keep quiet! This is where you will really hear what the client is thinking. You may believe you are a Wall Street wizard to get 9.5 percent in the current market, but the client could secretly be expecting 20 percent. Keep quiet and let the client talk. Whatever they say, take notes for your file. Always end with questions like: "Could you explain that more? Do you have any more questions? Is there anything else you would like for me to do?"

This kind of communication establishes the spoken expectations and where you stand in relation to them, and elicits feedback from the client. At least once a year, go through this exercise with each of the client's goals. This is also important because it reminds clients, who sometimes have short memories, what the rules of the game really are. You want to make sure they have not mentally changed the rules without letting you know.

The second approach addresses unspoken expectations by asking open-ended questions, such as "How am I doing?" Or you may want to state, "Is our relationship living up to your expectations? Is there anything I can do to improve my quality of service to you?" Be sure to thank them for their comments.

Once again, no matter what their comments are, write them down. If they are positive, they can help your mental attitude on a rough day. If they are negative, you want to be able to address them. Create a paper trail that shows you identified your clients' concerns early and you fixed them. In the unlikely event you are sued, your records showing how hard you worked to keep a client happy will go a long way toward winning your case.

A few years ago, a large mutual fund group presented their client research at the annual meeting of the Investment Company Institute. Their research found clients were most happy when returns matched their expectations. This was much more important to shareholders than investing with the top-ranked fund. There is a lesson here for everyone: Clients do not like surprises. The most successful planners and financial advisers are not necessarily the ones who pick the highest-performing investments, but those who meet the client's expectations.

Follow these guidelines to assure that both you and your client are in agreement as to goals.

◆ **Clearly label assumptions.** One of the painful lessons learned from *Oddi v. Ayco*[3] is that all financial advisers need to clearly label the assumptions used to make projections. In this case, the planner, who was working for Ayco, erroneously transposed numbers and recommended that the client, Oddi, take a lump sum withdrawal from his pension plan, as opposed to rolling it over into an IRA. Because she had erroneously transposed the numbers, it turned out this was actually the wrong recommendation and the client suffered significant damages. The court ordered Ayco to pay $483,088 plus income tax on the award to Oddi. Although there are a number of reasons this planner got into trouble, one main problem was not clearly labeling the assumptions she used to make projections.

Clearly labeling assumptions applies to investment recommendations, goals, planning, and insurance illustrations. If you project your clients will need to invest $1,200 a month at a 9 percent return to reach their goals, clearly mark it and make it plain that if returns are less, a larger monthly investment will be needed. Insurance illustrations should clearly show a worst-case scenario, a conservative projection, and a current interest rate projection.

◆ **Emphasize return variability.** When making projections and giving clients potential returns, it is important to give them as wide a range as possible. Instead of anticipating a particular mutual fund will average 12 percent per year, it is better to say, "The returns on this fund usually run between –10 and +20 percent." Then look straight at them and ask, "Can you live with this?" If they start to flinch over the thought they might be losing money some years, perhaps as much as 10 percent, you know this investment is probably too risky for them. Likewise, if the returns are not achieving the hoped for 12 percent, but are languishing around 7 or 8 percent after a couple of years, you can certainly point back to your original projections to state the fund is performing within the range you had anticipated.

It is particularly crucial to give a wide range of returns in more risky investments, such as limited partnerships, growth stocks, derivatives, and futures contracts. Frequently, clients see only the potential for high returns and forget there is also a potential for very low or negative returns. This is also a good approach to take with certain insurance products. If clients are advised of what the range is, they will be less surprised if they are requested to increase their premiums in order to reach their goals.

◆ **Describe investment risk.** Many financial advisers are much more likely to describe to a client the upside of an investment product rather than the downside. Perhaps it is because many financial advisers come from a sales background. Although it is important clients know about the upside potential of an investment, it is even more important that clients are not surprised. Let them know what can go wrong. It is difficult for a client to claim later they did not know some of the negative aspects of an investment if you had originally explained both the ups and downs in a letter confirming your recommendations.

Mark Bass of Lubbock, Texas tells every client the same thing: "I will only make you one guarantee. Something we do will lose money."[4] This is a great thing to tell clients up front. For one thing, it is true. You will not bat a thousand; you will make some recommendations that will lose money. Markets are unpredictable. That is why they can be opportunities for profit. This forthrightness also helps build trust with clients. When you are honest about potential outcomes, clients will respect and trust you.

Sometimes it is hard to call a client with the news their investment is down or interest rates are so low they will have to add premiums to their Universal Life policy. However, it is far better for clients to hear it from their adviser than from any other source. Bring bad news to clients before they read it in the newspaper or see it on the Bloomberg. It builds confidence and trust in the adviser.

Follow-Up Correspondence

FOLLOW-UP LETTERS AND MEMOS are another key ingredient of a successful practice. They not only let clients know you continually think about them and their needs but they also allow you to obtain feedback on what clients are thinking of you, your service, and your recommendations. It is one more way to let clients know you are serious about meeting their expectations. These communications are also important defense documents should you ever be sued.

At the end of each meeting with clients, take a moment to dictate a letter to them summarizing what you accomplished in the meeting, how the meeting related to their goals and expectations, and the date and purpose of the next meeting. This letter should list who is responsible for each follow-up action and what the deadlines are. File the letter on top of your correspondence file and it will make preparing for your next meeting easier. You probably will not have to review the entire file, but just take a minute to review the latest letter to remind yourself of the case's status and the next meeting's purpose. A letter is also a great way of putting clients on notice that they must let you know exactly what they require. If they think you misunderstood anything, they are obligated to advise you right away. This process underlines something that lawyers learn their first year in law school: clients love paperwork.

Whenever in doubt, send clients copies of any letters that pertain to them. If you are using a set of preformatted meeting agendas and notes, such as those discussed below, you can have the clients approve the minutes before leaving the office. This proves to your clients you are careful with their case and acting in their best interests.

TEXT LIBRARY SYSTEM As discussed in Chapter 11,

Ed Morrow has designed a software program called *Text Library System* to take the burden out of communicating with clients. This excellent resource can streamline your practice because it contains easy to modify templates for most of your needs, including client correspondence, checklists, forms, and contracts. Morrow has an almost limitless supply of letters covering the entire client process and a lot of helpful information on many subjects of interest to planners and financial advisers.

Morrow, knowing that communicating with clients is the secret to keeping them happy and avoiding lawsuits, has added many documents that most professionals know they should be using but have not taken the time to develop.

For example, in addition to providing clients with a follow-up letter after each meeting, Morrow goes two steps further: Before each meeting he sends the client an agenda of items to be covered and a reminder of the date and time of the meeting. Because he has an established agenda, he can deliver preformatted meeting notes that are already in his software program to the client at the close of the meeting.

This system is simplicity itself. The client shows up for the meeting with the agenda, knowing exactly what will take place and be discussed. This alone will streamline your time and demonstrate to the client your ability to organize and pay close attention to details. Because preformatted meeting notes matching the day's meeting are already in your computer, it takes only a few minutes to bring them up, make the few personalizations and corrections needed to make them accurate, and print them. Although you could mail them to the client after the meeting, it will save time to do this while your client is still in your office. Before leaving, the client can review the notes for accuracy, initial them, and take a copy home. Think how impressed all your clients will be as they leave your office with a sense of trust and confidence in your ability to provide the service they need.

A copy of one of Morrow's meeting agendas is included in Chapter 11. For further information on Morrow's *Text Library System,* call (800) 666-1656.

HAIKER LETTER SERIES Another planner, Fred Haiker of Swenson Anderson Associates in Minneapolis, has developed a series of letters that advise clients about the financial planning process and the status of their case and also build strong rapport. He uses these letters to let the client know how things are progressing and as a way of putting the client on notice if Haiker has misunderstood something. The client then will call Haiker with any concerns before they get out of control. Haiker also makes sure clients know they do not have to pay him until they are completely satisfied. Haiker has kindly allowed four of the letters in his series to be reproduced here.

Following 1st Interview In My Office

Date _____

Client _____

Address _____

City State Zip _____

Dear _____ :

I wish to thank you again for taking time out of your busy schedule to visit with me in my office. After a brief overview of our services and a short discussion concerning your situation, we agreed to the following:

1 To meet again in my office on _____ at _____. This appointment will last approximately.

2 You are to complete the information pages I gave

you, and also bring along any items on the check-list provided.

3 As a result of this second meeting, I will analyze the data gathered and provide a written profile of your situation to include a net worth evaluation and a clarification of your goals and objectives. This will be presented to you in a brief third meeting. I will also provide at that time a summary of what we believe to be appropriate for your financial situation and a written fee quote for the additional planning.

4 It is at this time that you will determine whether to engage our services. If agreeable, one half of the quoted fee is billed to you immediately. The second is billed upon the completion of the plan, and your complete satisfaction.

It was a pleasure meeting you. We look forward to seeing you again soon.

Sincerely,

Following Fact Finder

Date _____

Client _____

Address _____

City State Zip _____

Dear _____ :

Our last visit was very productive and therefore a good beginning. Although compiling this data is somewhat tedious, its accuracy is essential to proper comprehensive planning. I would now like to recap that meeting and outline what is ahead.

We have gathered a great deal of factual and subjective financial information from you. We deter-mined your goals, timing parameters, and risk tem-perament. We also know what assets, discretionary income, and other potential resources we have to work with.

If I understood you correctly, your current major areas of concern are:

1 _____

2 _____

3 _____

I am now in a position to assess your personal financial profile. I will also determine what areas need to be addressed first and prioritize them for you. Our next meeting is scheduled for _____ _____ at _____, and will take approximately one-half hour. At that time, we will review your profile and I will outline the specific services I will provide for a disclosed fee. If you agree with the written assessment, we will proceed by determining a convenient time for our next session.

I am comfortable that we communicate and work well together. I am also confident we can provide the needed planning strategies required to reach your goals. We look forward to seeing you again soon.

Sincerely,

Letter to Remind Clients to Call With Go-Ahead On Plan

Date _____

Client _____

Address _____

City State Zip _____

Dear _____ :

We wish to thank you again for visiting with us in our office last _____. After reviewing together your financial profile, we outlined those areas indicated where we could be of service to you. We quoted a fee of $_____ for preparation of a comprehensive written plan that would target those given areas for further analysis and recommendation.

We would now like to clarify once again your options with us at Swenson Anderson Associates. You may choose to proceed with this initial recommendation of having a written financial plan prepared for you. A second option is to utilize our services to find and implement financial products appropriate to your current needs. The second option requires no fee as we are compensated through commissions.

Finally, we agreed that you would call us with your decision within three business days. We are confident that we can be of valuable service to you.

We look forward to hearing from you by

_____ .

Sincerely,

Following Plan Presentation

Date _____

Client _____

Address _____

City State Zip _____

Dear _____ :

Just a brief letter to summarize our recent meeting and to outline our next session scheduled for

_____ at _____ .

We have now presented to you an initial plan which best focuses on your objectives given the resources available. As you recall, after our brief introductory meeting, we met again and gathered considerable financial data as well as determined your immediate and long range goals. We also determined your risk level to aid us in selecting the appropriate planning alternatives.

In our last meeting, we summarized your situation in a Financial Profile. After you advised us that this summary was accurate and we would not need to add anything, we proceeded to cover various plan strategies. The following factors were all taken into consideration:

1 Dollars available   **5** Taxation
2 Your goals   **6** Income protection
3 Risk temperament   **7** Potential growth
4 Necessary liquidity

We have given much thought to our recommendations and believe the ideas shared best fit your needs as well as fall within your comfort zone. On _____ , actual vehicles will be presented that may be used to implement your plan. We will focus on:

1 _____
2 _____
3 _____

The meeting will take approximately _____.
You are now beginning the first steps toward achieving some rather important and exciting financial objectives. Please remember to bring your Financial Plan Book.

We look forward to seeing you again on
_____ .

Sincerely,

German WonderCar Tactic

THE AUTO INDUSTRY HAS figured out something financial advisers should have been doing years ago— using customer satisfaction questionnaires to build rapport and develop good client relations. Have you ever purchased a German WonderCar? The Germans have built a high level of customer satisfaction in an industry that consistently rates low on the consumer trust and confidence index.

Here is how they do it. The day you pick up your new car, you will be scheduled for a two-hour orientation session with your salesperson to explain all the gizmos and whizzbangs (by the way, it takes at least this long, and you will only remember about 10 percent of the wonderworkings of your WonderCar).

Before you start the orientation, the salesperson will hand you a piece of paper with the words "Client Satisfaction Survey" in large type across the top. The salesperson will then explain that within a few days an independent consultant will be calling you for your opinions. At that time you will need to rank your salesperson in four different areas on a scale of 1 to 5.

At this point the salesperson will explain that 5 is a perfect score and anything less than your perfect satisfaction will not be satisfactory. To him a 4 or less will be abject failure. He will then look you directly in the eye and say, "If there is anything I can do to increase your satisfaction, will you promise me you will stop me and let me know? Also, here is my private number and my beeper. You can call me anytime of the day or night if you need help." By this point, you will have a hard time keeping a straight face.

Two days later, when the consultant calls, you will find yourself happily giving your salesperson a perfect score of 5 in every area. This is the exact same thing we want our clients to do for us. You can use the same technique with the same results.

Client Satisfaction Survey

BRING A CLIENT SATISFACTION survey out at the beginning of each relationship and at the annual reviews. Tell clients you will not be happy unless they are completely satisfied, and get a commitment from them that they will communicate any dissatisfaction to you first. Give them a copy so they know the ground rules and will be prepared for the phone call.

Remember, there is nothing in here about achieving specific investment returns. You cannot promise that, and clients need to know up front there are no guarantees.

If you can afford to hire a college student or someone else to follow up on the survey, you will probably get more candid results. If not, you should call the clients personally to make sure you are getting a perfect score in every area. Make sure the only purpose of the call is to get feedback on how you can serve them better. This is not the time to be promoting another investment.

You can use the sample survey developed below or construct your own using the information you learn from your clients. Though you should find most clients want the same things, the index should be designed to elicit individual needs and concerns.

SAMPLE CLIENT SATISFACTION INDEX Rate the following on a scale of 1 to 5, with 5 being completely satisfactory and 1 being completely unsatisfactory.

◆ My planner (adviser) carefully and accurately explained all investments and confirmation statements

☐ 5   ☐ 4   ☐ 3   ☐ 2   ☐ 1

◆ My planner (adviser) took the time to thoroughly understand my financial goals and temperament

☐ 5   ☐ 4   ☐ 3   ☐ 2   ☐ 1

◆ My planner (adviser) is accessible to answer questions

☐ 5   ☐ 4   ☐ 3   ☐ 2   ☐ 1

◆ My planner (adviser) handles my affairs in a timely manner

☐ 5   ☐ 4   ☐ 3   ☐ 2   ☐ 1

◆ I feel comfortable with my planner's (adviser's) recommendations

☐ 5   ☐ 4   ☐ 3   ☐ 2   ☐ 1

◆ My planner (adviser) did a good job making recommendations that fit my goals and my investment temperament

☐ 5   ☐ 4   ☐ 3   ☐ 2   ☐ 1

Do you have any comments about our service?

_____

_____

Is there anything we can do to serve you better?

_____

_____

Is there someone we should thank for taking good care of you? _____

_____

If you have not received the service you think you should, please let me know personally so we can address your concerns immediately. _____

_____

_____

QUARTERLY SURVEY J. Floyd Swilley, CEO and President of Investment Opportunity Corporation, has taken the survey process one step further and requests a quarterly review. He has generously allowed his form to be reprinted here.

In order to assure that we are providing you with the highest quality of service we periodically ask for feedback from you, our client. Please complete and return to our home office in Greenville as soon as possible. Thank you for your assistance in helping us make Investment Opportunity Corporation the best in the business.

Please Use Back of Page or Additional Sheets if Needed.

A) In what ways have we not met your expectations of the services we described to you when you became a client?

B) How can we improve the quality of services we are providing you?

C) What do you like best about the services provided you by IOC?

D) What additional services would you like to see IOC provide?

E) Have you been pleased with the services provided by IOC?   ☐ **YES**   ☐ **NO**
If no, what are you not pleased about?

F) Have you been kept informed as to your investments and their performance relative to your stated goals and objectives?   ☐ **YES**   ☐ **NO**
If no, what investments do you need more information on?

G) Do you feel the quality of services provided by IOC would merit your recommendation of IOC to someone you felt could benefit from our services?
☐ **YES**   ☐ **NO**
If not, why?

H) Have there been any changes in your goals or financial condition which we should know about?

_____
Signed   Date

Thank you for providing us with this information. We look forward to continuing to serve you.

UNHAPPY CLIENTS CAN be outrageously costly. It is not unusual for small law firms to charge $15,000 to $25,000 or even more to represent an adviser or broker at arbitration. Larger firms in New York, Washington, D.C., or Los Angeles might charge two or three times this amount. If the matter goes to court trial, the range is even more extreme. It might cost $30,000 just in pre-trial costs and an additional $30,000 if a small law firm takes the case to trial. Large broker-dealers have reported it is not unusual to spend $100,000 to defend a single court action. These costs will be incurred no matter what the outcome. [1]

Clearly, one lawsuit can put a small or medium-sized broker-dealer out of business and bankrupt the adviser.

Legal costs can be just the beginning. One E&O carrier found that for every dollar spent in legal fees, advisers spent an additional $4 to $10 in other ways. These included lost time, lost production, use of administrative staff, investigation, expert witnesses, and travel.

There are other costs to having an unhappy client that are hard to quantify. In addition to the obvious loss of income while preparing a case, it is hard to put a value on a damaged reputation or on the stress of preparing for a public confrontation regarding your ethics and abilities as a financial adviser. Unhappy clients are time-consuming and emotionally draining.

In short, unhappy clients do not add to the bottom line, they detract, and we want to avoid them at all costs. That is what this chapter is all about: identifying unhappy clients, satisfying them, and—when nothing else works—peacefully separating from them.

Identification of the Difficult Client

SOME CLIENTS WILL CAUSE you difficulty no matter what you do. Spotting the difficult client before trouble occurs was reviewed in Chapter 11. If at all possible, you want to screen these people out before they become clients. Although the following groups may not necessarily be ones you want to avoid, they will require you to pay close attention to details. You should at least recognize they have a greater than average probability of becoming unhappy clients.

◆ **The elderly and the infirm.** There are a number of reasons the elderly and the infirm can be difficult clients. Sometimes these clients are very lucid when you start working with them, but a few years later their mental capacity may fluctuate or be slowly eroding.

This can be particularly troublesome if you are not sure they always comprehend your recommendations and the risks. The elderly are also more likely to be targeted by aggressive law firms looking for unhappy investors, and they seem to have an easier time winning certain cases. Take extra care with the elderly and infirm, and if there is any question at all as to whether or not they understand the implications of your recommendations, you may want to involve a family member in all of the decisions.

◆ **Risk takers.** These are people who love gambling for high stakes and seem addicted to the adrenaline rush of risk. It is highly unlikely that these people will ever be happy with your service. Why? Because most financial advisers, insurance agents, and brokers are in the business of sleepy returns. They are not involved in helping clients make millions overnight; they want clients to get rich slowly, steadily, and safely. The more these risk-hungry clients push you for higher returns, the bigger your problems will be.

◆ **Clients with a lengthy litigation history.** There are a few clients who make a business out of suing their brokers. The best way to avoid them is by asking a number of questions in your initial interviewing process, including how many advisers they have had in the past and why they terminated each relationship. The client that has had one previous adviser may not raise any red flags, but the potential client who has a long history of previous advisers and even lawsuits would definitely be one to avoid.

◆ **Clients who do not want to get involved.** Occasionally you will find a client who will say something along the lines of, "Don't tell me. I don't want to know. I trust you," or "I'll do whatever you recommend." It is absolutely imperative that clients understand their investments and the risks and that they make the decisions. After all, it is their money. Clients who want to pass on the responsibility for this decision making at the beginning of the relationship may be quick to sue when things go wrong, claiming they did not understand the risks.

◆ **Clients who are constantly changing their minds.** This type of client will be in every few months or years to change the beneficiaries of their policies and investments. They want high returns one year and low risk the next. This can be a lawsuit waiting to happen. Once your client finally dies, the previous unhappy beneficiaries who are now excluded are likely to sue you to recoup their bequests. It is becoming more common for children and heirs to sue their deceased parents' advisers for not making more money.

Difficult Client Graduation

INTO EVERY PRACTICE, an unhappy client will fall despite all your prior screening and diligent efforts to communicate honestly, clearly, and frequently. You do not want these clients to go away mad, you just want them to go away. If they go away mad, they are likely to pass along their anger to other potential or current clients. No one needs to generate bad public relations.

Whenever possible, "graduate" your difficult clients. Two planners from New Jersey have shared their wonderful method for detaching themselves from the difficult client. It goes like this: About a year in advance, they set the stage with a series of comments, such as "You know, about a year from now, we expect your portfolio will be in such good shape you probably won't need our services any longer." At the next meeting, they may say, "One way that we will be able to increase your income in retirement is to eliminate our fees. Once we get your affairs straightened out, you will be able to manage them on your own, without us." Another meeting might include the comment, "We are getting close to getting your portfolio on automatic pilot."

The beauty of this system is the client is mentally prepared for the transition and feels comfortable with it. They can take pleasure in being graduated.

Other clients need to be forcibly graduated. If you have set the stage correctly at your initial interview (reviewed in Chapter 11), you can now approach them with this script: "When we first started doing business together, I mentioned that I have a few expectations of my clients, too. One is that they are scrupulously honest with me. I have found that you have consistently withheld important information from me, and it has kept me from doing my best work for you. I do not think I can continue to work with you under these circumstances. I would like to refer you to another planner if you would like me to do that. If not, tell me how you would like me to proceed in closing out your file."

Finally, there are certain circumstances under which, no matter how difficult the client is, you do not want to fire them. These are the smoking gun cases. Perhaps an investment went bad, or you have done something clearly wrong and it could come back to haunt you. You do not want to separate yourself from this type of client.

The painful truth is that you want to keep these clients close to you, where you can keep an eye on them. You do not want them to go to the adviser or broker down the block who will go through their file and prepare the case for a lawsuit. It is best to keep an eye on these clients and try to keep them happy, even when they are really difficult.

Warning Signals

SPOTTING PROBLEMS BEFORE they erupt is always the best offense. Even though you have focused faithfully on fulfilling your client's expectations, obtained good feedback, and educated your staff about compliance issues, all may not be well in your relationship. You need to be able to recognize the symptoms of an unhappy client early. You want to stop these clients from walking right into the courtroom and, instead, cause them to walk right back into your office and continue to invest with you. Taking an unpleasant situation and turning it into something positive will not only be good for you, it will be good for the client as well.

First, look at the early warning signals. Sometimes financial advisers get so wrapped up in their day-to-day business they ignore the obvious signs of an unhappy client. Here are a few common ones.

◆ **Unusual questions, phone calls, and letters.** Anything out of the ordinary may signal trouble.

◆ **Requests for files, prospectuses, or detailed investment history.** If your clients want a copy of the prospectus for a limited partnership you recommended six years ago, you can be sure they are preparing a case.

◆ **More or fewer phone calls.** If you have clients who are typically calling you all the time and suddenly you do not hear from them, that can mean trouble. The opposite is also true if you start receiving a lot of phone calls from the clients who never used to call you in the past.

◆ **Unusual questions about statements.** For example, the client you have been working with for many years suddenly says, "Could you explain this statement to me again? How does it work?" It may be a red flag if they are asking you about things they should have known from the very first week you started working with them.

◆ **Large sums of money missing from their accounts.** You may not be aware that anything is amiss until you get copies of their statements and notice that $50,000 is missing from their money market account. It could mean nothing—or it could mean they are unhappy and do not want to talk to you about it.

You may have missed the early warning signals, but the next stage is impossible to ignore: clearly ringing alarm bells.

There are two kinds of alarm bells. The first includes letters from attorneys or regulatory bodies such as NASD and SEC. If you start getting requests for information or notice of complaints from a regulator or investor's attorney, you will want to contact your compliance department immediately. You will also need to clear your calendar and work on the issue right away because it is extremely important. You will not want to talk directly to the client, the attorney, or the regulator until you have a strategy that has been reviewed with your legal counsel and compliance department.

The second kind of alarm bells are from clients or their close relatives. These can be threatening letters or phone calls or even visits where the clients say openly they are not happy with your service or their returns. The rest of these suggestions deal with this second type of wake-up call, before things have escalated to the attorney or regulatory stage.

Client Conciliation

WHEN DEALING WITH THE angry client, avoid making excuses. Do not belittle, condemn, or criticize other people who may be involved, such as your secretary, your home office, or the product sponsor. Never use humor or make light of the situation. Losing money is a serious issue to a client, and humor will make them believe you do not view their concern with the proper amount of respect. Avoid using technical terms or turning the tables, trying to make it look as if it was really the client's fault in the first place. This is not the time to start debating the facts.

Always avoid an admission against interest. An admission against interest is tantamount to a confession in a criminal case. For example, if Jerry Planner said to

Ursula Unhappy Investor, "I committed a serious error in handling your case and I am completely responsible," it would be an admission against Jerry's interest. These admissions can be damaging to your case later when the client gets on the witness stand and says, "Yes, when I confronted Jerry about this issue he said, 'You know, I really messed up here. I should have done more due diligence and I always was worried about that general partner'." It is almost impossible to win a case after you have made these damaging comments.

When the clients confront you with their dissatisfaction, you are likely to become angry. It is a natural response. After all, here is a client you valued and have worked very hard to satisfy, and now that client is threatening to take away your sense of financial security and damage your reputation.

However, it is important to control that anger, particularly in front of the client. Admit to yourself that anger is a matter of choice and that you can choose not to be angry—or at least not to be angry in front of your client. Let a little time pass before addressing the issue, but not too much time. You want the client to know you are being responsive, but it may take a few days to calm down so that you can come across in a positive manner. Be sure to diffuse your anger in a safe way.

If all of your prevention techniques have not worked and you still have unhappy clients, there is one major message you want to convey to the clients at every opportunity: "We want to make sure you are satisfied. There is no need to panic." When you talk to them, do so calmly and deliberately, all the while letting them know you value them and their business.

It is important to differentiate between telling a client you want them to be satisfied and saying, "I am really sorry I made a serious error in your account." Wanting to keep the client satisfied is not an admission against interest, and that is why it is the appropriate script to keep rephrasing and restating to the unhappy client.

Nine-Step
Conciliation Process

FINALLY, HAVE A PLAN to bring about resolution. The most comforting thing for you will be the realization of being able to get this issue resolved. The following nine steps guide you through a conciliation process.

It is extremely important to follow all nine steps in order. In the emotionally charged and stressful experience of dealing with an unhappy client, many people want to rush right to Step Six and state "What will it take to keep you satisfied?" and then cut the client a check. This can be a big mistake for a number of reasons. One, your E&O carrier will probably not cover you for settling this matter without contacting them. More important, without a chance to vent feelings and to be sure you do indeed understand the complaint, the client is not likely to be satisfied. Doing each step sequentially sets up the entire process for soothing the client, so that he or she is in a good position to want to resolve the matter amicably and move on.

STEP 1. Notify your compliance department and E&O carrier immediately. This is probably required in your agreement with your broker-dealer, but it is an important step in any event. You want the compliance officers on your side, working with you to make sure your client is satisfied. Ask for suggestions. The compliance officers have probably seen hundreds of cases just like yours. They are extremely experienced and will have a lot of thoughts on how to quickly bring the matter to conclusion.

It is equally important to notify your E&O carrier that trouble is brewing. Frequently, E&O carriers can refuse to pay a claim if you have handled the matter on your own without involving them from the very beginning.

STEP 2. Schedule a face-to-face meeting with the client. This step will not work well by letter or over the telephone. It is important for the client to sit with you across the table to see personally that you are sincere, concerned, and desperately eager to make this situation right.

STEP 3. Listen, listen, listen. The entire process will not succeed without this key element. Many clients just want to vent their feelings and frustrations. They do not really want to go to the expense, hassle, and emotionally draining procedure of suing you. They just want to make sure you are listening to their frustrations. Do not interrupt the client. Just keep nodding your head and saying, "Tell me more" or "Please elaborate on that last point."

This is not the time to offer your views. Just allow the client to continue dumping. When you think the client has finished, take a deep breath before you speak because he or she is likely to start up again. Once the client seems to have run out of steam, you should ask the next question, "Is there anything else that is bothering you?" Almost always you will find that there is something else. Keep asking this question until the client finally says, "No, I think that is it." While you are listening, remember never to interrupt. Also, *do not* offer your own views of the situation. Resist the temptation to jump in and defend yourself or go on the defensive.

It is amazing how many clients just want the chance to vent their frustrations. Sometimes this is all the client really needed to do, and it completely solves the problem.

STEP 4. Empathize. It does not hurt to say "I know this must be hard for you." Let the client know you are concerned and realize how difficult it is to bring this matter to your attention. You might say, "I really appreciate your talking with me about this. I know how difficult it must be for you, and I want to make sure we get things resolved to your satisfaction." Keep reminding yourself that this entire incident may have nothing at all to do with you. The client's unhappy marriage, difficulty with relatives, or a job loss may be the real problem.

STEP 5. Restate the client's position. By rephrasing comments, you are letting the client know that you do in fact completely understand the point. If the client does not believe you understand, let the client explain it again until he or she is convinced you thoroughly understand the client's point of view.

STEP 6. Ask "What will it take to keep you satisfied?" The next thing you do, and this is critically important, is to *keep quiet*. Experts in the art of negotiating will tell you, "He who speaks first loses." Keeping quiet at this stage may be the hardest part. It is highly likely that your client does not have a clue as to what he or she wants or would find satisfying, particularly if the client is just angry and wants to let off steam. It is important that you do not start offering suggestions on how you can fix concerns. Financial advisers will frequently offer more than what the client really wanted in the first place.

If you ask, "What will it take to keep you satisfied?" and you hear nothing from across the table, resist the temptation to start making suggestions. Keep your mouth closed as long as possible. If you are having a hard time doing that, you might say, "Well, why don't you think about it for a few minutes while I go get us a cup of coffee." Do a few laps around the office, pick up the coffee, open a letter or two, and then amble back into the meeting room and repeat the question, "What will it take to keep you satisfied?" If the client still does not have a suggestion, ask the client to take the night to think it over and meet with you face-to-face the next day. You can reiterate that you want to keep the client satisfied, but it is important for you to know exactly what he or she had in mind. Sometimes clients are already satisfied because they have had the opportunity to ventilate all of their feelings. It may take them a few minutes or hours to realize it.

STEP 7. Request time to review possible alternatives. Then set a specific date for getting back to the client. One of the worst things a planner or adviser can do at this stage is to come up with a solution at the meeting. Although you may not realize it, these meetings are emotionally charged. You may not be thinking of all the ramifications of different solutions. Or, the client could propose a solution that appears fine to you on the surface but may violate certain rules with your broker-dealer. Requesting a future meeting gives you a chance to buy time, gather your thoughts, and review the consequences of different alternatives.

STEP 8. Review the options for resolution with your compliance department, E&O carrier, or attorney. One key factor to take into consideration when settling with an unhappy client are the NASD settlement rules and disclosure requirements. Any settlement with a client in excess of $5,000 must be reported on your U-4. Consequently, it is far better to settle a case for $4,999 because it does not have to be reported.

STEP 9. Agree on a plan of action. In order for any plan to succeed, it must be acceptable to both sides. Clarify who is going to do what and by what date. If necessary, and you are making a financial settlement, make sure you have a release from the client that confirms the client will not sue you over this issue.

Complaint Strategies

CLIENT COMPLAINTS CAN usually be divided into three categories. The first category is the scurrilous or completely unjustified. These are the cases where there is absolutely no basis in law or fact for what clients are asserting. They have no legal grounds— they just want a lot of money.

The best strategy in these cases is to review all claims carefully, then write back a detailed letter rebutting each and every claim with specificity. At the end of your letter, conclude by throwing down the gauntlet. The language might be, "If you still want to proceed, go ahead, and take your best shot," or, "If this letter does not completely satisfy all your concerns, we will see you in court." More than 80 percent of all claims of this kind should disappear with this strong approach.

Category two involves cases that are justified. In these matters, there is no question that the representative or adviser made some error or committed some misconduct. A good strategy to resolve these cases is to work with the client to make them whole as soon as possible. You want these cases to go away and go away quickly. You will never win them. The sooner you can resolve them, the less expensive they will be. Dragging these cases out tends to make clients even more angry; their demands rise and your attorney fees escalate.

Category three involves the partially justified. These are the most difficult cases to resolve because there may have been some negligence or wrongdoing on the part of the adviser or representative, but the client may have been guilty, too. Typically, the client did not disclose all the facts. Or, the client was thoroughly aware of the risks and now claims complete ignorance. These cases are difficult because there are iniquities on both sides. These are the ones you will want to negotiate to find an acceptable compromise. Before sending any responses, review them with your compliance department and attorney.

Good communication does pay. Many wonder why there are not more lawsuits. In fact, clients can be amazingly forgiving with bad investments, particularly if you communicate with them using the steps outlined in this chapter. In addition, it is expensive for unhappy investors to sue. Many clients with losses of $50,000 or less will have a difficult time finding any attorney to represent them. Finally, it is difficult for investors to find an attorney who thoroughly understands this area. Unfortunately this last point cuts two ways: it can also be hard to find an attorney to defend these cases.

BUILDING A
GOOD
DEFENSE

SOMETIMES EVEN THE best offense cannot save the game. When it comes time to play defense, learn what you can do to calm angry clients, avoid lawsuits even if a client has already engaged an attorney, and survive a regulator's audit.

The remaining chapters acquaint you with claims clients make and responses available to you. Having appropriate insurance coverage is vital. Knowing the pros and cons of mediation, arbitration, and litigation enable you to determine what is at stake and how you should react. Even in a worst-case scenario, it is possible to save thousands of dollars in legal fees and damages.

WHEN CLIENTS SUE

THERE ARE TWO KINDS of financial planners, says J. Michael Dryton, a Kansas City attorney: those who have been sued and those who will be sued.[1]

One thing is certain: clients never complain about a well-performing investment, no matter how many rules their adviser may have violated in selling it. Given a significant market downturn, even the most agreeable clients may rush to their attorneys to seek reimbursement for losses.

As you start remaking your practice to become a world-class adviser, keep in mind there is a big difference between committing an action that could compel a client to sue you and actually getting sued. You may have done everything perfectly and still find yourself subject to a lawsuit or arbitration.

Lawsuits and arbitrations against brokers and advisers do track the market. However, even if the primary motivator for an investor to sue is losing money, this by itself is not sufficient legal grounds to succeed in court or arbitration. Why? Most investments do not guarantee profits. Therefore a court would dismiss a case that only alleges the investor lost money, because no one is responsible or legally liable for making the investment profitable.

In order to recoup losses, attorneys will frame the case using legal theories that are likely to succeed. These might be: the plaintiff is entitled to reimbursement because the broker was negligent and failed to disclose the investment's risks; or the plaintiff is entitled to be made whole because the broker committed fraud, failed to disclose material facts, and recommended an unsuitable investment. If the broker had truly made an unsuitable or negligent recommendation, but the market went up, a lawsuit would be only a slight possibility.

Although clients are free to file claims with their state securities department or insurance commission, or with the SEC and NASD, they sometimes press a claim on their own. The Investment Advisers Act, however, does not provide a means for the client to sue under a private cause of action for damages lost in investments. In *TransAmerica Mortgage Advisers Inc. v. Lewis,* [2] the Supreme Court held that a client's private right of action under the Act was limited to recision of the investment advisory agreement. This means that, although clients cannot receive any compensation for investments that have gone sour, they could receive reimbursement of all their fees paid to the adviser under a theory of recision. Nevertheless, it has become commonplace for clients to sue under a negligence theory and use the provisions of the Act to define the standard of care. Using this method, a client can indirectly achieve compensation for damages, even though damages are not allowed under the Act.[3]

Remember the three-step process for bullet-proofing your practice:

1 **Keep clients happy.** If that does not succeed, then:

2 **Aggressively work to satisfy your clients' concerns.** If that does not succeed, then:

3 **Prepare every file for the worst.**

Preparing every file for the worst means being able to say to yourself: Even though I have done nothing wrong in this case, if I am sued on the common legal grounds, I have written evidence that will exonerate me. Some of the most common causes of action—unsuitability, conflicts of interest, violating a fiduciary duty, and failure to disclose risks and sales charges—are covered elsewhere in this book. This chapter covers fraud and other common theories. As you review each one, ask yourself what written evidence would be necessary to defend this kind of claim. Then make sure you include that in every file.

Motivations

MOST PLANNERS AND ADVISERS assume the biggest motivation in filing a complaint is financial reimbursement. Although that can be a large factor, frequently it is not the guiding force in investor actions. Often, investors just want to vent their frustrations. They are angry that their investment went down. They may even be upset with themselves for not having a clearer picture of the risks involved, although they will rarely admit this. They may feel deceived and cheated. Sometimes they just want an apology.

Giving investors a chance to express their feelings can go a long way toward resolving a dispute before it gets out of hand. Keep reminding yourself: The investor may want something other than just dollars. It is well worth your time to let clients vent and see if there are other things, such as an apology or even a fee reduction, that would satisfy them. Your clients' real motivation may surprise you. This issue was covered in greater detail in Chapter 14.

Realize that the attorney representing you in this matter may not be in touch with the deep emotional issues motivating unhappy investors. Some attorneys see solutions only in terms of dollars and cents. If your attorney has not brought up this subject, feel free to ask her to explore it. Satisfying an investor's real motivations can bring a situation to a quicker resolution.

An attorney's motivation for assisting an investor is easy to determine. Attorneys want fees, lots of fees. Most attorneys handling cases against advisers or other financial professionals work on a contingent fee basis. That means three concepts are important to you:

1 The attorneys do not get paid unless the investor receives an award or settlement. The larger the settlement, the higher the attorneys' fees.

2 The attorneys want to work as little as possible to get the award and get paid.

3 The well-prepared defendant is an unpleasant and costly nuisance to contingent-fee attorneys. Soon attorneys begin to fear they might not get paid at all, or not enough to justify their time. This works to your advantage, because it will motivate the lawyers to recommend a quicker and smaller settlement.[4]

Negligence Theories

ALTHOUGH FRAUD AND THEFT cases are certainly the most entertaining and interesting to the media, they are few and far between. Even though NASAA calculated that fraud and abuse by financial planning professionals cost customers at least $90 million a year, IAFP estimates actual fraud and abuse among all planners at less than 2/100 of 1 percent.[5] Of course, any fraud at all is too much, yet it is far more likely for clients to suffer from the incompetence or negligence of their adviser than from outright theft.

The following points cover areas in which careless work or negligence can lead to legal action.

FAILURE TO PERFORM THE WORK WITH THE APPROPRIATE STANDARD OF CARE As Eli Bernzweig said: "Every person is responsible for conducting himself in a reasonable and prudent manner. When someone fails to conduct himself in this required manner and causes harm to another, he is 'negligent' and can be held liable for the damages his action, or inaction, cause. The failure to meet the required standard of care is professional negligence or malpractice."[6]

The standard a planner or financial adviser will be measured against is the standard of care provided by reasonably prudent planners or financial advisers. However, planners or advisers who hold themselves out as having additional expertise or as a subject matter expert will be held to a higher standard of care.

The standard of care can also be derived from the Codes of Ethics of the CFP Board of Standards, IAFP, NAPFA, NASD, and similar organizations. Courts or arbitration panels may also look at SEC regulations, prior cases, inner office memos, and even home office compliance manuals to establish the appropriate standard of care. As the court observed in one case, "The alleged violation of the NASD Rules of Fair Practice is relevant . . . not to form the basis of an action, but to suggest what duty the defendant had to the plaintiff."[7] Generally, for a case to succeed on this theory the plaintiff must prove:[8]

1 A legal duty or requirement to conform to a certain standard of conduct.

Malpractice Risk Test

TO IMPROVE YOUR chances of winning a suit, take the following test. Be totally honest with yourself. For a firm yes, score 2 points; for a weak yes, score 1 point. Give yourself 0 for a no response.

I keep detailed written notes in my files of all conversations, without exceptions, that I have with clients and others pertaining to active and prospective cases.

☐ **FIRM YES**　　☐ **WEAK YES**　　☐ **NO**

I periodically review (and document) with active clients the status and progress of their financial goals and plans. I use a tickler system to make sure I do not miss any review.

☐ **FIRM YES**　　☐ **WEAK YES**　　☐ **NO**

I always start every client relationship by establishing the client's expectations and documenting them in my file.

☐ **FIRM YES**　　☐ **WEAK YES**　　☐ **NO**

I regularly review clients' expectations of me and their level of satisfaction with my work.

☐ **FIRM YES**　　☐ **WEAK YES**　　☐ **NO**

If a client is angry and threatening, I always call my compliance department first. (Give yourself full credit if you have never had any unhappy clients.)

☐ **FIRM YES**　　☐ **WEAK YES**　　☐ **NO**

My compliance director knows me by name, and I

read everything submitted from that department cover to cover. I have personally interviewed the person in charge of due diligence at my broker-dealer and am satisfied that their systems and review are the best possible. If I do not have a compliance director, I subscribe to different publications to make sure I stay on top of this area.

☐ **FIRM YES** ☐ **WEAK YES** ☐ **NO**

If a client called me today about an investment I sold to her five years ago, I could find a copy of the original prospectus within 30 minutes.

☐ **FIRM YES** ☐ **WEAK YES** ☐ **NO**

I use a checklist in every case to make sure nothing falls through the cracks.

☐ **FIRM YES** ☐ **WEAK YES** ☐ **NO**

I am familiar with my own personal abilities, strengths, and limitations. I do not exceed my own limitations. I ask for help from an expert when necessary or decline cases that are beyond my ability. I continually study and take programs to improve my skills and stay current.

☐ **FIRM YES** ☐ **WEAK YES** ☐ **NO**

I work with my staff to educate them regarding our legal and ethical requirements. I carefully supervise them to make sure they do not exceed their limitations and training.

☐ **FIRM YES** ☐ **WEAK YES** ☐ **NO**

At least once a year I reread the code of ethics for

(continued on following page)

the associations to which I belong.
☐ **FIRM YES** ☐ **WEAK YES** ☐ **NO**

I never promise a client specific investment returns
(unless they are specifically guaranteed in writing).
☐ **FIRM YES** ☐ **WEAK YES** ☐ **NO**

I ask every question on the new account forms and
never guess at the answers. I ask the client to sign
the form and let me know if there are any changes
in their financial condition.
☐ **FIRM YES** ☐ **WEAK YES** ☐ **NO**

At the end of every discussion with a client or
prospective client, I make sure there is no doubt
as to what was discussed and the agreed on
action.
☐ **FIRM YES** ☐ **WEAK YES** ☐ **NO**

All my client files are neat and orderly.
☐ **FIRM YES** ☐ **WEAK YES** ☐ **NO**

I explain the risks and sales charges of every
investment. I explain about the financial strengths
of every insurance company I recommend. If suitability is questionable, I err on the side of caution.
☐ **FIRM YES** ☐ **WEAK YES** ☐ **NO**

I use prospectus receipts and risk receipts.
☐ **FIRM YES** ☐ **WEAK YES** ☐ **NO**

Before I begin any work for a client, I always disclose in writing how I am compensated.
☐ **FIRM YES** ☐ **WEAK YES** ☐ **NO**

If I am a financial planning practitioner, I am registered with the SEC or my state as an investment adviser, or I am affiliated with one. If I am relying on an exclusion or exemption (from registration), I have a written letter from my attorney or compliance department advising me this is appropriate.

☐ FIRM YES ☐ WEAK YES ☐ NO

Give yourself 2 points if you have been in business for five or more years and you have never had a client file a complaint against you with your state securities/insurance commissioner, SEC, or NASD.

☐ 2 POINTS

Also give yourself 2 points for the dismissal of any complaints that were made because the complaints were unsubstantiated or unfounded.

☐ 2 POINTS

TOTAL SCORE _____

Scoring

33 AND ABOVE	You are truly awesome! Your compliance department loves you.
25—32:	Tightening up some areas will help you sleep better and improve client relations.
16—24:	Immediate action is necessary! Schedule one day a week for revising your practice until you can get a handle on all of your areas of exposure.
BELOW 16:	How can you sleep at all? Cancel all your appointments next week and focus on getting your files and systems in shape.

2 The requirements of the standard of care.

3 A failure to conform to the standard.

4 A connection between the conduct and the resulting harm.

5 Actual losses or damages.

FAILURE TO SUPERVISE EMPLOYEES Many planners and advisers do not realize they can become responsible, both legally and financially, for the work of their paraplanners, assistants, and secretaries. Under the common law doctrine of *respondeat superior,* the master had to answer for the servant's actions. Financial advisers, as employers, can be held strictly liable for the negligent or wrongful actions of an assistant, paraplanner, or other subordinate, if that action causes injury and it occurred during the scope of employment. Although it is almost impossible to be in the financial services business without delegating some authority, there is a certain amount of risk involved, particularly when the delegated tasks are highly technical in nature.

To protect your clients from harm, make sure all your subordinates know exactly what you require of them and the deadlines for those actions. Do not delegate any activity unless you are absolutely sure your employee or assistant is capable of doing the job well. Make sure your subordinates know the limits of their activities. For instance, it is never appropriate for unlicensed people to give clients advice regarding insurance or securities.

Spot-check employees' work carefully. Question them regarding their ethics and make sure they understand all the legalities of your practice. Invite them to compliance workshops. It is important they have the skills necessary to check your work. They might see something you have missed. Have your subordinates read all your office compliance manuals, signing a statement that they not only read them but also understood the contents. Review the issues with them on a frequent basis. Remember, if they violate a security or insurance law during the course of their employment with you, you will be held responsible.

MISREPRESENTATION Another common claim against financial advisers is that an investment or insurance policy was misrepresented. Claiming that the planner or broker lied is common, because it can lead to substantial awards for punitive damages. This theory is similar to the common law action for deceit. These claims can be difficult to fight because it becomes your word against the clients'. In order to succeed, the plaintiff must prove: [9]

1 The defendant made a false representation.

2 The defendant knew, or should have known, the representation was false.

3 The defendant intended the plaintiff to act or refrain from acting based on the misrepresentation.

4 The plaintiff relied on the misrepresentation in taking action or refraining from acting.

5 The plaintiff suffered losses or damages due to the reliance.

Take care when describing the risks and the possible returns or benefits of an investment. Never portray either the risks or the rewards differently from the prospectus, or highlight or mark up the prospectus. Review the risk section of the prospectus in detail with the clients, encouraging them to make notes in their own handwriting in the margins as you go along. Do not, however, mark the prospectus for them. Attorneys have argued that the areas marked on were the only sections the clients were told to read.

DILEMMA

RANDY REP IS TOUTING a high-tech company stock to his client. He does not mention that the company has operated at a deficit or that during the entire period he was recommending the stock the company was insolvent. Instead, Randy tells the client that the company is a winner and will make money. It has fabulous potential and will double or triple, making Netscape or Microsoft look like they are standing still. Randy says he has purchased the stock for himself and he will be able to get rich on it and retire. It has possibilities of skyrocketing and will probably double in price within six months. Randy does not mention any of the company's many problems. The client loses money and sues for misrepresentation.

Question: How would you decide?

Answer: This is a clear case of misrepresentation. In one federal case,[10] four securities salesmen were permanently barred by the SEC from further association with any broker or dealer for fraudulent conduct. The conduct consisted of optimistic representations made without disclosure of information which rendered them materially misleading. In other words, they did not give the clients the downside of the investment. The court held: "Brokers and salesmen are under a duty to investigate, and their violation of that duty brings them within the term 'willful' in the Exchange Act. Thus, a salesman cannot deliberately ignore that which he has a duty to know and recklessly state facts about matters of which he is ignorant . . . Where the salesman lacks essential information about a security, he should disclose this as well as the risks which arise from his lack of information." Note the standard here was for a *salesperson*. It is reasonable to assume, if you have a higher duty as a financial planner or investment adviser, there would be an even greater responsibility to disclose the downside of an investment.

FAILURE TO DISCLOSE MATERIAL FACTS An issue similar to misrepresentation is the failure to disclose material facts. With misrepresentation there is the element of deceit, a sin of commission. Failure to disclose a material fact is more a sin of omission: failing to inform clients of important information that would have a significant impact on their decision to invest.

Rule 10b-5[11] states it is unlawful, in connection with the sale of a security, to make any untrue statement of a material fact or *omit to state a material fact*. Although it is difficult to generalize on how material is material, look to all your clients' circumstances. The more elderly, less sophisticated, and less educated your client, the greater the duty to inform. More information will be required for complex and high-risk investments than for simple, conservative ones. Always make sure you give the client a prospectus and get a signed delivery receipt. A copy of one is included in Appendix B.

You should also review the client's goals and relate how each investment will fit into those goals. Discuss the track record of the investment promoters and always show the downside potential in every case, making sure the client understands that there are no guarantees.[12]

NEGLIGENT SOLUTIONS OR RECOMMENDATIONS Although this can be extremely difficult to prove, sometimes a client will claim the planner's forecasts, solutions to problems, or recommendations were so out of the norm that they are entitled to damages for losses. Plaintiffs must prove other prudent professionals would have made substantially different recommendations based on the same facts at that point in time. The fact that tax laws or market conditions changed later, making an investment less valuable, is not a consideration. Financial advisers can defend these actions by proving they exercised the required degree of prudence and care in arriving at their conclusions and recommendations and that other competent professionals would have come to the same conclusions.

BETSY PLANNER RECOMMENDS an investment for her clients which has significant tax benefits. Betsy fails to consider the Alternative Minimum Tax when computing the potential tax advantages for the clients. The IRS later disallows the favorable tax treatment because of the Alternative Minimum Tax.
Question: Has Betsy been negligent?
Answer: Yes. The standard of care regarding recommending tax investments includes consideration of all the common tax treatments that may result from a tax-favored investment.

FAILURE TO CONSULT WITH AN EXPERT Because this industry is complex and rapidly changing, incompetence is one of the major reasons clients suffer loss. It is all too easy for financial advisers to get in over their heads, not even realizing they are beyond their level of competence. No planner, agent, or broker is required to be an expert in every area of financial planning, insurance, or the securities markets. However, you are expected to spot problems if you encounter them and obtain the proper assistance for your client.

If you are presented with any technical issue that seems out of the norm, have an expert review the situation and give you an opinion on how to proceed. Should the investment later go south, you will have helped protect yourself with the expert's opinion. Note it is equally important to select your expert with care. If you are looking to an incompetent expert to bolster your case, you may find you are both going down together.

NEGLIGENT CASE PROCEDURES AND MANAGEMENT One of your key responsibilities is to stay on top of things and make sure a customer's matters are handled expeditiously. Failure to meet critical time factors such as tax deadlines, processing insurance applications or investments promptly, or even updating critical legal documents can create serious financial losses for your clients. These cases are almost impossible to defend. Either you processed the information necessary to meet the tax deadline or you did not. There is no gray area. Take the time to set up internal procedures to make sure nothing falls through the cracks and all matters are processed in a timely fashion. A sample checklist to help you do so is included in Chapter 12.

ABANDONMENT OF THE CLIENT Seasoned planners or financial advisers have all worked with clients they would like to avoid. However, failing to handle the client's affairs in a timely manner can be deemed abandonment. Abandonment occurs when planners or advisers withdraw their services at a time when it is likely to prove harmful to the client's interests.

DILEMMA

MR. AND MRS. SMALL BUSINESS Owner retain Tony Planner to make recommendations on the allocation of certain assets. This information is needed to make changes before the end of the tax year, and Tony knows it. Tony fails to review the plan and does not get around to returning the clients' letters and phone calls. The clients sue because of the disastrous tax consequences of making investment changes in the following year.
Question: How would you decide?
Answer: This seems to be an open and shut case in the client's favor. Furthermore, Tony is unable to show any attempt at getting the work done on time. Tony will be personally responsible for the losses.

How do planners and advisers get into a position of ignoring a client or being irresponsible with critical deadlines? Certainly, there are some relaxed types who always miss deadlines, and were probably late for their own weddings, but there may be a deeper cause in most other situations. Lawyers have identified the same problems in their ranks, where failure to handle a client's case in a timely manner can have disastrous results. Lawyers have now set up programs nationally to get at the root issues of many of these delays: alcohol and substance abuse. If you know a fellow professional is abusing alcohol or other substances, it is not only a problem for him and his family, but for his clients and the industry. This can be a particular problem if the troubled adviser is one of your partners or colleagues. If you can take action to help him, you will be helping his clients, too.

There are only three ways to safely terminate a client relationship: death—either the adviser or the client dies; discharge—with or without cause, the client ends the relationship with the adviser; and withdrawal—after written notice to the client, preferably with the client's consent, the adviser withdraws.

Whenever terminating a client relationship, make sure the client's interests are not jeopardized and the client has ample time to find another professional.[13] More information on how to separate from the difficult client is covered in Chapter 14.

FAILURE TO PERFORM ADEQUATE DUE DILIGENCE In a *Forbes* magazine article, it was reported that a successful financial planner had been subject to numerous lawsuits and extensive fines by NASD. One of the major claims alleged in these suits was that the planner failed to perform due diligence by failing to carefully review an investment before recommending it to clients. In one case, the planner received an 8 percent commission for recommending the investment, plus an additional 2 percent for doing due diligence. This case provided particularly strong grounds for the clients to sue. Because the planner was paid to perform the due diligence, but did not do it properly in the client's opinion, the client was entitled to a refund when the risks were misrepresented. The client alleged the planner would have known the risks in the investment if proper due diligence had been performed.[14]

Failing to do due diligence is far more common than most realize. Regrettably, many financial advisers rely only on the information given them by wholesalers to clearly understand products. This is a particularly important issue if you are a member of a small broker-dealer that does not have the staff necessary to thoroughly research all the investments on its approved list. In that case, your own personal records should also reflect the time you have spent in reviewing the product and its sponsors. Include all the notes on your research with the original prospectus and sales literature that you keep on every investment you recommend.

Other Causes of Action

OTHER CAUSES OF ACTION can arise from situations over which you have little control or in which you feel you have acted correctly. The trend toward asset protection, for example, creates all sorts of problems. So, too, do divorce situations and ERISA rules. Finally, while you may think you have correctly read a covenant not to compete, a firm may often disagree with you. These areas are discussed below.

ASSET PROTECTION Savvy investors, particularly successful entrepreneurs and those with inherited wealth, are becoming more infatuated with the trend toward asset protection. Whether they fear a divorce or an action from a competitor, they are looking for ways to protect their assets in the event of a lawsuit. These techniques can be simple, such as transferring property to the spouse, or extremely complex, such as establishing a series of offshore trusts.

Because of the complexity and the vast amounts of money involved in these arrangements, they can expose the financial planner or adviser to severe personal liability. "This area is fraught with perils," says Barbara McInerney, General Counsel at Royal Alliance in New York. "A little knowledge can be dangerous."[15]

There are a number of ways a planner can be exposed, as described below.[16]

◆ The client may sue the planner for negligence if the recommended asset protection device failed or is later set aside by a court.

◆ The client's own creditor or adversary may sue the planner for assisting the debtor in secreting assets.

◆ Some clients may claim they were injured because their adviser did not recommend asset protection strategies.

◆ Criminal charges may be pending if the transfers violate the Bankruptcy Reform Act of 1994.

HERE ARE SOME TECHNIQUES for protecting your own assets.

◆ **Understand the law on fraudulent transfers.** Although there are differences in every state, it is generally illegal to assist debtors to transfer assets with the intent to hinder, delay, or defraud creditors. Sometimes fraud is found if the assets were transferred without receiving fair value. The key is whether a creditor or claim existed at the time of the transfer.

◆ **Be careful with your recommendations.** Send the client a letter stating there are a number of different possible courses of action given his situation, and then list the positive and negative consequences of each.

◆ **Bring in a skilled attorney to evaluate the alternatives.** This takes the burden off your shoulders and places it where it belongs.

DILEMMA

GEORGE GOODBODY OWNS a large network marketing company and made megamillions of dollars with his weight-loss formula. George is concerned that his former employer, Lean Bodies Incorporated, will sue him for starting "Good Bodies by Goodbody." He comes to you, his longtime financial planner, and asks if he can do something to protect his assets from the suit he knows will be filed against him soon.

Question: Should you help George protect his assets?

Answer: This probably does not pass the smell test. Although in some states George might win on the theory that Lean Bodies had not actually pressed a claim or been granted a judgment by a court, other jurisdictions would hold that he knew Lean Bodies would sue him, so any transfer was made to defraud his creditors. "A contingent action may be considered the same as one that already exists when determining whether a transfer is fraudulent," says Ted Moscowitz, a New Jersey attorney. [17] Your best bet is to pass this case on to a competent attorney who specializes in this area.

DIVORCE SITUATIONS: YOURS OR THEIRS The following situation seems to be prevalent in the South. A financial adviser's spouse, pursuant to their divorce, accuses the adviser of unauthorized trading in their joint accounts. This unfortunate situation could also occur when you have two clients who are divorcing. The clients could then allege that the adviser who followed the instructions of one spouse violated the rights of the other spouse by making unauthorized trades.

The best way to protect yourself here is to look at your New Account Forms and brokerage agreements. Make sure that trading for one spouse binds both. This matter can also be addressed in an engagement letter. Many broker-dealers can also provide you with a Limited Trading Authorization form, which should be signed by the spouse, giving trading authority to the adviser. If the spouse makes his or her own investment decisions, a letter to that effect should be signed and kept on file.

NONCOMPETE COVENANTS Sometimes even your own broker-dealer can sue you. As brokers and planners have become more mobile, making frequent changes in their broker-dealers, it has become increasingly common for representatives to be sued by their former firm for violating a covenant not to compete. Ignoring your employment documents can be costly.

DILEMMA

PRIOR TO LEAVING IDS, a planner copied the files of his best clients, sometimes taking original documents. He then sent a letter on IDS letterhead to 250 clients, enclosing a map to his new offices. The letter stated: "We are moving into space that will allow us to better serve your needs over the coming years . . . [w]e look forward to our continuing relationship and wish you a prosperous new year. Please call on us if you have any questions." The letter failed to inform the clients that the planner had already decided to leave IDS and had signed an agreement with another broker-dealer. IDS sued the planner for a temporary restraining order, injunctions, and other relief.

The planner claimed, among other things, that the restrictive covenant was overly broad and did not apply to him as an independent contractor. He also alleged that many of his clients were friends and were acquired through his own hard work and long hours.

Question: How would you decide?

Answer: The court did not find any of these arguments persuasive, stating:"[The planner] cannot complain that IDS's contract forced him to do what he agreed to do in the contract. The hard work and long hours were engaged in for the benefit of IDS and were an essential part of his agreement with IDS. If the planner did not like the arrangement offered by IDS, then he should not have accepted it." The court granted IDS the preliminary injunction with minor restrictions.[18]

ERISA RULES The Department of Labor or the client may bring a civil suit against the adviser to restore any financial loss occasioned by the adviser's failure to discharge his fiduciary duties and solely represent the interests of the pension plan participants and beneficiaries.[19] In addition, financial advisers should proceed with caution if they are earning a fee and a commission when working with retirement plans of publicly held corporations. It is best to check with your own attorney, as this may be a violation of the ERISA statutes.[20]

Taped Calls and "Securities Bankruptcy"

THE FOLLOWING ARE TWO other areas with which you should be familiar.

1 Taped phone calls. It has become more common for unhappy investors to surreptitiously tape phone calls with their brokers and advisers. The clients will then submit these tapes to NASD to be used in an investigation or as part of an arbitration. In many states it may be illegal for clients to make this tape without your consent. However, in some states these tapes may be perfectly legal. It has been reported anecdotally that even though these tapes may have been obtained illegally, NASD will, on occasion, use them against a representative.

If you think you are being taped, it is important to get off the telephone as soon as possible. Ask your client straight out, "Are you taping this conversation?" If the client says yes, then you want to respond with: "You must be awfully upset about something. Tell you what I'll do. I'll clear my calendar, have you come into my office and we will sit down right away and talk this over." Do not let this conversation go on. Instead, the message you have conveyed is that you want to keep them satisfied and see them face to face.

The client may be lying, though, and say they are not taping the conversation. If that is the case, then the lie will show up at the arbitration or later on and put the client in a bad light.

Occasionally a client will ask if they can tape an entire appointment because they are afraid they are going to forget what you said. If you are using pre-formatted agendas and meeting notes, you can assure the client that taping will not be necessary because you will be giving them detailed notes about the meeting.

2 "Securities bankruptcy." There are a number of advisers who sold bad investments, particularly limited partnerships, who are trying to purge their past by dropping their registered representative licenses and becoming RIAs and fee-only planners. Their mistaken belief is that this wipes out the past and they can move on by clearing the slate. Nothing could be further from the truth. In fact, this could be the worst thing they could do as dropping their licenses and leaving their broker-dealer can effectively terminate their E&O coverage. Not only could they be sued while they are a fee-only planner for past actions that occurred while they were in the brokerage business, but they will also have no E&O coverage.

ACTION ITEMS

◆ IF YOU ARE CITED with a legal complaint by a client, a notice to appear before an arbitration panel, or even a letter from a client who threatens legal action, contact your attorney, E&O carrier, and broker-dealer as soon as possible. Invariably, the financial adviser/defendant has only a short amount of time to respond to a civil complaint or arbitration petition. Failure to respond in a timely manner could allow the court or arbitration panel to decide the case completely in the client's favor.

◆ BEFORE YOU LEAVE your current broker-dealer, check your contract for a covenant not to compete. It may be worthwhile to have an attorney give you an opinion on how you would fare defending this kind of case in court or in NASD arbitration against your broker-dealer. If you are sure you want to take the risk, you may want to request that your new broker-dealer indemnify you should you have to face any claims from the old firm.

COMMON
COMPLAINTS

TWO OF THE MOST common complaints you could face in a lawsuit or arbitration proceeding are an investment's unsuitability and failure to disclose an investment's risks or sales charges. While you may not be able to stop clients from suing you on these grounds, you can carefully document your files to win these cases. This chapter gives an overall review of these two common complaints and how you should defend yourself.

Suitability, in particular, is viewed by some lawyers as a gold mine. "The good news is that claims of this nature tend to be difficult to sustain, absent bad faith on the part of the financial professional; the bad news is that you can go broke defending your-self."[1] That is the advice from Bud Bigelow. He is pres-ident of Cambridge Alliance, which operates as pro-gram manager for Financial Service Mutual Insurance Company. The sheer number of these complaints will only increase as lawyers for investors continue to take out full-page advertisements, now common in Florida, and encourage elderly investors to believe they may have a case if their investments have suffered losses.

Investment Suitability

ALMOST 50 PERCENT OF ALL claims made to one profes-sional E&O carrier involved an allegation of unsuitable investments.[2] As discussed in Chapter 15, very few investors are really concerned with suitability claims; they are simply unhappy with the performance of their investments. However, as there are rarely any guaran-tees as to performance, clients need another legal the-ory to advance their claim. One of the most common legal grounds is alleging that the investment was not suitable, meaning that it was not appropriate given the investor's return objectives and aversion to risk.

Although the obligation to recommend only suit-able investments may arise from a number of sources, Kathryn McGrath, former head of the Investment Management Division at the SEC, says it is the states, more than the SEC, that are scrutinizing suitability issues.[3] In addition to the states and the SEC, NASD has set standards for suitability as expressed in the NASD Rules of Fair Practice:

"In recommending to a customer the purchase, sale or exchange of any security, a member shall have reasonable grounds for believing that the recom-mendation is suitable for such customer upon the basis of the facts, if any, disclosed by such customer as to his other security holdings and as to his finan-cial situation and needs."[4]

Some investments carry their own suitability requirements. For instance, it is not unusual for a particular limited partnership to be sold only to investors with a minimum annual income of $75,000 per year and net worth of $100,000, exclusive of home and furnishings. This is an attempt by regulators and program sponsors to limit the sale of riskier investments to those who are better able to tolerate the risk.

AVOIDING A CLAIM Although suitability claims are extremely common, there are a number of things you can do to completely avoid them. If they do arise, you can have your files in such good shape that the case is easy to defend.

◆ **Scrutinize every investment before you recommend it to your client.** Use this checklist[5] as a guide for making notes about every investment you recommend.

Does the client meet the investment's minimum stated financial suitability standards without any creative accounting? If the client does not clearly fall within the guidelines, do not stretch the compliance limits. This not only destroys your reputation for integrity with the client; because the client really was not suitable, these are the very cases that go bad and come back to haunt you.

Does the investment meet the client's written, overall financial objectives? This simple criteria can help defeat even the toughest suits. Many brokers and advisers get into trouble transacting business that is clearly outside the client's stated and written objectives. Another common occurrence is a large portfolio that is geared for low risk but has one higher-risk investment for balance. Sometimes the client's objectives have changed, but the written document in the file reflects the old objectives. Frequently the objectives are the same, but the client wants to deviate from them "just this once." Always make sure the recommendations match the goals and that you can prove it by having complete notes. If this is one investment outside the norm, get a statement from the client acknowledging it is more risky than the client's stated objectives, but appropriate in these circumstances. Another possibility is to check all the boxes on the New Account Form from low risk to high risk, if that honestly describes the client and is allowed by your broker-dealer.

Does the client truly understand the risks as well as the rewards of the investment? This can sometimes be a hard call, particularly with elderly clients who may be slowly moving into dementia. If you are not sure the client understands the risks and the rewards, do not proceed. Since proving the client actually understood the riskiness of the transaction is difficult after the fact, it is good to have the client sign off on a statement that says he or she knows the investment will fluctuate in value and may be worth more or less than the purchase price.

Does the investment fall within the client's risk tolerance range and time horizon? Once again, if you have used a tool to determine risk tolerance, make sure the investment is within the guidelines.

Does the client understand the difference between an illiquid and liquid investment? Is the client comfortable with holding an illiquid investment for an extended period of time? Does the client understand the terms "thinly traded" and "no secondary market?"

Does it pass the Wall Street Journal *test?* When it comes to suitability, or any questionable issue, picture yourself in an article on the front page of the *Journal.* If you could make a good argument that would satisfy the *Journal's* reporter, it would probably satisfy your state regulators or the court, too. If, on the other hand, it might seem questionable in national print, leave it alone. If you have a questionable recommendation or a bad gut feeling about whether an investment is suitable for a particular client, choose another product in which you have confidence. These investments seem to breed the type of clients who sue their planners or financial advisers.

◆ **Keep your New Account Forms up to date and signed by the client.** This simple document can go a long way in helping you defend a suit.

One suggestion: have clients fill out the document in their own handwriting. If you fill it out, have the clients initial all the answers. Make sure it is the clients' signature on the document and not yours or your assistant's best rendition of the clients' signature. If your clients refuse to provide income and net worth, or offer financial data, show them the door. Although the clients may consider it private and confidential, their attorneys will be loudly publicizing it in arbitration.

Finally, remind clients of the importance of maintaining current information in the New Account Form. Ask them to update it at least annually or upon a sudden change in circumstances such as a death, divorce, or loss of job.

◆ **Adopt these guidelines, suggested by Bud Bigelow,[6] as companywide policies to avoid suitability claims.**

Adhere to conservative investment principles.

Recommend only those investment instruments that you understand.

Be cautious with discretionary investment authority. Although discretionary investment authority may ease the administrative burden, the higher returns advisers associate with discretionary authority need to be assessed relative to the adviser's increased risks. In many cases it also makes the representative a fiduciary with even a higher degree of responsibilities and obligations. Leaving the authority with the client allows the financial services professional to share the risk with the client, a much better position in the event of litigation.

Use loss limitation techniques, such as a stop loss for publicly traded securities, if appropriate.

Carefully document your clients' investment objectives. The higher the return objective, the more carefully they need to be documented. Carefully documented objectives and risk tolerance are the first line of defense in the event of a claim.

Pick your clients with care. Avoid clients with unrealistic expectations, questionable integrity, or a history of contentious relationships.

◆ **Keep detailed notes of meetings, always summarizing what was discussed.** Make sure the notes indicate you discussed the risks and how the investment matches the client's goals and temperament.

◆ **Avoid making the bad case worse.** According to W. A. Jackson of Lancer Claims Services, the following factors were found to make it difficult to win suitability claims, even when the facts were favorable to the broker:[7]

Abnormally high commissions. Frequently, a registered representative's recommendations, even taken in the best light, are questionable. Where the representative has consistently recommended investments that paid higher than normal commissions, it is hard to defend a suitability claim because it looks much worse than just ill fortune or poor insight. This can take a questionable case and push it over into the loss category.

Kickbacks. Although sometimes criminal and roundly condemned by the SEC, a surprising number of brokers pay undisclosed kickbacks or finder's fees to other professionals, such as accountants and attorneys. This practice can provide support for a securities fraud theory. Clients will argue that they would not have followed the recommendations if they had only known of these offensive practices.

Marginal training and experience. As mentioned in Chapter 5, many registered representatives and brokers have inadequate training and little experience. This, too, can push the questionable case over to the claimant's side, particularly in a failure to supervise suit.

Selling away. Registered representatives are limited to offering securities on their broker-dealer's approved list. To make recommendations outside that list is called "selling away," discussed more fully in Chapter 7. Sometimes the portfolio recommended by the representative includes securities not on the broker-dealer's approved list. This can infect and destroy the entire defense. Note the securities that were "sold away" will not be covered by the broker-dealer's E&O policy. This means it will be difficult to win this case and the costs of defending it may not be fully covered by insurance.

Theft and fraud. Although outright theft and fraud are always excluded from an E&O policy, fraud is frequently linked with a straightforward suitability claim to create a punitive damages award. Theft or an obvious lack of honesty, even if it involves another investment or claim, can make it impossible to defend a suitability claim.

Falsified suitability forms. A suitability questionnaire to accompany a purchase application is commonly required to ensure the investor meets the guidelines. Some representatives view these questionnaires as unfairly depriving the small investor of an exceptionally good investment opportunity. Whether representatives falsify the information on their own or with the investor's tacit approval, it is impossible to win these cases.

SUITABILITY VIOLATIONS Occasionally, unscrupulous financial advisers will do outrageous things in order to meet suitability requirements. One broker treated a future stream of Social Security payments as a capital asset for the sole purpose of qualifying to invest, even though the client was too young to qualify for any Social Security payments. If the client loses money on the deal, this broker is likely to be liable for the losses and may have committed a felony.

In one large case, the arbitrators found that a single investment in a limited partnership was suitable for the client's portfolio; however, subsequent investments in limited partnerships overloaded the portfolio and hence were not suitable. The arbitrators reached this conclusion even though each limited partnership investment looked upon individually was suitable. Consequently the company, in an internal memo that was leaked to the press, urged its representatives to use care when selling limited partnerships.[8] A high concentration of limited partnerships, even if they are diversified between oil and gas, cable, leasing, and real estate, can be unsuitable.

W. A. Jackson has noted that the following fact patterns are common in suitability cases.[9]

◆ **Stretching for yield in retirement.** Cal-Surance Associates, Inc. noted that many claimants are retired clients on limited incomes. They need the highest possible yield on their investments because it is their rent and grocery money. This can be a tempting situation for a representative to downplay the risks of a high-yield investment. These clients are frequently emotionally and financially incapable of handling the risk and panic at the first signs of trouble.

◆ **Investing the windfall.** Once again, these clients are typically of modest means and have little financial experience. Suddenly they receive a substantial sum of money from an inheritance or an insurance settlement. With little or no investment experience, they seek advice on how to invest. It is common for them to have a big emotional investment in making sure this money grows or at least does not decline in value. If these investors lose all or even a large part of their windfall, they become traumatized and head for the nearest attorney's office to see if they can get it back.

◆ **Starting late in the game to do retirement planning.**
These claimants have reached the age of 55 and suddenly realize the $25,000 they have accumulated in
their 401(k) accounts will not get them through retirement. Their instructions to their broker or planner are
clear: "Turn this into $500,000 by the time I retire in
10 years." The broker knows that only a high-risk
investment has any chance of reaching this unreasonable goal. According to Jackson, "If he succeeds he is a
hero, if he loses, he is a defendant."

◆ **Sanitizing the memory.** Cal-Surance notes that
some claimants are in fact rich, sophisticated, and
savvy. They have a clear picture of what they want to
accomplish with tax shelter or highly leveraged investments. If the investment takes a tumble, their memory
quickly changes and they calmly swear they requested
only conservative investments.

SUITABILITY DETERMINATION There is an important distinction between RIAs determining suitability
and other financial advisers making the same determination. For stockbrokers, insurance agents, registered representatives, or other financial services professionals without a fiduciary duty, suitability is
determined at the point of sale. If the investment was
suitable on the day you sold it, it will pass the suitability
screen. If it later declines substantially in value, you still
look back to the date of sale. However, an RIA has an
ongoing responsibility to monitor suitability. The same
investment that may be suitable when you recommended it could become unsuitable years later. An
RIA, as opposed to a registered representative, may
have an ongoing duty to monitor investments and take
steps to make sure they continue to be suitable.

Some attorneys believe that planners, with their
inherent fiduciary duty, also have an ongoing responsibility to assess suitability. If the client's physical or
mental health deteriorates suddenly, it may make the

investment inappropriate. Planners' fiduciary duties will require them to advise clients when suitability is no longer appropriate and help their clients take steps to extricate themselves from the investment.[10]

Many insurance agents are concerned about how to apply the suitability requirement in states which require that only suitable insurance products can be sold. Their fear is that insurance commissioners will favor term products and find all permanent insurance unsuitable. The top attorneys at one state department of insurance review the entire client file to determine how much information the insurance agent had on the client. They look for a paper trail to prove the agent knew the specifics on the client, such as assets, goals, and investment temperament level. They want to see this recommendation is in the client's best interest. Clearly, the same defensive measures that can help you win an unsuitable securities claim can also be used for an unsuitable insurance claim.

Although suitability violations used to be more flagrant, such as investing all of an elderly widow's net worth in a highly leveraged limited partnership, it is now becoming more common to see gray areas.[11] Cal-Surance even reported, "Brokers who make no recommendations may have a duty to warn customers who make an imprudent investment decision entirely on their own."[12]

Failure to Disclose

A SECOND COMMON AREA of client complaints is the financial adviser's failure to disclose the risks, fees or sales charges, or conflicts of interest associated with an investment or insurance product. As with suitability complaints, clients who are unhappy with the performance of an investment often use these theories to press their suit. As a few clients seem to have a very limited memory when their investments underperform, careful financial advisers should not skim over these disclosures in their haste to have the clients sign the application.

RISKS As detailed in Chapters 12 and 13, it behooves the careful adviser to make sure the client clearly understands that, with most investments, what goes up can also come down. Make sure the client realizes there are no written guarantees, if that is the case. To protect yourself, as well as thoroughly advise the client, it is usually best to explain these risks in writing. This can be done in a number of ways: in the engagement letter, follow-up letters, memos, and meeting notes.

SALES CHARGES It is not uncommon for clients to seek reimbursement of their entire investment because they were not advised there were sales charges. As sales charges are discussed in the prospectus, this argument is harder for investment clients, as opposed to insurance clients, to prove. Nevertheless, it is important to explain in detail the sales charges and how they affect performance. If there are front-end sales loads, contingent deferred sales loads, or even hidden loads, disclose them thoroughly, preferably in writing. It is recommended that you do not mark upon or highlight this section of the prospectus. It may be deemed unfair to the client as they are expected to read the entire document.

A good place to disclose loads is Form ADV, giving a range of possible compensations. Also include this information in the letter of recommendations you make to the client. Sample phrasing might be: "You may recall, there is a 4 percent sales charge on this investment, described on page three of the prospectus. This means 4 percent of your initial investment will be used to pay the distribution charges, the broker-dealer, and to cover my expenses and compensation." Remember it is not enough to direct the client to read the prospectus. The burden is on the adviser to thoroughly explain the sales charge to the client.

Again, it is absolutely crucial that this disclosure be carefully documented in your files. If it is not documented, at trial the case becomes merely your word against the client's. A good form of documentation is the prospectus receipt. A copy of one is included in Appendix B.

DILEMMA

JANE APPROACHES her financial adviser with a request to maximize the return on her portfolio so she can retire in ten years. Artie Adviser recommends dividing her portfolio between two funds. He gives her a prospectus on each fund: one is a conservative balanced fund and the other an aggressive growth fund. Artie verbally explains to Jane there are no guarantees, but given the history of these funds, he thinks it is highly likely she will reach her goals on time. Artie also explains that 5 percent of her initial investment will be deducted to pay for sales charges. Three years later, Jane files a complaint against Artie alleging she did not know about the sales charges, and that the investments were so risky she had lost 15 percent of her portfolio. She also states she did not receive a copy of the prospectus.

Question: Who wins?

Answer: Even though in this situation Artie did everything correctly, he is in the unfortunate position of being unable to prove it. Because his statements were given verbally to Jane and the only written documentation he has is the prospectus, there is a good chance an arbitrator or a jury would take Jane's word above Artie's.

CONFLICTS OF INTEREST Conflicts of interest are situations in which trusted advisers can use the influence from their position to benefit their own private interests, usually at the expense of the client. Usually agents and representatives can negotiate an arm's-length business transaction without concern about a conflict of interest. However, a fiduciary, such as a financial planner or an RIA, is held to a higher standard of care than most registered representatives and insurance agents.

One of the greatest areas of potential danger for planners is self-interested advice. In extreme cases this would constitute fraud. For financial planners this includes advising the client to make a purchase or sale only because the planner benefits. If planners recommend the wrong kind of insurance or an unsuitable investment just because they will make a large commission, they could be breaching their fiduciary duty and other rules.

Although fee-only planners may escape criticism for self-interested advice, a *Wall Street Journal* article exposed the practice of fee-only planners organizing partnerships and selling the interests to clients. Some fee-only planners condoned the practice, others condemned it. One planner confessed he took too long to give up on some troubled ventures he assembled. "It's awfully hard to stay objective. If it hadn't been my deal, I probably would have cut the losses and walked away from it. The investors would have lost less money." [13]

Fee-only planners have also been criticized for another potential conflict of interest: asset management fees. [14] When financial planners are paid a fee to manage assets, it may become difficult for them to fire themselves when their performance is down.

It is important to note that some conflicts are so extreme they should be avoided at all costs, even if the client does not object. These could include entering into a business transaction or relationship with clients which would impair the planner's objectivity and make it impossible for the planner or investment adviser to give disinterested advice.

Although a fiduciary's duty to disclose is always high, it is especially high when there is a conflicting self-interest. Conflicts should always be disclosed at the beginning of the relationship or the conflict, and the planner should decline the engagement unless the client waives the conflict in writing.

ACTION ITEMS

◆ OBTAIN COPIES OF suitability requirements from your broker-dealer and your state departments of securities and insurance. Read and review them with your staff. Be conservative with your recommendations and always document your files. Although suitability may be the most common complaint clients have against their financial services professional, it can be the easiest to win.

◆ CAREFULLY DOCUMENT all your client disclosures in your files. Also note the date you gave the client a copy of the prospectus and have the client sign a prospectus receipt. Chapter 11 contains a sample financial adviser disclosure form you can use to document all your disclosures, and a copy of a sample prospectus receipt is included in Appendix B.

◆ DO YOU FIND YOURSELF in a conflict of interest at the present time? It is best to disclose that conflict to the client now, before it is too late. To protect yourself, keep a written verification in your client's file of the date the conflict was not only disclosed but also waived. Question yourself on all your recommendations that involve commissions:

Are they in the client's best interests? Carefully document your reasons in the file. Make sure clients know the difference between fees and commissions. Commissions are for the sale of a product; fees are for services.

◆ CAREFULLY EXAMINE your motives and your business practices. Are you recommending products because they are right for your client or because they are right for you? Disclose up front if you will be receiving fees and commissions. If clients want you to disclose the amount of your securities commissions, refer them to the prospectus or broker-dealer commission schedule. If they request the amount of your insurance commissions, tell them.

◆ AVOID RECOMMENDING any business transaction that could impair your objectivity. For most planners, this means not organizing or managing any partnerships.

◆ TAKE THE EMPHASIS OFF returns by telling your clients you cannot guarantee performance but you can guarantee a high level of service. Getting the client to focus on service instead of returns will help satisfy their expectations.

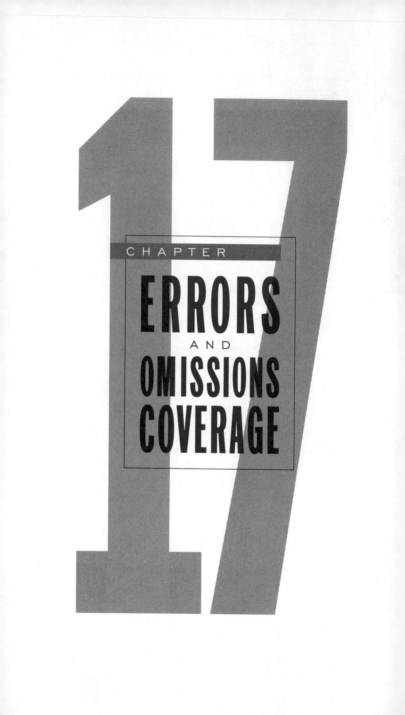

ERRORS

AND

OMISSIONS
COVERAGE

IT IS NOT UNCOMMON to hear financial planners and other advisers resist the idea of purchasing E&O insurance. Planners whose only income is derived from fees sometimes feel they are above lawsuits, and do not need any liability coverage.[1] Other excuses run the gamut from "I have no assets to protect" to "insurance is a lightning rod for lawsuits."

These views are shortsighted and dangerous for a number of reasons. First, lawsuits track the market. In any prolonged downturn, clients will seek to recoup their losses from both product sponsors and their advisers, regardless of whether the adviser is compensated by fees only or fees and commissions.

Second, most clients assume all advisers have liability insurance, so the issue never affects their decision to press a claim. In addition, they will have to sue you to reach the broker-dealer or product sponsor. You will be involved whether or not you have insurance.

Third, the First Specialty Program reports that defense costs comprise approximately 50 percent of all costs, with damages comprising the other 50 percent. This is consistent with the experience of most professional liability carriers.[2] It is important to realize you will still owe your attorney the costs of defending a suit, even if all the damage claims are completely withdrawn or settled in your favor.

Fourth, even if you have no assets to protect, you could find yourself in an expensive litigation proceeding to avoid having your wages or commissions garnished or from having judgments filed against your homestead.

Fifth, it may shock you to know that as a financial planner or adviser, you have a 10 percent chance of being sued in the next five years.[3] In 1995, more than 6,000 arbitrations alone were filed with NASD.[4] The time to review your E&O coverage is now, before any claims are filed.

Finally, if you are ever in the unfortunate position of being sued, you will briefly see your entire life pass before your eyes. You will wonder how quickly it will take to go bankrupt and if you will ever be able to work again. If you have E&O insurance, these thoughts will go away as you remind yourself that you are covered and your children will still be able to eat in the morning. Think of E&O coverage as medicine that allows you to sleep at night.

Carrier Considerations

USE THESE QUESTIONS to help you select a carrier best suited to your needs.

◆ **How is the carrier rated by A.M. Best and other reputable firms?** You want your insurance company to be in business when you need them. Select only firms that have the highest ratings.

◆ **What lines of insurance does the carrier write?** Do financial advisers and planners constitute a significant portion of their writings? Do they have long-term experience and a commitment to insuring the profession? Look for firms that have been in the business during both up and down markets, when most of the claims originate. They should also have significant experience with the profession.

◆ **What references can the carrier supply?** Reputable firms will have had dealings with ICFP, IAFP, NAPFA, and other professional groups.

◆ **How is the policy rated?** Are claims-made step factors used on a renewal rating? Look for companies that do not use claims-made step factors, but use a renewal rate structure that is based on the number of financial advisers covered, the gross annual revenue, the limits and deductible chosen, and the nature of the practice. Claims-made step factors are increases in premium that are not based on revenues or staff counts. Their purpose is to increase the premium in each of the first several renewals, leading to a rate that is typically two to three times higher than the first-year rate.

◆ **Are any discounts available to you?** Some firms offer a multiple adviser discount where the aggregate limit is shared by more than one adviser. Some firms also offer a fee-only discount to practices that do not engage in product sales or discretionary asset management. If gross annual revenues are high, it is also possible to get a higher deductible.

Policy Considerations

USE THESE QUESTIONS to help screen your choices for policy coverage.

◆ **What is your retroactive date?** If you are replacing existing coverage, make sure that your retroactive date on your expiring policy is preserved on the replacement policy to ensure your continuous claims-made coverage for prior acts.

◆ **Do you have a contractual right to purchase a "tail" if your policy is canceled or not renewed by your insurance company?** A tail is an extended reporting period endorsement that extends coverage under the policy. This can be a particularly troublesome area if you leave the business, switch firms, or change broker-dealer affiliations or if your broker-dealer changes insurers. You may be surprised to learn that your E&O coverage stops the day you walk out of your old firm, even if a claim is later made against you. The ideal situation would be a policy that you can take with you wherever you go. If that is not possible, explore the costs of a tail to cover you for acts committed while working at this firm. Look for a policy that offers a tail of at least one year.

DILEMMA

GEORGIA GOODPLANNER works for Best Ever Broker-Dealer during 1992 and 1993 and has E&O coverage through the firm. During that time she prepares a written financial plan for Clayton Client and recommends The Very High Risk Mutual Fund, which Clayton purchases in 1993. In 1994 Georgia changes her broker-dealer to Really Fine and obtains a new E&O policy through Really Fine. Clayton reregisters his Mutual Fund to list Really Fine as Georgia's broker-dealer.

The market takes a tumble and Very High Risk

Mutual Fund loses 30 percent in 1995. In 1996 Clayton consults with his attorney and files suit against Georgia, claiming the investment was unsuitable when she recommended it and she breached her fiduciary duty as a planner by not performing the proper due diligence on the fund. Georgia contacts the E&O insurance carriers that covered Best Ever broker-dealer and Really Fine broker-dealer. Both refuse to cover her defense costs or to pay any claims to Clayton. Georgia sues both carriers to force them to cover her.

Question: Who wins?

Answer: Neither carrier is responsible for this claim. Really Fine is not liable because the act that gave rise to the claim occurred before their policy was in effect. Best Ever is not responsible because Georgia effectively dropped this policy when she switched firms and did not purchase a "tail," a policy from the first carrier that would have covered later claims. Georgia's most expensive errors were not reading both policies to know what was covered and not inquiring about E&O coverage before a claim was made.

Coverage Considerations

USE THESE QUESTIONS to review what is to be covered in your policy.

◆**What professional services are included and excluded?** Does the policy cover you for financial planning, budgeting advice, fiduciary responsibilities, and RIA activities with your own RIA? It can be a shock to review your E&O coverage and discover it does not cover any of your financial planning activities. This is not an uncommon provision in policies provided through broker-dealers or life insurance companies wanting to cover their own agents. Look for policies that will cover financial planning, including both fees and commission business, if that defines your business.

◆ **If you are reviewing a broker-dealer policy, how high is the aggregate limit, and how many claims has your broker-dealer had in a bad year?** Although an aggregate limit may be quite high for a broker-dealer, remember you are sharing it with all the other representatives of the firm. If the firm has had a bad claims year and reached the aggregate limit before your case is decided, you could be without coverage. If possible, look for individual coverage that applies only to your practice.

◆ **Is the policy portable?** Look for a policy that moves with you as you change broker-dealers or the nature of your practice. Remember, most broker-dealer policies end when you leave the firm.

◆ **Should you have dual coverage?** It may make sense for you to maintain your coverage through your broker-dealer or insurance company and also to carry a separate policy that covers just you. This is analogous to group versus individual medical insurance and will allow you to take the coverage with you if you leave the firm. Also, it could protect you if the broker-dealer policy does not cover your activities. If you decide to do this, read the "other insurance" clause carefully. Make sure your individual policy is excess over any other valid and collectible insurance.

◆ **Who is covered?** You, your corporation, your partnership? Are your unlicensed employees covered? Many firms rely on paraplanners, accountants, and other employees and advisers to provide clients a team approach. Are all team members covered or only those licensed in securities and insurance?

Terms and Provisions

REVIEW YOUR POLICY for the following terms and provisions before purchasing coverage.

◆ **"Right and the duty to defend."** This is the strongest defense provision possible. Other clauses used in the industry are the "option to defend," which allows the insurance company to decide whether it will defend you, or a provision that provides defense on an indemnity basis. In the latter case, you may also be required to manage and pay for the defense; the insurance company would then reimburse you. This indemnity clause also relieves the insurer of an implied warranty of providing an adequate defense.

◆ **"Defense within the limits."** This means that defense costs paid to defend against a claim reduce the amount available for payment of damages. This can significantly affect the amount of funds you have available for claims, because defense costs, as mentioned above, typically comprise 50 percent of the entire claim.

◆ **"Claims made."** This means that the policy must be in force at the time a claim is made, and the transaction or act that gave rise to the claim must have been rendered after the retroactive date. The retroactive date is identified on the policy declaration page and is usually the inception date of the first policy for which coverage has been continuously in effect. Nearly all professional liability policies are written on a claims made, defense within the policy limits form.

◆ **An incident trigger in the definition of claim.** An incident trigger allows you to report not only written demands for damages or claims, but also incidents that might reasonably be expected to give rise to a claim at a later date.

Exclusions

FINALLY, AS YOU REVIEW your E&O policy, you will note it has exclusions. These exclusions are typically found in any professional liability policy for financial advisers:

— fraud or the allegation of fraud
— discrimination

— employer/employment liability
— trustee activities
— guaranteed investment performance
— economic forecasts
— market value fluctuations
— selling away
— return of fees paid by client.

Take a careful look at the fraud provisions in your policy. Note the differences of exclusions for *fraud* and for *allegations of fraud*. Although no policy will cover *fraud* (because fraud is alleged in approximately 50 percent of all cases before NASD and E&O policies never cover unlawful acts), it is important to find a policy that covers *allegations of fraud*. This will ensure coverage until the allegations of fraud have been disproved. Otherwise, this claim will not be handled by the carrier until fraud has finally been disproved, long after much of your litigation expenses have been incurred.

DILEMMA

RALPH AGENT HAS received a number of reports from his home office compliance department warning agents against calling any life insurance product a private pension plan. The company has made it clear that such activities are considered a misleading sales practice and false advertising. Ralph continues to use sales materials describing insurance as a private pension plan. A client sues Ralph for refund of premiums, claiming the variable life insurance policy underperformed and that she did not know it was insurance. Ralph claims his activities were merely a negligent, but honest, mistake and should be covered by his insurance policy. His carrier claims that because Ralph had numerous notices about these activities being prohibited, his actions were not negligent but fraudulent and therefore not covered by his E&O policy.

Question: Will the E&O carrier be forced to cover Ralph's claim?

Answer: No, according to insurance compliance experts Dennis M. Groner and Mary B. Petersen. Under these circumstances a court might determine that Ralph intentionally, and not negligently, used inappropriate and unapproved sales tools.[5] This would constitute fraud under the policy and be excluded from coverage.

The author is grateful to Bud Bigelow, who represents Financial Service Mutual Insurance Company as Program Manager, for his considerable help with this chapter and for allowing an adaptation of material appearing in his white paper on What Should Financial Planners and Registered Investment Advisers Ask About Professional Liability Insurance? *(Financial Services Mutual Insurance Company, 1995).*

MEDIATION

18

IF THERE COMES A DAY when you have tried everything and you are still not able to satisfy the unhappy client, do not panic. Consider mediation as a last-stop measure for resolving your dispute before it escalates into the expensive and traumatic arenas of litigation or arbitration.

Mediation is one of the techniques designed to avoid costly litigation and known as Alternative Dispute Resolution. It is a voluntary process in which a neutral third-party mediator helps the parties find common ground and negotiate a final settlement. As mediation is nonbinding, the parties must contractually agree to accept the final settlement. Otherwise, they may continue their dispute through arbitration or the court system. NASD, IAFP, ICFP, NAPFA, and the CFP Board of Standards have all endorsed mediation as an alternative means to resolve disputes.

When you approach mediation, you must change your mind-set on resolving disputes. It is completely unlike arbitration and litigation—both of which require you to establish your position as being on the side of the angels, all the while disparaging your opponent. In mediation, you will instead agree to sit down calmly and concede that your position may not be as holy as you first believed and that indeed your opponent is not an adversary, but a human being who needs to vent his frustrations. There is no winner or loser in mediation. Instead, the emphasis is on finding a solution that satisfies all the aggrieved parties.[1]

What differentiates mediation from arbitration and litigation is that the mediator will not impose a solution but will assist the parties in creating their own resolution. Although mediators may not be technically expert in the securities industry, they are trained to smooth over hostile attitudes and miscommunications while helping to craft a suitable compromise solution. The mediator often helps the parties see things about their own case they did not want to see or gives them a clearer view of the entire situation that may have previously been distorted by anger and high emotion.[2] As a result, mediation is efficient and quick, with NASD reporting that 85 percent of its first 125 cases resulted in a settlement, usually within a one-day session.[3]

Mediation Benefits

THERE ARE MANY BENEFITS to mediation.[4]

◆ **Greater control.** Most parties appreciate being able to help craft a suitable resolution as opposed to having a solution imposed upon them by a third party, as in an arbitration or litigation proceeding. The parties also control the entire process, including the scheduling and the costs, in addition to the outcome of the dispute.

◆ **Less adversarial.** With parties focusing on creating a mutually acceptable solution, the entire process is not only less formal but also less adversarial and confrontational than arbitration or litigation. There is much less "He done me wrong" and a lot more "How can we get along?"

◆ **Options protected.** Parties can enter into mediation without jeopardizing their positions at a later arbitration or litigation proceeding. Nothing disclosed to the mediator may be revealed to the other side without the disclosing party's consent. Nor may anything that is disclosed during the mediation process be used in a later arbitration or court trial. Although discussions during mediation are confidential, a fact that is disclosed during the mediation process, as opposed to a rejected settlement offer, is not protected from disclosure in a subsequent proceeding if the fact was otherwise discoverable.[5]

◆ **Swift settlement.** As mediation is frequently used early in the dispute process, settlement can be reached sooner than in arbitration and litigation. Once all the documents are received, it is typical to schedule a mediation hearing within three to six weeks.[6]

◆ **Lower cost.** Mediation is significantly less expensive than arbitration and litigation. Frequently the parties handle the matter themselves without legal assistance. This quick resolution also helps reduce expenses.

◆ **Relationship preserved.** Reaching an early resolution to a client's claim, without undue financial or time strains on either party, can sometimes help preserve your long-term business relationship.

◆ **Privacy protected.** All meetings are strictly confidential, thereby offering even greater confidentiality than arbitration.

◆ **Creative solutions.** Because the parties themselves are helping create suitable solutions, the process can allow creative alternatives that would not be available to arbitrators or judges in a courtroom setting.

◆ **Low risk.** With an 85 percent chance of settlement, there is no reason not to mediate. The mediation process will not delay an arbitration or court case. Even if the mediation is not successful, the parties may have successfully resolved certain parts of their dispute, which will make arbitration and litigation more efficient.

Mediation Steps

THE AMERICAN ARBITRATION Association's *A Guide to Mediation for Financial Planning Disputes*[7] lists five steps in mediating financial planning disputes.

THE PARTIES AGREE TO MEDIATE As mediation is entirely voluntary, financial advisers and their clients must first agree in writing that the dispute will be mediated. This can be done in any one of the following three ways.

1 Future disputes clause. The financial adviser and client can incorporate a clause into their contract that provides for mediation in the event of a future dispute. (Note, however, a Registered Investment Advisory Agreement cannot require a client to mediate *and* waive all other dispute resolution alternatives, such as arbitration and civil litigation.[8])

2 Submission to mediation. Even if a financial adviser and client did not provide for mediation in their original contract, they may submit an existing dispute to mediation by filing a submission to mediation form with the American Arbitration Association (AAA), NASD, or another mediation service.

3 Alternative submission process. Either the client or the financial adviser may contact AAA, NASD, or another mediation service and request that the service contact the opposing party to encourage their participation in a mediation proceeding.

The document initiating mediation will include a brief description of the case and the appropriate administrative fees. Typically there is a $150 filing fee.

SELECTING A SUITABLE MEDIATOR Upon receiving the proper request for mediation, AAA will assign the case to a case administrator who will appoint a mediator. Both the financial planner and client will receive a biographical sketch of the proposed mediator and be allowed to notify AAA if they object to the appointment. AAA will replace any mediator that is not acceptable to both parties. NASD has similar procedures. It is also possible to avoid these services entirely and choose a mutually acceptable third party to mediate.

PREPARING FOR THE MEDIATION SESSION To be properly prepared for mediation, both a financial adviser and client should:

◆ Define and analyze all the issues involved in the dispute

◆ Identify and prioritize the needs and interests of all parties in settling the dispute

◆ Identify and evaluate the strengths and weaknesses of each party's case

◆ Gather all necessary facts, documents, and support to validate the claim

◆ Determine a course of action and possible compromises or trade-offs

◆ Determine initial proposals, fall-back proposals, and bottom-line positions

◆ Anticipate the other party's position, needs and demands, and version of the facts

◆ Focus on the interests of each party in reaching an acceptable solution.

ATTENDING THE MEDIATION CONFERENCE As the mediation begins, the mediator will meet with each party privately and then, usually, with all parties together. The private sessions are called caucuses. The parties may be accompanied by an attorney, although that is certainly not necessary. Once the parties are in their separate caucuses, they may discuss their cases freely with the mediator. During these confidential meetings, the mediator will speak frankly about the strong points and vulnerabilities of the party's case and their chances of winning if they went to arbitration.[9]

It is not unusual during the caucuses for the mediator to discover the parties are ill informed, with each believing their case is much stronger than it actually is. Both the clients and their attorney may have been pumping each other up to an unrealistic position.[10] The mediator will work to clarify each party's version of the facts and their priorities and positions. Part of the mediator's job will be to soften a rigid position and explore alternative solutions and possible trade-offs. Using both separate and joint sessions, a mediator will assist the parties in crafting a workable resolution and negotiating the final terms for a written settlement. It is also the mediator's responsibility to make sure both parties are clear on the terms of the agreement.

ONCE A SETTLEMENT HAS BEEN REACHED, IT WILL BE REDUCED TO WRITING AND WILL INCLUDE MUTUAL RELEASES If the parties fail to reach a mediated settlement, they may still continue their dispute through arbitration or litigation. If they have reached a partial solution during mediation, the contested issues will be the only ones to be resolved in arbitration or civil litigation.

The parties are required to maintain the confidentiality of the mediation process. This means they may not introduce into evidence at a later arbitration or court proceeding any admissions, proposals, or suggestions made during the mediation process, nor may they introduce the views expressed by the mediator or other parties.

With the reduced costs and stress of mediation, there is no question that it will be used more frequently in the future. E&O carriers have also found that mediation is less expensive than arbitration and litigation. As a result, one firm, First Specialty, encourages mediation by reducing an investment adviser's or a planner's deductible up to 50 percent if mediation is used.[11]

Mediation can be a terrific way to resolve client disputes, even if the matter is not concluded satisfactorily. Most parties report they are happy with the mediation process. At the very least, you get to see your opponent's case before arbitration or trial. In short, you have nothing to lose and everything to gain.

ACTION ITEMS

◆ CONSIDER PLACING the following language in your engagement letters: "If a dispute arises from our engagement and cannot be settled through negotiation, the parties agree to try in good faith to settle the dispute first by mediation administered by the American Arbitration Association, NASD, or another suitable group before resorting to arbitration, litigation, or some other dispute resolution procedure."

◆ FOR AN EXCELLENT comparison of mediation and arbitration, see NASD's publication on "NASD Mediation: An Alternative Path to Resolving Securities Disputes."

CHAPTER

ARBITRATION

19

ALTHOUGH SECURITIES arbitration is more than a century old, its exponential growth did not occur until the Supreme Court's 1987 decision in *Shearson/American Express, Inc. v. McMahon.*[1] That case held that customers who sign predispute arbitration agreements with their brokers could be compelled to arbitrate claims. As a result of *McMahon,* most individual investors who transact business with broker-dealers, and virtually all individual investors who use margin or option accounts, must resolve claims with member firms in Self Regulatory Organization (SRO) sponsored arbitration.[2]

McMahon transformed securities arbitration from a voluntary alternative to civil litigation into the principal means of resolving securities disputes. It has led to a sharp increase in both the number and duration of cases. By 1995, NASD had received more than 6,000 new cases for arbitration in that year alone.[3] Those cases average three days of hearings; in 1980, most sessions were concluded in a half day.[4]

Although all 10 SROs have an arbitration procedure, NASD receives 85 percent of all arbitrations involving securities claims.[5] NASD arbitration hearings are conducted in 46 cities nationwide. More than 7,000 hearing sessions were logged during 1995.

In addition, claims between members themselves, or between a broker-dealer and a registered representative, are required to be arbitrated. Many registered representatives may not be aware their employment agreement compels them to resolve disputes in NASD sponsored arbitration, even if the matter is not securities related.

Notice of Arbitration

WHAT SHOULD YOU DO when the dreaded statement of claim arrives?

First, take a deep breath and remind yourself that this is not the end of the world. Then:

◆ **Run, do not walk, to your compliance department and advise them of the pending action.** This is not only a requirement in all firms, it makes good sense. These people have been through many cases before, and their experience can be invaluable to you.

◆ **Notify your E&O carrier.** Failure to do so may result in denial of your claim. This is also a good time to get out your policy and see exactly what it covers and which areas are excluded.

◆ **Review appointment of legal counsel.** Depending on your policy, you may or may not have the option to choose your own legal counsel. The most critical factor is to select an attorney with extensive NASD arbitration experience. Even your own E&O carrier may unknowingly provide you with an inexperienced lawyer. Ask for extensive details about the attorney's qualifications and background. Do not accept a lawyer who has not had numerous cases before NASD. Engage one who has had significant experience handling cases like yours. If you are not happy with the choice of your E&O carrier, speak up and request a different attorney. You have too much at stake to be underrepresented.

◆ **Get your files in good shape.** Note, this is not the same as manufacturing evidence. Creating or destroying evidence is a crime and could lead to your incarceration, a fate much worse than losing an arbitration claim.

Second, and perhaps most important, read the remainder of this chapter.

NASD Arbitration Process

THE FOLLOWING PRESENTS a brief, seven-step review of the NASD arbitration process, starting with the initial claim and ending with the arbitrator's decision.

STEP 1. Claim initiation. The current NASD arbitration process begins when the investor/claimant initiates proceedings by filing a statement of claim with the NASD Director of Arbitration and Mediation. The claim describes the controversy in dispute and outlines the remedies sought.[6] The claimant is required to file a fee based on the amount in controversy and a deposit to cover the cost of hearings. The filing fee ranges from $15 to $300, and the hearing deposit can go as high as $1,500, depending on the amount in dispute and the number of arbitrators needed. According to NASD records, most deposits fall within the range of $400 to $750.

In order to proceed, the claim must arise from the

investor's relationship with the broker-dealer and it must involve a member broker-dealer or a person associated with the member, typically a registered representative.[7]

STEP 2. Eligibility limitation. Current eligibility rules, the equivalent of statute of limitations in a court system, state that a claim may not be eligible for arbitration if more than six years have elapsed since the occurrence or event giving rise to the dispute. The purpose of the rule is to prevent stale claims. Six years was chosen because it coincided with many broker-dealer recordkeeping requirements.[8]

This rule has become one of the largest areas of controversy in the entire process. Investors want the time extended so their claims are viable for as long as possible. Respondents want to shorten the time to reduce their exposure. The Director of Arbitration will usually pass the issue on to the designated arbitrators to determine. As the arbitrators themselves frequently have no legal background, the answers to this controversy have been uneven. Sometimes a panel will use six years from the date of the original transaction and sometimes six years from the date the investor learned or should have learned of the grievance. Other panels may apply underlying state laws, which may invoke one- to seven-year rules, depending on the theory used. Still other panels may apply the law of the home state of the broker-dealer, which could be different from the home state of the investor/claimant.

It is extremely common for a broker-dealer to file a collateral claim in court if it appears the arbitration panel will not make a favorable eligibility decision. Frequently, these cases are brought in New York courts, even though the investor or the transaction may not have any connecting link to that state.[9] One reason New York has been so popular is that the courts there generally interpret the eligibility period to commence from the date of the transaction (usually the date of purchase),[10] thereby eliminating many investor claims.

This issue alone has served to greatly increase the expense, complexity, and timeliness of the arbitration process. Investors, expecting an inexpensive solution to their disputes, may find themselves simultaneously in a local arbitration panel and in court, hundreds or thousands of miles from their hometown. If the matter is taken up out of state, the claimant will be forced to retain legal counsel in the state the broker-dealer files suit, making the process impossibly expensive for most small investors.

STEP 3. Respondent notification. The Director of Arbitration serves the Statement of Claim on the responding party, although experienced counsel have usually provided this information to the claimant in advance as a courtesy. The respondent is almost always a broker-dealer or a registered representative/employee of the broker-dealer, or both. The respondent has 20 days to answer the claim and set forth any defenses and facts he will rely on to prove the case at hearing. Sometimes the respondent will bring a counterclaim against the claimant.[11]

Depending on the amount in controversy, the case may then proceed in one of three ways. If the claim is for $10,000 or less, the matter will be resolved through simplified arbitration procedures where a single arbitrator is appointed. Sometimes these cases are decided just by reviewing the written evidence and statements, because it is up to the investor, not the respondent, to request a hearing.

Complex cases and large claims of more than $1 million are handled under enhanced and flexible procedures that incorporate elements of civil litigation. Arbitrators may rule on motions to dismiss, and, upon mutual agreement of the parties, the arbitrator's final decision may be accompanied by a statement of reasons. Other cases that do not fit the guidelines for large and complex cases may also use these procedures if the parties mutually agree.[12]

STEP 4. Document collection. All cases other than those described above are handled under the standard procedures. At this stage, the parties may request documents and other information helpful to proving their case in a process called "discovery." In theory, any party may request information or documents from the other party, and these must be produced or formally objected to within 30 days. This has been another area of controversy, as it has become more common for one party to use the vacuum cleaner method of discovery—requesting huge volumes of material, sometimes to harass the other party. It is not uncommon to have parties ignore these requests or produce documents that are illegible or so late in the process that it is not possible to use them effectively. Sanctions, if any, for this behavior have been unevenly applied, thus encouraging these abusive tactics.[13]

STEP 5. Arbitrator selection. Selecting the arbitrators is the next step in the process. Arbitration panels in standard arbitration involving public customers consist of three people: two public arbitrators and one industry arbitrator. The public arbitrators are people with little or no securities industry background; the industry arbitrator is a person who has been associated with a broker-dealer within the previous three years or is retired from such a position. The chair of the panel is almost always one of the public arbitrators. Parties are allowed to challenge selected arbitrators for cause, if there is some conflict of interest or other reason the person is ineligible. There is no limit to the number of challenges for cause either party can make. Each party is also allowed one preemptory challenge, to remove one of the arbitrators from the list without providing any reason.[14]

After a hearing date is scheduled, the Director may

also schedule a prehearing conference to resolve discovery disputes, determine stipulations, and narrow the scope of disputed issues.[15]

STEP 6. Hearing procedure. Although many arbitration hearings last one or two days, in complex cases they may go several weeks or even months. It is not unusual for long sessions to be scheduled for nonconsecutive days and stretch over several months. The sessions may be held in hotel rooms, NASD offices, or the offices of one of the arbitrators. All are tape-recorded.

At the hearing, the arbitrators will introduce themselves and relate any interest they may have in the case. Parties are free to be represented by legal counsel at all stages, and counsel will also introduce themselves at this time. The arbitrators then take an oath of fairness and impartiality.[16]

Beginning with the claimant, each party makes an opening statement. Then the claimant presents her case through witnesses and evidence. As the arbitration hearing is not subject to the same rules of evidence used in court proceedings, the parties may present whatever evidence the arbitrators consider trustworthy and relevant. Witnesses take an oath of truthfulness and may be cross-examined by adverse parties. The arbitrators may also ask questions. Once the claimant has finished the presentation of her case, the respondent has an opportunity to present her side of the controversy. Finally, each side presents a closing argument summarizing the key points of their case.

Once the closing arguments are concluded, the arbitrators deliberate in a closed session to reach a consensus on the final decision, known as the "award." A majority vote prevails.

STEP 7. Award announcement. The Report of the Arbitration Policy Task Force to the NASD Board of Governors summarized the process arbitrators use to come to a decision by stating: "As arbitration is an equitable proceeding, arbitrators are not bound by the same statutes and case law that would be applied in a court. Although arbitrators may not disregard controlling case law and should make an effort to conform their decision to its general principles, they may ultimately decide the case based on whatever equitable principle they consider appropriate."

The arbitrators provide only a written report of the final award, specifying the amount awarded to the prevailing party and any nonmonetary relief. They are not required to provide any legal reasons, theories, or written opinions explaining the award. The award is considered final and binding. Subsequent litigation over the same dispute or issues is also barred. An award is only subject to court review for a few specific reasons. These include fraud, arbitrator partiality, or manifest disregard for the law.[17] As the arbitrators do not provide any explanation of their awards, it is almost impossible to prove these criteria for appeal.

Advantages and Disadvantages

ARBITRATION, WITHOUT the many legal requirements of a court trial, was designed to be more efficient and less costly for both parties. There are certain advantages for a claimant who chooses arbitration:[18]

◆ **Less expensive.** The proceedings are less formal, quicker, and less expensive than taking the same case to a court trial.

◆ **Expedited process.** The process is expedited for a number of reasons: there are no lengthy pretrial motions or discovery procedures.

◆ **No jury.** Because there is no jury, both parties can eliminate the time involved in selecting a jury.

◆ **No securities expert.** These people are not required to explain complicated transactions to a jury, as the panel chosen should be familiar with industry practices.

◆ **Convenient location.** Claimants are more likely to

have the arbitration held in a city convenient to them; in many court cases they may be required to travel to another state to press their claim.

THERE CAN ALSO BE DRAWBACKS for both parties: [19]
◆ **Limited discovery.** Although the parties are allowed some discovery, they are denied the extensive discovery procedures of court litigation. This can be critically important where the claimants need extensive records from the broker-dealer files to prove their case, the respondent needs copies of the investor's documents to defend a claim successfully, or where either party needs to take a deposition, especially of third parties.

◆ **Questionable evidence.** Because the formal rules of evidence do not apply, the arbitrators will frequently allow into evidence items that would be disallowed as hearsay or as prejudicial in a court of law.

◆ **Limited appeals.** Also, arbitrators rarely give their legal reasoning when rendering a decision, making it almost impossible to appeal a panel's decision. The lack of a meaningful review is actually a purposeful intent of the arbitration process. In *Bavarati v. Josephthal, Lyon & Ross, Inc.,* [20] the court held, "By including an arbitration clause in their contract, the parties agree to submit disputes arising out of the contract to a non-judicial forum, and we do not allow the disappointed party to bring his dispute into court by the back door, arguing that he is entitled to appellate review of the arbitrator's decision." Another appellate court stated "[o]verly technical judicial review of arbitration awards would frustrate the basic purposes of arbitration: to resolve disputes speedily and to avoid the expense and delay of extended court proceedings." [21]

Concerns about Arbitration

IN RECENT YEARS, MANY OF the advantages of arbitration have eroded, making the process at times cumbersome, time-consuming, and unfair. Concerns about the overall fairness of arbitration and limited due process have brought into question whether the increased speed and efficiency of arbitration are worth the potential risks. [22]

In addition, the belief that a broker or investment adviser fares better in arbitration is predicated on the assumption that the awards, or final settlements, are likely to be the same in arbitration or court and that arbitration is thus quicker and incurs fewer legal fees. This assumption is probably not reasonable for a number of reasons. [23]

First, the awards are most likely not the same. We know that claimants win their arbitration cases about 60 percent of the time, receiving about 60 percent of what they claimed. [24] Court cases, on the other hand, are far more likely to be settled prior to trial. Although this makes it harder to compare the outcomes and awards statistically, it is entirely possible that given a good set of facts, a respondent would fare better in court: either in having the matter dismissed outright, or receiving a significantly reduced judgment.

Second, one expert estimated that more than 90 percent of all civil lawsuits are settled prior to trial, while only about 50 percent of arbitration proceedings are carried through a hearing. [25] This could mean a respondent may incur more legal fees by going to arbitration, because there is a higher likelihood of needing legal advice throughout the entire process, as opposed to using an attorney to take a court case that will probably settle before trial.

Third, the entire arbitration process may be comparable in time to a court case in certain jurisdictions. It now takes, on average, 11.2 months to go through an arbitration hearing.[26] The arbitration case may even take longer than a straightforward court case in some jurisdictions, particularly if one party files a collateral lawsuit to determine certain eligibility issues.

Fourth, elaborating on the previous point, unsuspecting claimants may find themselves simultaneously in court and arbitration, where a broker-dealer respondent files a court action to clarify an arbitration issue. These cases are frequently brought in New York regardless of where the claimant lives. This practice can drastically increase not only the case time but the expense, if the claimant and respondent are required to seek additional legal counsel for an out-of-state court case.

Fifth, as lawyers have become more involved in the arbitration process, it now looks more like traditional litigation. Burdensome requests for voluminous documents and tactical delays are commonplace and add to the time and expense of defending an action.

Finally, as many procedural safeguards are missing in arbitration, respondents can find themselves before an arbitration panel defending a claim that would have been thrown out of court—either because it was past the statute of limitations or relied solely on hearsay or other inadmissible evidence. In particular, NASD has been much more reluctant to dismiss cases outside the statute of limitations than civil courts.

According to Terrence J. Fleming, a Minneapolis attorney specializing in securities arbitration, there are three fundamental problems with arbitration:[27]

1 Cases are tried rather than settled. Far more court cases than arbitrations are settled, and the reasons may relate to the speed and informality of the arbitration process, the limited discovery, and the absence of meaningful opportunities to discuss the matter face-to-face with the opposing party prior to the hearing. The bottom line is that financial risks to all parties are increased when matters are tried rather than settled. [28]

2 There is no meaningful appellate review. Appellate review of arbitration decisions is only allowed in rare and limited circumstances. Further, it is frequently impossible to facilitate a meaningful review, because the arbitrators generally do not provide any legal or factual basis for their decision. Limited and infrequent review also means arbitrators are not accountable for their decisions in the same manner that judges are accountable. [29]

Fleming goes on to state: "Perhaps the biggest problem with arbitration today is the ability of arbitrators to award punitive damages without any articulated factual or legal basis and in any amount, with limited judicial review. . . . It is possible for a runaway arbitration panel to award huge punitive damages in an unjust and unreasonable manner, and the party burdened with the award would have virtually no recourse." The fact that punitive damages were awarded in only 1 percent of the cases did not alleviate Fleming's concern.

3 The law to be applied is uncertain. Parties in arbitration usually assume that arbitrators apply the law in a manner analogous to how judges apply the law in court. For a number of reasons, nothing could be further from the truth. Most arbitrators have no formal legal training and do not approach the hearings using the same legal, logical, and methodical principles that would be used during a trial. Instead, they approach the matter from a business point of view or make their decisions more like juries than lawyers and judges. [30]

Parties and legal counsel at arbitration hearings often assume that the state's law or federal law of their geographical Circuit Court of Appeals will be applied to the claims and issues. However, in the absence of a contractual provision addressing this issue, arbitrators are free to apply any law they choose or no laws at all. As there is limited judicial review of the decisions, there is little, if any, recourse if the arbitrators apply the wrong law or no law to their decisions.

The two cases below were both decided in the broker's favor. However, in order for the arbitrators to have ruled (correctly) for the broker, in one case they had to apply state law and in the other they had to disregard state law.

DILEMMA

A LARGE WALL STREET firm terminated Agron, a Kansas broker, for forging a customer's signature (even though the customer had consented to the action), because the action violated firm and NASD rules. Agron commenced an NASD arbitration proceeding, required by his employment contract, for wrongful termination, damages, and other remedies. The arbitrators ruled in favor of Agron, and the firm appealed on the grounds that Kansas law should apply. Kansas had an employment-at-will doctrine that allowed the firm to terminate Agron at any time, with or without cause.

Question: What law should be applied? Who wins and why?

Answer: The Court of Appeals found for Agron by disregarding Kansas law.[31] They reasoned, "If the broker's employment was purely at will, the arbitration procedure designed to interpret that employment relationship would serve no identifiable purpose." (Note, if Agron had not been required to arbitrate this matter, but sued in state court, he probably would have lost because the state court would have been obligated to follow Kansas law.)

DILEMMA

IN RECENT YEARS, many brokers who have been terminated involuntarily have sued their former broker-dealers for libel or defamation. The basis for these suits is the broker-dealers have placed false or defamatory information about the broker's termination in the Form U-5. Broker-dealers must file this form with NASD. Some courts have determined that there is an absolute privilege safeguarding statements made in a Form U-5, even if the information is false, misleading, or inaccurate. In such cases, an aggrieved broker could face the difficult position of being unable to find other employment because of false statements in the U-5 and be unable to require the broker-dealer to change the form.

A large broker-dealer terminated broker Bavarati and stated on his Form U-5 that he was under investigation by the firm for fraudulent and wrongful taking of more than $7,000 of the firm's property. The broker commenced an NASD arbitration proceeding claiming the statements in the U-5 were false and defamatory. In fact, according to the broker, he was terminated because he blew the whistle to the SEC about the firm defrauding its customers.

Question: What would you do?

Answer: An NASD panel awarded the broker $180,000, including $120,000 in punitive damages. The 7th Circuit Court of Appeal affirmed, using the law of Illinois (which did not allow an absolute privilege to extend to false and defamatory statements) as their basis for decision.[32]

Current Status

THE RISE IN ARBITRATION claims and the questions about the usefulness and efficiency of the process prompted the creation of an arbitration policy task force, headed by former SEC Chairman David Ruder. In January 1996, it issued more than 70 recommendations concerning the arbitration of securities claims.[33] Although these recommendations have not been activated as this book goes to press, it is likely that many will in the near future.

Some of the recommendations are:

◆ **Arbitrators.** The task force recommended expanding the available pool of qualified arbitrators through improved training, increased compensation, and other measures. This change alone would help reduce the burdensome discovery requests and ensure more even application of the appropriate laws.

◆ **Eligibility/statute of limitations.** The present rule requires claims to be brought within six years of the event that gave rise to the dispute. This rule would be suspended for three years, during which time procedures would be implemented for enforcing the appropriate statutes of limitations more rigidly. Under the new proposal, arbitrators will decide which claims are viable, based partly on the statutes of limitations in the state involved or appropriate federal rules. They will also take into consideration when the alleged wrongdoing was discovered. This should bring clarity to an issue that has triggered long and costly collateral litigation in court.

◆ **Punitive damages.** An investor would be able to seek punitive damages wherever such damages are available in the investor's judicial forum. Such damages, however, would be limited to the lesser of twice the amount of compensatory damages awarded or $750,000.

◆ **Simplified arbitration.** The use of simplified arbitration procedures under a single public arbitrator, in which most disputes are resolved without a hearing, would be expanded to include all claims in which the total damages sought do not exceed $30,000.

◆**Simplified discovery.** Most document discovery would be limited to specified essential documents which would be required to be produced early in the process.

◆**Mediation.** NASD would expand its mediation program and also initiate a two-year pilot program of early neutral evaluation, under which a percentage of cases would be required to participate. The neutral would provide the parties with an assessment of the strengths and weaknesses of the case early in the proceeding.

Arbitration Clauses

IF YOU ARE A BROKER, there is a good chance that your firm's New Account Form requires clients to arbitrate all disputes. Even with the numerous problems inherent in NASD arbitration, the Ruder Commission declined to recommend eliminating mandatory arbitration clauses. However, some industry authorities believe it makes sense to eliminate them. Stan Hargrave, a frequent expert witness at NASD arbitrations, recommends eliminating the clause altogether.

There are a number of good reasons for this. First, a client can always force a broker to NASD arbitration, with or without an arbitration clause. Second, if arbitration later appears to be a better choice, it is still possible to arbitrate with court approval if both parties agree. Third, if you do not have the clause, and you do not wish to arbitrate, you may have the chance for a court trial, where in certain cases you might fare better. In short, you could eliminate the clause and increase your options.[34]

Fleming takes just the opposite view. In his opinion, broker-dealers who eliminate the arbitration clause give all the power to the investor to decide the forum for settling disputes. He reasons that it is better for the broker-dealer to make the decision than to pass it on to an unknown investor. Also, he believes it is possible to opt for a court case, if the investor agrees. One reason Fleming favors arbitration clauses is that he believes there are cases that are better resolved in arbitration.[35]

ACTION ITEMS

◆ RECONSIDER MANDATORY Arbitration Clauses. Check with your law firm to get an opinion on retaining predispute resolution clauses. If the arbitration cases in your area seem to be fair, equitable, and efficient, you may want to continue requiring investors to use this process. If arbitrators have been capricious or consistently unfair, you may want to eliminate the clause. Remember, any investor signing a New Account Form today may not file a case for up to a decade; it is hard to tell which forum will be better then.

◆ EVEN IF YOUR FIRM decides to retain mandatory arbitration clauses, check with your attorney about including language requiring arbitrators to use the laws of a particular state or judicial district.

◆ INCLUDE A MANDATORY Mediation Clause. As most clients are interested in venting their frustrations, a mediation clause makes a lot of sense and is far less expensive. You can have some control over the outcome, and resolution is quicker and more likely. If your mediation case is one of the few that is not resolved, you will have lost nothing and will have gained the opportunity to preview your opponent's case.

The author is grateful to Terry Fleming of Lindquist and Vennum for his considerable help with this chapter.

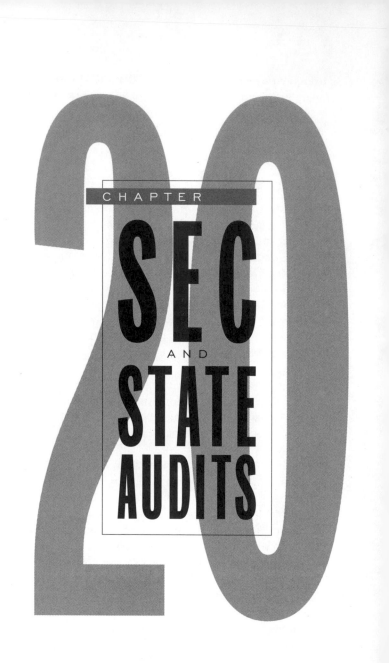

SEC

AND

STATE

AUDITS

IF THERE IS ONE THING that strikes fear into the heart of any planner or investment adviser, it is the possibility of an SEC or state audit. Until recently, that fear was almost groundless. Between 1980 and 1987, for example, the SEC inspected an average of only 12.16 percent of all investment advisers.[1] In 1992, then SEC Chairman Richard Breeden stated that most small investment advisers could anticipate being inspected at the rate of only once every 30 years.[2]

The passage of the Investment Advisers Supervision Coordination Act in 1996 has completely changed the picture. With fewer SEC RIAs and a larger budget, the SEC will be performing more audits. State audits will also increase. No longer required to monitor large firms, state agencies can focus on smaller firms where there are more likely to be problems.

This chapter tells you how to be prepared for an audit and what to expect should one occur. The most important thing to remember is if you have neat, clean records that are easy to retrieve, you have nothing to fear from an audit. The corollary, of course, is that if your records are a mess, you should make it a high priority to clean them up; you will sleep better at night, even during an audit. While the following focuses on the SEC audit, the information and suggestions can be used to prepare for state regulators as well.

Background Information

THE SEC AND STATE SECURITIES administrations are empowered to inspect any RIA, affiliate, or RIA representative. If, however, you are affiliated with your broker-dealer's RIA, it is most often the home office, not you, that can expect a surprise visit from SEC examiners. State examiners, on the other hand, sometimes make no distinction regarding whether it is the home office or the individual in the field who is actually registered as an adviser. In Illinois, any RIA, affiliate, or RIA representative can expect a surprise visit.[3]

If you live in or near one of the nine cities where the SEC has a regional office, you are likely to have the SEC appear at your office unannounced. Those cities are Atlanta, Boston, Chicago, Denver, Fort Worth, Los Angeles, New York, Philadelphia, and Seattle.

If you live in East Overshoe, Missouri, you have a better chance the SEC will call in advance to announce their arrival. They do not want to travel a great distance and discover you are on an extended fishing trip.

Most SEC examiners are likely to be very young.

Many have been out of college for just two years. They are smart, with GPAs of 3.5 or higher, but they have limited experience in the securities industry. Rarely are they attorneys or accountants.[4]

There are few limits on the SEC's inspection powers. Two of the more important are that the SEC cannot mislead a registrant, and examiners are limited to requesting only copies of books and records listed in Rule 204-2.

◆ In *SEC v. ESM Government Sec., Inc.*,[5] the registrant was assured he was being inspected as part of the routine inspection process. Later, it turned out that the SEC had actually targeted him for a criminal enforcement action. The court dismissed the case because the SEC had lied about the purpose of their inspection.

◆ Examiners are entitled to only copies of the books and records covered in Rule 204-2 (and described under "Required Record Keeping" in Chapter 8). This is important for two reasons: You do not have to produce anything not on the list, and, technically, you do not have to answer questions. However, refusing to answer questions is likely to raise the ire, if not the suspicions, of the SEC examiners and make them dig further looking for violations. Generally, it makes sense to answer their questions, even if it is not legally required. Records, as noted in Chapter 8, may be stored on computer, magnetic disk, or tape.[6] It is not unusual for examiners to come with a portable computer and download the necessary information onto their computers for review back at the SEC office.

There are few procedural safeguards available to advisers. The SEC does not need a search warrant to come to your office and go through your records. Also, advisers cannot plead the Fifth when under examination to avoid producing incriminating records.[7]

Types of Exams

THERE ARE TWO TYPES of exams: routine and for cause. Routine exams are part of the regular cycle, where the SEC may not be looking for anything in particular. The dreaded exams are for cause. "For cause" means the staff is concerned about a particular violation of law, or they have had a tip, complaint, or rumor of trouble. Occasionally staff will use for cause audits to look into industry practices. Although staff must advise you the exam is for cause, they do not have to tell you who made the complaint or what the cause is. However, you will probably be able to discern the scope of their exam by the type of questions they are asking.

Exams for cause are troubling because they can lead to enforcement proceedings in which the SEC can fine, suspend, or publicly reprimand advisers or even bar them from the industry. In certain cases staff can refer an adviser over to the appropriate authorities for criminal prosecution. No matter what the outcome, the publicity can be humiliating and costly.

Prior to the audit, the examiners will review all of your filings and correspondence with the SEC. They will look at the reports of previous examinations and any deficiency letters in addition to any newspaper or magazine articles about your firm.

There are a number of things the SEC must notify the registrant at the time of the audit.[8] These include: SEC authority for requesting the information and whether providing it is mandatory or voluntary; the purpose of gathering the information; the routine uses of the information; the effects, if any, of failing to produce the requested information; and if gathering the information is pursuant to routine inspection powers or law enforcement powers.

Red Flag Areas

THE FOCUS OF AN EXAM often depends on which SEC regional or state office is conducting it; however, there are certain red flag areas that are likely to cause scrutiny no matter where you are located. These are as follows.

◆ **Suitability.** As 50 percent of all E&O claims involve suitability, this area is likely to be reviewed.

◆ **Know your client.** Staff will also be reviewing your files to see if there was adequate client information obtained before recommendations were made and that the recommendations match the client's goals.

◆ **Compensation.** All areas of compensation are open to review. One important area is charging a percentage of assets under management. Fees of 3 percent may be deemed too high by SEC staff.[9] Examiners will also check if you are charging full brokerage fees or using discount brokerage schedules when also charging RIA fees.

◆ **Trading practices.** This area may include churning, insider trading, obtaining best price in execution, and front running. Examiners will also look at your personal securities transactions to make sure they are not at odds with your clients'.

◆ **Cash referral fees/solicitors.** If you have a third party who is not an employee soliciting business on your behalf as a solicitor, you must comply with additional rules. Some of these are covered in Chapter 8. Examiners will want to look at the solicitor's separate brochure and verify that the clients knew the solicitor was going to receive compensation for making the referral. Staff particularly wants to know clients were aware that this arrangement increased their costs, if that was the case.

◆ **Conflicts of interest.** The magic words for conflicts are: eliminate them. If not, at least disclose them.[10]

◆ **Receipts for delivering the prospectus and the ADV**

Part II or brochure. Although there is no rule mandating receipts, the SEC infers this requirement from the rules that require delivery of these documents. A sample prospectus receipt is included in Appendix B.

◆ **Sales practices, particularly performance advertising.** If you use performance figures, make sure you can verify their accuracy. More information about RIA advertising restrictions is contained in Chapter 8.

◆ **Insider trading policy.** Some advisers may not be aware of a relatively new rule that requires a separate insider trading policy for the RIA. It is not permissible to rely on the broker-dealer's policy. [11]

◆ **Written offer to deliver the brochure.** The SEC staff will look for a list of all clients who received the offer and all who responded.

◆ **Fiduciary duty.** Any breaches of fiduciary duty will be closely scrutinized.

◆ **Impartial advice.** Staff will try to determine whether the adviser has rendered disinterested and impartial advice.

◆ **Supervision.** Procedures for supervision of advisory representatives are also reviewed.

◆ **Trades against recommendations.** Evidence that the adviser made personal trades against recommendations will require a closer look. [12]

◆ **General partner issues.** Instances where the adviser functions as a general partner for an investment partnership and receives compensation in violation of the incentive fee provision of Sec 205(1) may be targeted. [13]

◆ **Switching mutual funds.** Make sure you have written evidence that the limitations, drawbacks, and fees of switching mutual funds have been disclosed. [14]

◆ **Brokerage transaction rates.** Keep records that show the adviser obtained the best price in executing brokerage transactions.

◆ **Advisory contracts.** Are there any hedge clauses that

limit the clients' right to sue the adviser?[15] Are the other requirements for these contracts being followed?

◆ **Custody or discretion authority.** As more than 50 percent of all enforcement actions involve theft of client funds, staff takes a close look at this area. If you are currently running your practice in a way that allows access to client funds, you can save yourself a lot of time and trouble by eliminating this procedure.

◆ **Derivatives and other confusing or trendy investments.** Sometimes staff will do a series of examinations just to determine industry trends. Be careful with investments that are high risk and difficult to explain. Staff will want to see that clients not only understood the underlying investments, but that they also comprehended the risks involved.

◆ **Recommendations matching actions.** One planner who reported beating the odds with three examinations in the last few years noted that each time staff was looking for the same thing: Did the client's investment actions match the planner's recommendations? Perhaps staff is concerned with bait-and-switch.

◆ **RIA actions that match established policies and procedures.** Recently the SEC has brought several enforcement proceedings against investment advisers who failed to establish and maintain the required policies and procedures or who failed to adhere to them.[16]

Survival Techniques

AS DISCUSSED IN CHAPTERS 11 through 13, the key to any successful client relationship is determining the client's expectations and then meeting or exceeding them. It might help to think of the SEC or your state examiner as "The Client." There is no question that you want to meet or exceed the expectations of the examiners, because they can put you out of business if you do not. However, they are much easier to read than the average client, because all of their expectations are a matter of public record. You already know what you have to do to please them.

The two most critical factors in surviving an exam are neat records and a good attitude. Examiners form an opinion about your firm within the first few minutes of arriving at your door. If you can quickly provide the requested records and they are neat and in order, you are sending the strong message examiners like to hear: "We take compliance seriously here." If you have trouble finding records, stall for more time, or produce documents that are incomplete and messy, examiners will be thinking "trouble" and dig in deeper to find some problems. Neat records are absolutely essential to surviving an audit.

Attitude is the second most important factor in surviving an SEC audit. Everything about you should exude the philosophy, "We are very careful to follow all of your rules." Be cooperative, positive, responsive, and courteous. Avoid being overly friendly or smarmy.

With these two absolutely crucial principles in mind, put into practice the following survival techniques. With them, you will find you have nothing to fear should the examiners arrive unannounced at your offices.

BE A BOY SCOUT: ALWAYS PREPARED Even if an audit was not a fact of your business life, you would still want to have efficient filing systems, a functioning compliance program, and a trained staff to maintain the profitability of your practice. Excellence in all three areas not only reduces the time and anguish often associated with an audit but also increases the efficiency and profitability of your practice.

AREA 1. Filing Systems. The following guidelines should help you create a top-notch filing system.

Review list of required records. Get copies of what your state is looking for by contacting your broker-dealer or your state securities department. SEC requirements are listed in Chapter 8. Knowing what you need to have on hand is the first step to simplifying.

Create a separate file drawer for audits. After reviewing the list, make at least one folder for each item on the list and put it in a file drawer labeled "SEC/STATE AUDITS." Once you know the SEC is going to ask for your compliance manual, ads, and check stubs, your procedures should include making an extra copy for the Audit file. Whenever you send a client a letter, make two copies and put one in an audit file marked "client correspondence."

Color coordinate your client files. Separate insurance business from planning, brokerage, and general client information using different colored folders or labels for the same client. Although the SEC is limited to requesting items on their list, if your filing is sloppy, you may find examiners reviewing your insurance plans, an item that is normally left to state insurance departments. Clean filing will keep auditors focused on what they should be reviewing.

Although it may take some time to set up this kind of system, it will save you hours of frustrations when examiners arrive without notice demanding to see all your client correspondence for the last three years. Think how impressed the SEC will be when you can walk over to your dedicated file drawer and retrieve these documents in less than a minute.

AREA 2. Compliance Program. Now is the time to have those long-delayed compliance meetings with all your colleagues and staff. Once a year, take your RIA compliance manual and divide it into sections, assigning homework. Give everyone an advance reading assignment to be completed before the meeting. At the meeting, take attendance and good notes. This is an excellent way to make sure everyone is following the same procedures.[17]

When the examiners arrive, they will hand you a list

of items they need to review. Before you retrieve them, hand the examiners a copy of your compliance manual, your signed attendance sheets, and the notes of all of your compliance meetings. This will give the examiners something to look at while you are finding your files, and it sets the tone for the examination. You want them to know you take compliance very seriously.

Be sure to fix problems before the auditors arrive. If you have uncovered some areas that are not in compliance, it only makes sense to fix them as soon as possible. Do not wait until you receive a deficiency letter.

AREA 3. Staff Education. Part of being prepared is teaching staff and colleagues what to say in those crucial first few minutes when the examiners arrive. Make sure your receptionist does not get on the intercom or yell down the hall, "Geooooorge, they're heeeeeeere!" This can alarm clients and make them wonder what you have done that is so dreadful you deserved an audit.

Explain to your receptionist that he should take the examiners' business cards and calmly walk back to your office and notify you in person, even if you are in a meeting. This gives you a few moments to collect your thoughts and present yourself in a poised and confident manner.

It is also important to give your receptionist a script, in case you and all the partners in your RIA are out of town when the examiners arrive. The receptionist should say something along these lines:

"George is currently out of town and will be back next Tuesday. Unfortunately, I am not authorized to release any company records. May I schedule you to return on Wednesday? That will give George the entire day to clear his calendar to make sure you can make the most efficient use of your time." The receptionist could even offer to get you on the phone, long distance, to confirm the time if the examiner is skeptical about your whereabouts. This is important, because if the SEC staff perceives this as a stalling technique, they will treat you accordingly.

Prepare colleagues and staff on how to answer questions beyond those first minutes. Think of it as preparing a witness for trial. This is no time to say, "I am so glad you are here, I have been having a lot questions about our advisory contract. Would you please take a look at it and let me know if you can find any problems?"

Staff education also includes performing regular reviews and mock audits. Periodically go through your files to make sure everything is in order. If you have other members in your firm, you could take turns doing surprise audits on each other. Also, there are a number of consulting companies that will conduct mock audits for you in advance and let you know how you would fare in a real audit.

BE AN EFFICIENT HOST The SEC staff will expect complete cooperation and appropriate work space. You want to get this audit over as quickly as possible. The longer the staff is in your office, the more likely they are to find trouble. Your entire process should be geared to efficiently gathering all the necessary information so staff will vacate the premises in record time. To make their stay as smooth and as short as possible, consider the following.

◆ **Liaison.** It can be critical to have one person, the liaison, communicating with the SEC staff at all times. The liaison accompanies staff around the office and is present at every interview. The liaison makes sure that, for every copy staff requests, an extra one is made, so you have an exact record of what staff took back to their offices for further review. At the end of the examination, the liaison should dictate a lengthy memo on what occurred during the audit, the kind of documents requested, and a detailed summary of every interview.

This system is important for a number of reasons. It helps you get a good picture of exactly what the examiners are looking for. It also assures your firm will be giving uniform answers to the same questions. If, on the other hand, you tell the examiners the files are over there, help yourself and feel free to talk to anyone in the office, you will have no idea what they took or what everyone is saying. A liaison will reduce the amount of conflicting information, because you will have one person who sees and hears everything.

◆ **Parameters.** It is important to identify the senior person on the audit team. If you run into any problems, you know immediately to whom you can advocate your position. After meeting the senior member of the team, ask about the scope of the exam. Although the examiners may not tell you this information, it does not hurt to ask. Use this script: "So I can clear my schedule to make sure your time here is as efficient as possible, how long do you plan to be here and what is the scope of your exam?"

You will also want to set parameters. This is a difficult area to vocalize without sounding harsh and defensive. You do not want to be demanding by saying, "We have to have a few rules around here." Instead, try this: "To make your time more efficient and productive, we have appointed a liaison to help you out. Connie Compliance is terrific with compliance issues, and she is going to provide you with all of the documents that you request. If you need to question anybody in our office, she will help answer any questions. Connie will also accompany you if you need to go anywhere in the office and she will get you all of your copies." Translation: We do not want you wandering around on your own, making your own copies, or talking to anyone without Connie being there.

Request a daily status meeting. They may not want to grant this request, but it helps to see how things are going so you can fix any problems as you go along.

Last, always provide proper facilities. A conference room with electrical outlets is preferable. Do not put the audit team in a lunch room or out in a hallway.

THINK DAMAGE CONTAINMENT Your primary goal is to keep the inspection within the inspection staff. The inspection staff is not trained to prosecute enforcement actions. Consequently, you want to avoid a referral to the enforcement division at all costs.

To keep the matter with the examiners, follow these guidelines.

◆ **Produce records promptly.** Remember, the SEC staff is taught to be skeptical. If you start hedging about documents or cannot locate them, the staff will think the worst, a Ponzi Scheme, and dig in. Staff will in all likelihood request volumes of information. Pick a couple of easy things on the list to keep them busy. This will give you more time to find the more difficult items if you do not have your records in good shape. If a document cannot be found, however, request extra time to locate it. Give staff some idea of how long it will take and why you need the extra time.

◆ **Ask for help.** It does not hurt to tell them this is your first audit, if that is indeed the case. Let them know you do not understand exactly what they are asking for and you need an explanation. One East Coast planner reported that the more the planner requested an explanation, the more likely the auditor was to say, "Oh, we really don't need that. Let's scratch it off the list."

Similarly, ask the staff to narrow the scope of burdensome requests. Sometimes staff, particularly if they are young and inexperienced, have no idea of the amount of work required to fill a request. Staff may not want to review hundreds of files if a smaller number will give them the information they are seeking.

◆ **Ask for authority verification.** If a request does not

appear to be covered by a rule, ask the examiners for the specific rule that grants them authority to make the questionable request.

◆ **Have your legal staff review incriminating items.** Some planners or advisers may want an attorney to review every document before it is turned over. Although you have the right to do this, it is not a good idea in a routine examination. For one thing, you cannot prolong or delay the examination by having your attorney there. Also, it may make examiners nervous and wonder why you are having your attorney present.

However, if you are being audited for cause and there is a possibility of a serious enforcement action, you may want your attorney there so you do not make any incriminating statements.

◆ **Advocate your case when problems arise.** Tell the inspection staff the problem was inadvertent, isolated, and can be fixed right away. Better still, the problem has already been fixed. Many examiners take the position that, if the problem can be fixed before they leave the office, it never took place. If that approach will not work, or is not honest, explain why this practice is legal. Most examiners will feel obligated to find something wrong, even if it is minor. Respond back quickly in writing explaining how you fixed the problem.

CONTACT OUTSIDE HELP Shortly after receiving that long-awaited knock on your office door, contact your broker-dealer compliance department. These experienced professionals have probably been through numerous audits around the country. They have a good handle on how to deal with the SEC staff. In addition, they can become your behind-the-scenes coach, confidant, and consultant.

The first thing a good attorney will tell you is not to volunteer any information, and contain your answers to the questions that are asked. It is equally important not to speculate or draw legal conclusions. If you do not understand their questions, ask the examiner to explain in more detail.

If you find yourself in the unfortunate position of knowing you have some damaging information in your files, or that you have failed to comply with SEC or state rules, consult with your attorney in advance and in private. It is extremely important that you deal with an attorney experienced in the Investment Advisers Act of 1940. This is an area that calls for an expert.

Responses and Outcomes

MANY PLANNERS AND ADVISERS may hold the mistaken belief that once the examiners walk out of the office, their problems are over. Nothing could be further from the truth. In fact, examiners will be taking piles of information back to their offices so they can review it more closely. They may want to review questionable items with their superiors or legal counsel.

In general, there are four possible outcomes to an audit.

1 A clean bill of health. This would appear in the form of an official letter. It is highly unlikely that you will receive such notification, as the staff is loath to declare that any firm or individual has a clean shop.

2 An eerie silence. If you have nerves of steel, you might take the "let sleeping dogs lie" approach. If you do not hear anything, do not rouse the SEC staff by calling and asking for an opinion. If you do not have nerves of steel, you may want to wait 60 days before calling with the question, "Might I be expecting a letter from you in the near future?" It is always possible they lost your file.

3 A notice of deficiency. These are almost always in the form of a letter. It is comforting to note that the SEC has no monetary penalties for minor deficiencies.[18] Do not be surprised if they are exceedingly picky. One Denver planner reported the only deficiency found was that, on some documents, one of the planners did not use his middle initial. It is not uncommon to get a deficiency that you have no complaint file, even if you have never had a complaint. Solve this one by writing "complaints" on an empty file folder and putting it in the drawer you have set aside for SEC inspections.

If you receive a deficiency letter, you can expect a follow-up inspection within a year. Staff will use the second examination to verify that previously cited deficiencies have been corrected.[19]

4 Referral to the enforcement division. This worst-case scenario is actually quite rare, occurring in less than 3 percent of all SEC audits.[20] If it happens to you, call your attorney immediately. Most enforcement actions are decided by consent.[21] Contested actions go before an administrative law judge in a procedure similar to a trial to the court, without a jury.

Sanctions include censure, limitation of practice, suspension, revocation of registration, and civil fines up to $100,000 for individuals. A $500,000 fine is possible for trusts, corporations, and partnerships if fraud, deceit, manipulation, or deliberate or reckless disregard of a regulatory requirement occurred, which resulted in substantial gain to the violator.[22] In addition, the SEC can issue cease and desist orders,[23] injunctions, and money penalties. For criminal violations, the Act calls for fines of up to $10,000 and five years in jail, per violation. Similar sanctions are available on the state level.

ACTION ITEMS

◆ WHENEVER POSSIBLE, take steps to keep confidential information confidential. If that is not possible, request confidential treatment under the Freedom of Information Act. SEC staff or state examiners may request personal information about a client that you have within your files. This can be legally correct, but can create problems for you and your client if this sensitive information was later released pursuant to the Freedom of Information Act. For example, what if your client's chief competitor could request a copy of your client's corporate tax returns? Your client may be damaged, or at the least embarrassed, by the release of this information.

◆ NEVER LIE, MISLEAD, or alter documents. Any one of these actions could be a criminal offense and can get you into a lot more trouble than a deficiency letter.

◆ ONCE YOUR EXAMINATION is over and all your deficiencies are cleaned up, it is time to rethink your relationship with the SEC or state audit staff. They can be wonderful resources in the future. Take the time to develop a rapport with them and call if you have questions. This may be less expensive than retaining legal counsel for those quick telephone questions.

REGULATORS AND ASSOCIATIONS

THE FOLLOWING ARE CURRENT addresses and phone numbers as this book goes to press.

Associations

American Bankers Association
1120 Connecticut Avenue, NW   (202) 663-5000
Washington, DC 20036

American Institute of Certified Public Accountants
1211 Avenue of the Americas   (212) 596-6200
New York, NY 10036

American Society of CLU and ChFC
270 South Bryn Mawr Avenue   (610) 526-2500
Bryn Mawr, PA 19010-2195

Association for Investment Management & Research
5 Boars Head Lane   (804) 977-6600
Charlottesville, VA 22903

Certified Financial Planner Board of Standards Inc.
1700 Broadway   (303) 830-7500

Suite 2100
Denver, CO 80290-2101

International Association for Financial Planning
Suite B-300   (404) 845-0011
5775 Glenridge Drive, NE
Atlanta, GA 30328-5364

International Association of Registered
Financial Consultants
PO Box 504   (314) 530-7855
Chesterfield, MO 63006-0504   (800) 532-9060

Institute of Certified Bankers
1120 Connecticut Avenue, NW   (202) 663-5092
Suite 600
Washington, DC 20036

Institute of Certified Financial Planners
3801 E. Florida Avenue   (303) 759-4900
Suite 708
Denver, CO 80210

National Association of Insurance Commissioners
120 West 12th Street   (816) 842-3600
Suite 1100
Kansas City, MO 64105-1925

National Association of Enrolled Agents
200 Orchard Ridge Drive   (301) 212-9608
Suite 320
Gaithersburg, MD 20878-1978

National Association of Life Underwriters
1922 F Street, NW   (202) 331-6000
Washington, DC 20006

National Association of Personal Financial Advisors
355 West Dundee Road   (888) 333-6659
Suite 200
Buffalo Grove, IL 60089

Securities Industry Association
1401 I Street, NW   (202) 296-9410
Suite 100
Washington, DC 20005

Regulatory Agencies

U.S. SECURITIES AND EXCHANGE COMMISSION
450 Fifth Street, NW   (202) 942-8088
Washington, DC 20549

NATIONAL ASSOCIATION OF SECURITIES DEALERS
National Executive Offices
1735 K Street, NW   (202) 728-8000
Washington, DC 20006

NORTH AMERICAN SECURITIES ADMINISTRATORS ASSOCIATION
One Massachusetts Avenue, NW   (202) 737-0900
Suite 310
Washington, DC 20001

STATE SECURITIES AND INSURANCE ADMINISTRATORS
Alabama
SECURITIES CONTACT:
Director,
   Securities Commission   (205) 242-2984
INSURANCE CONTACT:
Commissioner   (205) 269-3550

Alaska

SECURITIES CONTACT:
Senior Securities Examiner   (907) 465-2549
INSURANCE CONTACT:
Director, Dept. of Insurance   (907) 465-2515

Arizona

SECURITIES CONTACT:
Director of Securities   (602) 542-4242
INSURANCE CONTACT:
Director, Dept. of Insurance   (602) 255-5400

Arkansas

SECURITIES CONTACT:
Commissioner,
    Securities Dept.   (501) 324-9260
INSURANCE CONTACT:
Director, License Division   (501) 371-2600

California

SECURITIES CONTACT:
Supervising Examiner   (213) 736-2741
INSURANCE CONTACT:
Commissioner,
    Dept. of Insurance   (916) 445-5544

Colorado

SECURITIES CONTACT:
Securities Commissioner   (303) 894-2320
INSURANCE CONTACT:
Commissioner,
    Dept. of Insurance   (303) 894-7499

Connecticut

SECURITIES CONTACT:
Division Director   (203) 240-8230

INSURANCE CONTACT:
Dept. of Insurance   (303) 297-3849

Delaware
SECURITIES CONTACT:
Securities Commissioner   (302) 577-2515
INSURANCE CONTACT:
Dept. of Insurance   (302) 739-4254, ext. 50

District of Columbia
SECURITIES CONTACT:
Deputy General Counsel
    for the Office of Securities   (202) 626-5105
INSURANCE CONTACT:
Insurance
    Commissioner   (202) 727-8000, ext. 3018

Florida
SECURITIES CONTACT:
Director, Florida Division
    of Securities and Investor
    Protection   (904) 488-9805
INSURANCE CONTACT:
Insurance Commissioner   (904) 922-3100

Georgia
SECURITIES CONTACT:
Assistant Commissioner
    of Securities   (404) 656-3920
INSURANCE CONTACT:
Section Director,
    Dept. of Insurance   (404) 656-2081

Hawaii
SECURITIES CONTACT:
Commissioner of Securities   (808) 586-2722

INSURANCE CONTACT:
Insurance Commissioner   (808) 586-2790

Idaho
SECURITIES CONTACT:
Securities Bureau Chief   (208) 334-3564
INSURANCE CONTACT:
Bureau Chief,
   Dept. of Insurance   (208) 334-2250

Illinois
SECURITIES CONTACT:
Director, Securities Dept.   (217) 782-2256
INSURANCE CONTACT:
Director, Insurance Dept.   (217) 782-4515

Indiana
SECURITIES CONTACT:
Securities Commissioner   (317) 232-6681
INSURANCE CONTACT:
Commissioner,
   Dept. of Insurance   (317) 232-3520

Iowa
SECURITIES CONTACT:
Superintendent of Securities   (515) 281-4441
INSURANCE CONTACT:
Commissioner,
   Dept. of Insurance   (515) 281-5705

Kansas
SECURITIES CONTACT:
Director of Licensing and
   Compliance   (913) 296-3307
INSURANCE CONTACT:
Agents and Brokers
   Supervisor   (913) 296-7860

Kentucky

SECURITIES CONTACT:

Investment Adviser
    Registration   (502) 564-3390

INSURANCE CONTACT:

Agent Licensing Division   (502) 564-6004

Louisiana

SECURITIES CONTACT:

Deputy Commissioner,
    Securities Commission   (504) 568-5515

INSURANCE CONTACT:

Commissioner,
    Dept. of Insurance   (504) 342-5900

Maine

SECURITIES CONTACT:

Securities Administrator   (207) 582-8760

INSURANCE CONTACT:

License Supervisor   (207) 582-8707

Maryland

SECURITIES CONTACT:

Assistant Attorney General   (410) 576-6365

INSURANCE CONTACT:

Associate Commissioner for
    Property/Casualty   (410) 333-6180

Massachusetts

SECURITIES CONTACT:

Director, Securities Division (617) 727-3548

INSURANCE CONTACT:

Commissioner,
    Insurance Division   (617) 727-3333

Michigan

SECURITIES CONTACT:
Examiner, Enforcement
   Division, Regulation Unit   (517) 334-6215
INSURANCE CONTACT:
Licensing Dept. Analyst   (517) 373-9273

Minnesota

SECURITIES CONTACT:
Director of Securities
   Registration   (612) 296-2284
INSURANCE CONTACT:
Commissioner,
   Dept. of Commerce   (612) 296-4026

Mississippi

SECURITIES CONTACT:
Senior Attorney,
   Securities Division   (601) 359-6363/6371
INSURANCE CONTACT:
Director, Division of Licensing   (601) 359-3582

Missouri

SECURITIES CONTACT:
Commissioner of Securities   (314) 751-4704
INSURANCE CONTACT:
Director, Missouri State
   Insurance Dept.   (314) 751-4126

Montana

SECURITIES CONTACT:
Securities Examiner/Analyst   (406) 444-2040
INSURANCE CONTACT:
Examiner IV,
   Commissioner of Insurance   (406) 444-2040

Nebraska

SECURITIES CONTACT:

Staff Assistant, Dept. of
  Banking and Finance   (402) 471-3445

INSURANCE CONTACT:

Director, Dept. of Insurance   (402) 471-2201

Nevada

SECURITIES CONTACT:

Director of Securities
  Registration and Licensing   (702) 486-2440

INSURANCE CONTACT:

Commissioner,
  Insurance Division   (702) 687-7668

New Hampshire

SECURITIES CONTACT:

Director, Dept. of State Bureau
  of Securities Regulation   (603) 271-1463

INSURANCE CONTACT:

Insurance Commissioner   (603) 271-2261

New Jersey

SECURITIES CONTACT:

Deputy Bureau Chief   (201) 504-3600

INSURANCE CONTACT:

Commissioner,
  Insurance Dept.   (609) 292-5360

New Mexico

SECURITIES CONTACT:

Licensing Manager   (505) 827-7140

INSURANCE CONTACT:

Superintendent,
  Dept. of Insurance   (505) 827-4500

New York
SECURITIES CONTACT:
Associate Accountant,
  Investment Advisory Unit   (212) 416-8233
INSURANCE CONTACT:
Director of Licensing Services   (518) 474-6600

North Carolina
SECURITIES CONTACT:
Deputy Securities Administrator   (919) 733-3924
INSURANCE CONTACT:
Commissioner,
  Dept. of Insurance   (919) 733-5633

North Dakota
SECURITIES CONTACT:
Commissioner, officer of the
  Securities Commissioner   (701) 328-2910
INSURANCE CONTACT:
Commissioner,
  Dept. of Insurance   (701) 328-2440

Ohio
SECURITIES CONTACT:
Licensing Supervisor   (614) 644-7381
INSURANCE CONTACT:
Director,
  Dept. of Insurance   (614) 644-2658

Oklahoma
SECURITIES CONTACT:
Administrator,
  Securities Commission   (405) 521-2451
INSURANCE CONTACT:
Insurance Commissioner   (405) 521-3916

Oregon

SECURITIES CONTACT:
Chief of Registration
& Licensing   (503) 378-4387
INSURANCE CONTACT:
Manager, Agents Licensing/
Continuing Education   (508) 378-4511
                               ext. 610

Pennsylvania

SECURITIES CONTACT:
Director,
Div. of Licensing
& Compliance   (717) 787-6828
INSURANCE CONTACT:
Commissioner, Pennsylvania
Insurance Dept.   (717) 787-2317

Puerto Rico

SECURITIES CONTACT:
Securities Investigator   (809) 751-7837/5606
INSURANCE CONTACT:
Commissioner of Insurance   (809) 722-8686

Rhode Island

SECURITIES CONTACT:
Associate Director &
Superintendent of Securities   (401) 277-3048
INSURANCE CONTACT:
Associate Director &
Superintendent of Insurance   (401) 277-2223

South Carolina

SECURITIES CONTACT:
Registrar   (803) 734-1087
INSURANCE CONTACT:
Director, State of South Carolina
Dept. of Insurance   (803) 737-6212

South Dakota
SECURITIES CONTACT:
Director, Securities Division   (605) 773-4823
INSURANCE CONTACT:
Director, Division of Insurance   (605) 773-3563

Tennessee
SECURITIES CONTACT:
Securities Examiner   (615) 741-3187
INSURANCE CONTACT:
Commissioner,
    Dept. of Commerce
    & Insurance   (615) 741-2241

Texas
SECURITIES CONTACT:
Director, Dealer Registration   (512) 305-8332
INSURANCE CONTACT:
Commissioner,
    Dept. of Insurance   (512) 463-6189

Utah
SECURITIES CONTACT:
Director of Securities,
    Dept. of Commerce   (801) 530-6600
INSURANCE CONTACT:
Licensing Supervisor   (801) 538-3827

Vermont
SECURITIES CONTACT:
Deputy Commissioner,
    Dept. of Banking,
    Insurance & Securities   (808) 828-3420
INSURANCE CONTACT:
Commissioner,
    Dept. of Banking,
    Insurance & Securities   (802) 828-3301

Virginia

SECURITIES CONTACT:
Chief of Registration   (804) 371-9610
INSURANCE CONTACT:
Supervisor, Agents Licensing
    Division   (804) 371-9631

Washington

SECURITIES CONTACT:
Securities Analyst,
    Dept. of Licensing   (206) 586-5068
INSURANCE CONTACT:
Deputy Commissioner   (206) 753-7300

West Virginia

SECURITIES CONTACT:
Director, Securities Division   (304) 558-2257
INSURANCE CONTACT:
Commissioner,
    Dept. of Insurance   (304) 558-3354

Wisconsin

SECURITIES CONTACT:
Administrator, Division of
    Market Licensing   (608) 266-3431
INSURANCE CONTACT:
Commissioner,
    Dept. of Insurance   (608) 266-0102

Wyoming

SECURITIES CONTACT:
Assistant Securities
    Commissioner   (307) 777-7370
INSURANCE CONTACT:
Insurance Commissioner   (307) 777-6887

SAMPLE STATE INVESTMENT ADVISER REQUIREMENTS

AS INDICATED THROUGHOUT the text, state investment adviser registration rules and regulations vary dramatically. The passage of the 1996 Coordination

CALIFORNIA SAMPLE

Registration Fees	Examination Requirements	Dual Registration Statue
$125 IA Part 7, Ch. 1, Sec. 25608(q), Cal. Stat.	Series 2, 7, 24, CFA or CIC OR have been actively engaged as a portfolio manager or securities analyst in the banking, insurance or securities industry during 3 of the past 5 years. (Note: All exams must be taken within 2 years prior to date of application unless actively engaged in business without interruption since passing the examination.) Title 10, Ch. 3, Art. 10, Rule 260.236(1), Cal. Code Regs.	Concurrent association prohibited unless: (1) such person gives written notice to both affiliates, (2) both affiliates consent to concurrent affiliation, (3) both affiliates establish procedures to guard against possible conflicts of interest, and (4) both affiliates assume liability for all acts of the agent. Title 10, Ch. 3, Art. 10, Rule 260.216.16, Cal. Code Regs.

Act could make this situation particularly fluid. Areas which are of concern include: registration fees, examination requirements, dual registration status, application procedures, capital requirements, bonding requirements, and *de minimis* requirements. The IAFP has provided information for two states, California and Florida, as an example. The data have been gathered from the respective state statutes, corresponding regulations, the 1996 Compliance International C-Text for Windows Blue Sky Law Reports, and subsequent clarification with the department of securities in each state.

Please be advised that this information changes constantly and neither the author nor the IAFP can be held liable for actions taken in reliance on this material. IAFP members may contact their national headquarters at (800) 945-4237 for current information on their state.

Application Procedures	Capital Requirements	Bonding Requirements	*De Minimus* Exemptions
Applications for investment adviser registration shall be filed upon Form ADV. Title 10, Ch. 3, Art. 10, Rule 260.231(a), Cal. Code Regs. IF the firm making the application is FIRST, a registered broker-dealer, then these items are required to register as an investment adviser: Submit Part II of Form ADV and; give the state's BD file number. Form BD, Item 10S = Yes	Investment advisers must maintain net capital of not less than $25,000. Title 10, Ch. 3, Art. 10, Rule 260.237.1(a) (!), Cal. Code Regs.	The commissioner may require the posting of a fidelity bond for those investment advisers with custody of client securities or funds. Part 6, Ch. 3, Sec. 25237, Cal. Stat.	5- Exemption not available if the investment adviser maintains an office in the state. Exemption is available only if the investment adviser is registered with the SEC and if the investment adviser has not previously had any registration in the state denied or revoked.

FLORIDA SAMPLE

Registration Fees	Examination Requirements	Dual Registration Statue
$200 IA, $40 IA rep. Associated persons not having current fingerprint cards filed with the NASD or a national securities exchange registered with the SEC shall be assessed an additional fee to cover the cost for said fingerprint cards to be processed by the department. Each dealer and investment adviser shall pay an assessment fee of $100 for each office in this state, except its designated principal office. Florida Blue Sky Sec. 517.12(10)	Principal—Series 2, 65, or 66 (w/80 score) within last 2 years; OR proof of passing within last 2 years appropriate exam relating to the position to be filled, administered by a national securities association or a national securities exchange registered with the SEC; OR proof of current membership in the AIMR with CFA designation or ICA membership with CIC designation; OR having remained continuously registered in the capacity to be filled with the State of Florida. Agent—Series 2, 65, or 66 (w/70 score) within last 2 years; OR proof of passing within last 2 years appropriate exam relating to the position to be filled, administered by a national securities association or a national securities exchange registered with the SEC; OR proof of current membership in the AIMR with CFA designation or ICA membership with CIC designation; OR having remained continuously registered in the capacity to be filled with the State of Florida. Rule 3E-600.005(2), Fla. Admin. Code	Multiple registration is allowed with more than one B-D so long as separate applications are filed. I-A reps. are allowed if compliance is paid by each firm, customer funds are maintained by dually registered dealer/inv. adviser or a clearing dealer, compliance with Chap 517 by firm, each firm registered with Dept. and each firm approves the other. Rule 3E-600.003, Fla. Admin. Code

Application Procedures	Capital Requirements	Bonding Requirements	*De Minimus* Exemptions
Applicants for investment adviser registration must submit Form ADV. Rule 3E-301.002, Fla. Admin. Code Applicants for registration as associated persons (investment adviser representatives) must submit Form U-4. Rule 3E-600.002, Fla. Admin. Code If the firm making the applications is FIRST, a registered broker-dealer, then these items are required to register as an investment adviser: Form ADV, Proof SEC effectiveness as an investment adviser and a statement: "All persons who will render investment advisory services to Florida residents will be properly registered with the CRD."	Investment advisers who have custody of their clients' funds or securities must maintain net capital of $25,000; while those who have no such custody must either (1) maintain net capital of $5,000 or (2) maintain minimal capital of $2,500. Rule 3E-600.016(3)(a)& (b), Fla. Admin. Code	There are no bonding requirements for investment advisers.	15—Exemption not available if the investment adviser holds itself out as an investment adviser to the general public. Exemption not available if adviser is registered with the SEC, as Florida views being registered with the SEC as "holding itself out" as an investment adviser.

CODES OF ETHICS

AUTHOR'S NOTE: Malpractice occurs when professionals do not act in accordance with the accepted standards of their profession and, as a result, the person to whom they owe a duty, such as a client, suffers harm. As the financial planning profession is so new and there are few, if any, case law or statutory standards, many experts believe the courts are very likely to turn for guidance to the standards adopted by professional organizations such as the International Association for Financial Planning and the Certified Financial Planner Board of Standards, Inc.

IAFP Code
of Professional Ethics

INTERNATIONAL ASSOCIATION FOR FINANCIAL PLANNING

Suite B-300
5775 Glenridge Drive, NE
Atlanta, Georgia 30328-5364
Voice: 404.845.0011
Fax: 404.845.3660
E-mail: daleb@iafp.org
http://www.iafp.org

≣IAFP
INTERNATIONAL ASSOCIATION
FOR FINANCIAL PLANNING

THE OBJECTIVE OF THE CODE of Professional Ethics is to specify and set forth the means to enforce the minimum ethical conduct expected of all members as professionals, and to facilitate voluntary compliance with standards considerably higher than the required minimums.

Accordingly, the Code prescribes two kinds of standards: Canons and Rules of Professional Conduct.

The Canons serve as model standards of exemplary professional conduct. They express the general concepts and principles from which more specific Rules are derived.

The Rules are specific standards of a mandatory and enforceable nature. They prescribe the absolute minimum level of conduct required of every member.

In addition to the Canons and Rules, the Ethics Committee has developed a set of Ethics Policies and Procedures to guide members, the committee and staff in the application and enforcement of the Code of Professional Ethics. A copy of the Ethics Policies and Procedures is available from the IAFP upon request.

Although the official Code of Professional Ethics consists of all Canons and Rules, only a violation of the Rules will constitute sufficient grounds for disciplinary action. The Canons and Ethics Policies and Procedures are used by the Ethics Committee to apply and interpret the Rules uniformly, with reference to the general principles and concepts they embody. The Ethics Committee may also refer to applicable rulings in previous cases brought before the Committee, as well as relevant published opinions of the Ethics Committee.

The following presents the Code of Professional Ethics, including the Canons and Rules of Professional Conduct as they existed at the time this book went to press and is reprinted with the permission of the IAFP.

THE CODE OF PROFESSIONAL ETHICS The reliance of the public and the business community on sound financial planning and advice imposes on financial planning professionals an obligation to maintain high standards of technical competence, morality, and integrity. To this end, the following Code of Professional Ethics serves as the guiding document.

CANON 1 Members should endeavor as professionals to place the public interest above their own.

Rules of Professional Conduct:

R1.1   A member has a duty to understand and abide by all Rules of Professional Conduct which are prescribed in the Code of Professional Ethics of the Association.

R1.2   A member shall not directly or indirectly condone any act which the member is prohibited from performing by the Rules of this Code.

CANON 2 Members should seek continually to maintain and improve their professional knowledge, skills, and competence.

Rules of Professional Conduct:

R2.1   A member shall keep informed on all matters that are essential to the maintenance of the member's professional competence in the area in which he/she specializes and/or claims expertise.

CANON 3 Members should obey all laws and regulations and avoid any conduct or activity which would cause unjust harm to those who rely upon the professional judgment and skill of the members.

R3.1   A member shall be subject to disciplinary action for professional misconduct and has the duty to know and abide by the laws and regulations and all legal limitations pertaining to the member's professional activities.

R3.2   A member shall place the needs and best interest of the client above the needs and interests of the member, the member's employees or business associates in all cases; and shall not allow the pursuit of financial gain or other personal benefit to interfere with the exercise of sound professional judgment and skills.

R3.3   In the conduct of business or professional activities, a member shall not engage in any act or omission of a dishonest, deceitful or fraudulent nature.

R3.4   A member shall not knowingly misrepresent or conceal any material limitation on the member's ability to provide the quantity or quality of service that will adequately meet the financial planning needs of the client.

R3.5   In marketing a product, a member shall not knowingly misrepresent or conceal any material limitations on the product's ability to meet the financial needs of the client, and shall scrupulously avoid any statements which are likely to mislead the client regarding to future results of any recommendation.

R3.6   A member has the duty to disclose fully and accurately the material facts representing the true costs, benefits, and limitations of any service or product recommended; and disclose any actual or potential conflict of interest that could impair objectivity.

R3.7 A member shall not disclose to another person any confidential information entrusted to or obtained by the member in the course of the member's business or professional activities, unless a disclosure of such information is required by law or is made to a person who necessarily must have the information in order to discharge legitimate occupational or professional duties.

R3.8 In the rendering of a professional service to a client, a member has the duty to maintain the type and degree of professional independence that (a) is required of practitioners in the member's occupation, or (b) is otherwise in the public interest, given the specific nature of the service being rendered.

CANON 4 Members should be diligent in the performance of their occupational duties.

Rules of Professional Conduct:

R4.1 A member shall competently and consistently discharge the member's occupational duties to every employer, client, purchaser, or user of the member's services, so long as those duties are consistent with what is in the client's best interests.

R4.2 In the making of oral or written recommendations to clients, a member shall (a) distinguish clearly between fact and opinion, (b) base the recommendations on sound professional evaluation of the client's needs, and (c) support the recommendations with appropriate research and adequate documentation of facts.

CANON 5 Members should assist in improving the public understanding of financial planning.

Rules of Professional Conduct:

R5.1 A member shall support efforts to provides lay persons with objective information concerning their financial planning needs, as well as the resources which are available to meet their needs.

R5.2 A member shall not misrepresent the benefits, costs, or limitations of any financial planning service or product, whether the product or service is offered by the member or by another individual or firm.

CANON 6 Members should use the fact of membership in a manner consistent with the Association's Rules of Professional Conduct.

Rules of Professional Conduct:

R6.1 A member shall not misrepresent the criteria for admission to Association membership, which criteria are (1) active participation in the financial services industry; and (2) a written commitment to abide by the Bylaws and the Code of Professional Ethics of the Association.

R6.2 A member shall not misstate his/her authority to represent the Association. Specifically, a member shall not write, speak, or act in such a way as to lead another to believe that the member is officially representing the Association, unless the member has been duly authorized to do so by the officers, directors or Bylaws of the national Association.

R6.3 A member shall not use the fact of membership in the Association for commercial purposes but may use the fact of membership for the following noncommercial purposes: in resumes, prospectus, and in introductions if the speaker clearly states that the opinions and ideas presented are his/her own and not necessarily those of the IAFP. [1, 2]

R6.4   A member or prospective member applying for Association membership shall not misrepresent any credentials or affiliations with other organizations.

CANON 7 Members should assist in maintaining the integrity of the Code of Professional Ethics of the Association.

Rules of Professional Conduct:

R7.1   A member shall not sponsor as a candidate for Association membership any person who is known by the member to engage in business or professional practices which violate the Rules of this Code.

R7.2   A member possessing unprivileged information concerning an alleged violation of this Code shall, upon request, reveal such information to the body or other authority empowered by the Association to investigate or act upon the alleged violation.

CFP Board of Standards
Code of Ethics and
Professional Responsibility

THE CFP BOARD OF STANDARDS, Inc. has established a Code of Ethics and Professional Responsibility, to which all CFP licensees are obliged to subscribe. The CFP Board administers disciplinary action up to and including revocation against those licensees violating its Code. The Code as well as the Disciplinary Rules and Procedures are periodically revised. Because of this, the CFP Board prefers not to have these materials published in this book. Current copies of these documents may be obtained, however, by accessing the CFP Board's Web site at www.cfp-board.org. Select "licensees" from the main menu. CFP licensees may also wish to write to their Board at 1700 Broadway, Suite 2100, Denver, Colorado 80290.

DOCUMENTS
AND SAMPLE FORMS

ALL FORMS AND AGREEMENTS contained in this book are for illustrative purposes and printed for your assistance only. They are not a substitute for your legal counsel, and neither the author nor publisher is engaged in rendering legal services.

Forms and agreements used by financial and investment advisers should be appropriately tailored to meet the individual needs of the advisers and their specific clients. They should also be drafted and subsequently reviewed on an ongoing basis by qualified legal counsel and the adviser's compliance department to ensure conformance with applicable state and federal laws.

The table of contents on the following two pages lists the forms in this appendix and gives a brief description of their purposes or uses. While the textual material contained in the original forms has been duplicated, there have been some design changes in the presentation. Specifically, while the original forms vary in their use of type, the material presented here uses only the typeface and style found throughout this book. In addition, color has been added so that the presentation is consistent with material in the earlier part of this book.

Forms Explaining Investments 434

The following are examples of documents providing written proof of an investment being fully explained to a client.

Receipt Forms 440

The following are examples of documents providing written proof of a client receiving a prospectus and being fully aware of its financial implications.

SEC Audit Request 442

This document is a copy of an actual request received by a firm.

INVESTMENT POLICY AND OBJECTIVE-SETTING QUESTIONNAIRE

WE WILL STRUCTURE and give advice concerning your investment portfolio based on the facts and preferences you provide below and on discussions with your Investment Adviser.

I. INITIAL FACTS ABOUT YOU AND YOUR INVESTMENT PORTFOLIO

1. What is the initial size of your investment portfolio? $ _____

broker-dealer_____

2. What percentage of your total assets (excluding real estate and tangible personal property) will this portfolio represent?

☐ 76 to 100% ☐ 25 to 50%
☐ 51 to 75% ☐ less than 25%

3. What is your projected time horizon for this portfolio (That is, how long do you expect the assets to remain in the portfolio until they are completely withdrawn for their intended purpose)?

☐ Up to 3 years ☐ 6 - 10 years
☐ 4 - 5 years ☐ More than 10 years

4. Describe (in terms of amount and probability) the contributions and/or withdrawals you anticipate making in the following time periods.

	Contributions	Withdrawals	High	Medium	Low
				Probability	
Near term (first year)	+$ _____	$ _____	☐	☐	☐
Mid-term (2 - 5 years)	+$ _____	$ _____	☐	☐	☐
Long term (over 5 years)	+$ _____	-$ _____	☐	⊓	☐

☐ None anticipated

5. Over the next several years, you expect your annual household income to:
  ☐ Stay about the same
  ☐ Increase moderately
  ☐ Increase substantially
  ☐ Decrease moderately
  ☐ Decrease substantially

6. Check the types of investments you have owned or presently own, and rate your knowledge of each type checked

	Good	Fair	Poor
		Knowledge	
☐ Certificates of Deposit (CDs)	☐	☐	☐
☐ Treasury bills	☐	☐	☐
☐ Money market funds	☐	☐	☐
☐ U.S. Government and corporate bonds	☐	☐	☐
☐ Domestic stocks and stock mutual funds	☐	☐	☐

	Knowledge		
---	Good	Fair	Poor
☐ Foreign stocks and stock mutual funds	☐	☐	☐
☐ Foreign bonds	☐	☐	☐
☐ Other	☐	☐	☐

7. Rate your overall investment knowledge and experience (of products, risk factors, return characteristics, etc.):

☐ No knowledge or experience   ☐ Good
☐ Poor   ☐ Very good   ☐ Fair

8. To what extent do you actively follow the markets?

☐ Not at all   ☐ Fairly closely
☐ A little   ☐ Very closely
☐ Somewhat

9. Over the next 5 years, how much would you like to increase your knowledge about investing?

☐ Not at all   ☐ A moderate amount
☐ A little   ☐ A substantial amount

10. What is your primary purpose for investing? (Check all that apply. If more than one applies, estimate the percentage applicable to each purpose.)

☐ Retirement   _____ %
☐ Education   _____ %
☐ Income   _____ %
☐ Emergency needs   _____ %
☐ Major purchase   _____ %
☐ Long-term wealth accumulation   _____ %
☐ Estate (probably will not need during retirement)   _____ %
☐ Grow assets faster than inflation   _____ %
☐ Maximize return over a specific time period   _____ %

☐ Charitable giving   _____ %
☐ Other_____   _____ %

11. If you found yourself without current income, how many months of current expenses could you cover with liquid assets?

     ☐ Less than 3 months   ☐ 13-24 months
     ☐ 4-6 months   ☐ More than 24
     ☐ 7-12 months   months

12. (A) How much income do you currently need per month? $_____

     (B) Do you have disability insurance?
                                ☐ Yes   ☐ No

If yes, how much would your policy pay you per month if you were disabled? $_____

II. ADDRESSING YOUR TOLERANCE FOR INVESTMENT RISK

13. Investment risk means different things to different people, and people have varying levels of risk tolerance. For each of the following possibilities, check the reaction that best reflects your risk tolerance:

(A) My portfolio may experience a negative return in 1 out of 4 years.

     ☐ Avoid at all cost.
     ☐ Permissible under certain circumstances.
     ☐ Acceptable in order to achieve my expected returns.

(B) My portfolio may experience a wide fluctuation in an individual security or several securities.

     ☐ Avoid at all cost.
     ☐ Permissible under certain circumstances.
     ☐ Acceptable in order to achieve my expected returns.

(C) My portfolio may experience a high degree of

fluctuation in value over a market cycle (usually 3-5 years).
- ☐ Avoid at all cost.
- ☐ Permissible under certain circumstances.
- ☐ Acceptable in order to achieve my expected returns.

14. If the value of your portfolio decreased by 20% in one year, how would you react?
- ☐ I would be very concerned and would find another way to invest my money.
- ☐ I would be somewhat concerned and would reconsider the aggressiveness of my portfolio.
- ☐ I would not be concerned about the temporary fluctuation in my portfolio.

15. If the stock market increased by 15% in one year, while the value of your portfolio, which primarily contains bonds and cash, increased by 5% during that same time period, what would be your reaction? (Remembering that the future performance of any investment is uncertain)
- ☐ I would replace the bond and cash portion of my portfolio with stocks.
- ☐ I would add more stocks to my portfolio, but stocks would not make up the majority of the portfolio.
- ☐ I would not change my portfolio.

16. Choose the statement that best describes yourself:
- ☐ I would prefer to be out of the stock market when it goes down rather than in the stock market when it goes up (i.e., the volatility of the stock market is too much for me to handle).

☐ I would prefer to be in the stock market when it goes down rather than out of the stock market when it goes up (i.e., while I may not like the stock market's volatility, I can live with it in order to earn market returns).

17. Which scenario would cause you the greatest amount of stress?
☐ Not owning stocks when the market goes up.
☐ Owning stocks when the value of the stocks drop.

18. Which of the following would you prefer?
☐ You win $80,000.
☐ You have an 80% chance of winning $100,000.

19. Which of the following would you prefer?
☐ You lose $80,000.
☐ You have an 80% chance of losing $100,000.

20. Which of the following scenarios would concern you the most (Rank 1 through 4 with 1 = most worrisome and 4 = least worrisome.)
☐ You did not achieve the return on your investments that you expected (i.e., your target rate of return).
☐ Your portfolio was worth less in real dollars due to inflation.
☐ Your portfolio dropped substantially in value over one year.
☐ Your portfolio dropped substantially in value over five years or longer.

21. What is the maximum percentage you would be willing to lose in any one year in your portfolio? A general (but not guaranteed) proposition for investing is that, over time, higher returns correspond with greater risks.

☐ 0 ☐ 20 ☐ 35
☐ 5 ☐ 25 ☐ 40
☐ 10 ☐ 30 ☐ 45
☐ 15

22. Due to a general market correction, one of your investments loses 14% of its value a short time after you buy it. What do you do?

☐ Sell the investment so you won't have to worry if it will continue to decline.

☐ Hold on to it and wait for it to climb back up.

☐ Buy more of the same investment, since at the new low price it looks even better than when you bought it.

III. UNDERSTANDING YOUR RETURN EXPECTATIONS

23. Over the past 15 years, the average annual rates of return for Treasury Bills, long-term bonds, domestic stocks and foreign stocks are: T-Bills: 6% (Consumer Price Index (CPI) + 1%); long-term bonds: 8% (CPI + 3%); domestic stocks: 11% (CPI + 6%); and foreign stocks: 13% (CPI + 8%). As stated earlier, a general (but not guaranteed) proposition for investing is that, over time, higher returns correspond with greater risks. Given this information, what is your long-term return objective **above** inflation?

☐ 1 - 2% ☐ 3 - 5% ☐ 6 - 8% ☐ Over 8%

24. How important is current investment income to you?

- ☐ Essential and the amount must be certain.
- ☐ Essential, but willing to accept uncertainty about the amount.
- ☐ Important, but other factors also influence.
- ☐ A modest amount is desirable.
- ☐ Irrelevant.

25. How important is beating the market over a market cycle?

- ☐ Irrelevant
- ☐ Not essential
- ☐ Important but other factors can take precedence
- ☐ Very important

26. The time period used in evaluating your portfolio performance has a significant impact on the probability of realizing a stated return objective. How long are you willing to wait for your account's performance to meet your rate of return objective?

- ☐ One year or less
- ☐ Three to five years
- ☐ More than five years

IV. A CLOSER LOOK AT THE RELATIONSHIP BETWEEN INVESTMENT RISK, TIME AND RETURN.

Before answering the remaining questions, please review the following basic propositions regarding investing:

◆ Generally and historically, there is a direct relation between risk and return. That is, the more return required, the more the investor needs to tolerate risk and volatility. (However, considerable risk-taking does not always ensure high returns, and low returns are not always the result of little risk.)

◆ Most experienced investors understand the importance of time in relation to risk. In short, in regard to some long-term investments, time may help lessen the impact of risk since the potential for higher returns over the long run may outweigh the effects of any short-term volatility.

◆ Any investment strategy involves risks. A common example is the risk that a traditionally low-risk investment strategy would fail to meet an investor's objectives by producing low returns that do not keep up with the rate of inflation.

27. If these were your only choices, which of these plans would you choose for your investment dollars?

☐ You'd go for maximum diversity, dividing your portfolio among all available investments, including those ranging from highest return, greatest risk to lowest return, lowest risk.

☐ You're concerned about putting all your eggs in one basket, so you would divide your portfolio among several investments with the highest rates of return and moderate risk.

☐ You would put your investment dollars into the investment with the highest rates of return and the most risk.

28. Assuming you're investing in only one bond, which bond would you choose?

☐ A junk bond that pays a higher interest rate than the other three bonds, but also gives you the least sense of security with regard to a possible default.

□ A treasury bond, which pays the lowest interest rate of the four bonds, but is backed by the United States government.

□ The bond of a well-established company that pays a rate of interest somewhere between the other three bonds.

□ A tax-free bond, since minimizing taxes is your primary investment objective.

29. Not including the Great Depression of the early 1930s, the longest time that investors had to wait to recover losses after a significant market decline has been 4 years for stocks, 2 years for corporate bonds and 1 month for U.S. Treasury Bills. Knowing this and that it is impossible for us or any financial advisers to protect you from ever having a loss, answer the following question:

If my portfolio yields a long-term return that enables me to meet my investment objectives, I am willing to endure the following time period before any loss of mine would be recovered:

□ Less than one year
□ One to two years
□ Two to three years
□ More than three years

30. Select the answer that best reflects your return expectation:

□ I cannot afford any possible loss of capital, regardless of the potential return.

□ While unable to risk my capital, I want the best return I can get.

□ If I can get high yields from bonds, it's not worth suffering through the ups and downs of the stock market.

□ Although equities historically earn better than other types of investments, I will forgo some future gains to reduce volatility and earn a steady stream of income.

☐ I believe in the power of compounding income and growth and want a combination of the two.

☐ Solid companies in growing businesses historically give very good results over time, with a level of risk I can tolerate.

☐ Higher risk investors generally earn higher returns, and I want higher returns.

☐ Smaller is better in the long run. Small companies' stocks may be more volatile, but will reward me with the best long-term results.

31. Choose the statement that best reflects your attitude toward varying annual returns:

☐ I want to emphasize limited variability and am willing to accept lower long-term returns.

☐ I want to match market returns over the long-term and am willing to accept temporary return fluctuations.

☐ I want to emphasize above-average long-term returns, and am willing to accept swings in the value.

32. Select the one choice that best represents how you feel about the following statement: "My portfolio should be managed for the long run and the volatility is less important than the end result."

☐ I disagree.

☐ I am willing to accept some variability of return, but never any loss of capital.

☐ I am willing to accept a reasonable amount of annual fluctuation and an occasional year of negative return, in the interest of building capital.

☐ I agree.

33. For your investment portfolio, how do you rank the following?

	Very Important	Somewhat Important	Not Important
(a) Preservation of purchasing power	☐	☐	☐
(b) Consistency of return	☐	☐	☐
(c) High long-term growth	☐	☐	☐
(d) High dividend yield	☐	☐	☐
(e) Low volatility	☐	☐	☐

V. SELECT THE INVESTMENT OBJECTIVE THAT'S RIGHT FOR YOU

34. You have taken a look at past investment returns, established your investment time horizon and considered the risk and return issues important to successful investing. Which one of the following investment objectives most closely meets your needs and circumstances?

☐ **Aggressive Growth** - Growth of capital through investments in common stocks of small, emerging growth companies. No income considerations. Little or no concern for volatility.

☐ **Long-term Growth** - Growth of capital through investments of common stocks of established Blue Chip companies. Little or no income considerations.

☐ **Balanced Growth** - Growth of capital through approximately equal investments in high quality common stocks and fixed-income securities.

☐ **Conservative Growth & Income** - Growth of capital through fixed income securities and stocks for growth and dividend yield.

☐ **Capital Preservation & Income** - Income and safety are the primary emphases, achieved through investments in Government and other investment-grade fixed-income securities.

_____

Client Signature

_____

Client Signature

_____

Date

This Investment Policy and Objective-setting Questionnaire should accompany your Asset Monitoring Agreement.

The author wishes to thank Arnold D. Abens, Jr., a Registered Representative of Royal Alliance Associates, Inc., and President of Abens Financial Services, Inc., a Registered Investment Adviser, for allowing this form to be reprinted here.

ENGAGEMENT LETTERS AND CONTRACTS

Financial Planning/Advisory Disclosure Agreement

THIS AGREEMENT SETS forth the financial and investment advisory engagement entered into by and between ARMSTRONG, WELCH & MACINTYRE, INC., a duly registered advisor, whose principal office is located in Washington, D.C., ("Advisor") and _____

("Client") with residence or place of business at

_____

_____ .

Advisor is in the business of providing financial services and investment advice and Client desires Advisor to provide financial services and investment advice. Therefore, in consideration of the premises and mutual promises contained in this Agreement, the parties agree as follows:

1. Services of Advisor Advisor shall provide the following service(s) to the Client:

   a) COMPREHENSIVE FINANCIAL PLANNING: Advisor will collect the pertinent data, conduct personal interviews with the Client, prepare computer-assisted analyses of the financial data, and present a written financial plan to the Client. The Advisor will be available to help the Client implement the recommendations.

b) **SPECIFIC FINANCIAL PLANNING:** Advisor will collect the pertinent data, conduct personal interviews with the Client, prepare computer-assisted analyses of the financial data, and present selected report(s) to the Client. The Advisor will be available to help the Client implement the recommendations presented.

c) **HOURLY FINANCIAL CONSULTATION:** Advisor will provide financial planning and/or investment advice on an hourly basis.

d) **PORTFOLIO MANAGEMENT:** Advisor will manage the Client's investment portfolio. Written portfolio reports are provided on a periodic basis as mutually decided by Advisor and Client.

e) **PORTFOLIO MONITORING:** Advisor will monitor the Client's investment portfolio. Written portfolio reports are provided on a periodic basis as mutually decided by Advisor and Client.

2. Responsibilities of the Client The Client agrees to provide, on a timely basis, information regarding income and expenses, investments, income tax situations, estate plans, and other pertinent matters as requested by Advisor from time to time. The Client also agrees to discuss needs and goals and projected future needs candidly with Advisor and to keep Advisor informed of changes in Client's situation, needs, and goals. The Client acknowledges that Advisor cannot adequately perform its services on the Client's behalf unless the Client performs such responsibilities on his/her

part and that Advisor's analysis and recommendations are based on the information provided by
the client. The Client agrees to permit Advisor to
consult with and obtain information about the
Client from the Client's accountant, attorney, and
other advisors. Advisor shall not be required to verify any information obtained from the Client,
Client's attorney, accountant or other advisors and
is expressly authorized to rely on the information
received. The Client is free at all times to accept or
reject any recommendation from Advisor and the
Client acknowledges that (s)he has the sole
authority with regard to implementation, acceptance, or rejection of any counseling or advice from
Advisor.

3. Confidentiality All information and advice furnished by either party to the other, including their
agents and employees, shall be treated as confidential and not disclosed to third parties except
as agreed upon in writing or required by law. Advisor is herein given absolute authority by Client to
disclose, provide copies of, and communicate
information obtained from Client or developed by
Advisor to _____

_____

_____

_____

4. Basis of Advice The Client acknowledges that
Advisor obtains information from a wide variety of
publicly available sources and that Advisor has no
sources, and does not claim to have sources, of
inside or private information. The recommendations developed by Advisor are based upon the professional judgment of Advisor and its individual
professional counselors and neither Advisor nor its

individual counselors can guarantee the results of any of their recommendations. Client at all times may elect unilaterally to follow or ignore completely or in part any information, recommendation or counsel given by the Advisor under this agreement.

5. Implementation The Client is free to obtain legal, accounting, and brokerage services from any professional source to implement the recommendations of Advisor. Client will retain absolute discretion over all investment and implementation decisions. Advisor shall cooperate with any attorney, accountant, or broker chosen by the Client with regard to implementation of any recommendations.

6. Purchase of Securities and Insurance Products - Additional Compensation It is understood by and between the parties hereto that employees of Advisor are also registered representatives with FSC Securities Corporation ("FSC"), a registered securities broker dealer, and in such capacity as registered representatives may, if requested by the Client, implement the decisions of the Client and execute the corresponding transactions. In such capacity such representative **WILL PARTICIPATE IN AND RECEIVE THE USUAL AND CUSTOMARY COMMISSIONS OR FEES ON THE INVESTMENTS IN WHICH THE CLIENT INVESTS** and may receive other commissions, considerations and fees from sponsors of investments or other brokers (real estate, securities, insurance, etc.). Employees of Advisor are also employed as independent insurance agents enabled to sell insurance products suitable for Client's needs and goals. In this capacity, representatives will receive commissions from the insurance products Client purchases through them.

In the event an employee of Advisor is acting in

the capacity of registered representative or insurance agent, his or her receipt of commissions, considerations, and fees for executing securities transactions or selling insurance products pursuant to rendering advice hereunder will constitute a conflict of interest. While such conflict could impair the rendering of unbiased and objective advice, it is the intent of the Advisor to act primarily for the benefit of the Client. Client may purchase products and execute transactions through other broker dealers and insurance agents/brokers. The services of Advisor and its employees hereunder are being performed independent from their employment as registered representatives of FSC. Client consents to Advisor's dual capacity as a registered representative. It should be emphasized that Client is under no obligation to purchase products through FSC Securities Corporation.

7. Legal And Accounting Services It is understood and agreed that Advisor and its employees are not qualified to and will not render any legal or accounting advice nor prepare any legal or accounting documents for the implementation of Client's financial and investment plan. Client agrees that his/her personal attorney and/or accountant solely shall be responsible for the rendering and/or preparation of the following: (i) all legal and accounting advice; (ii) all legal and accounting opinions and determinations; and (iii) all legal and accounting documents.

8. Fees to Advisor In consideration of the services rendered by Advisor, the Client shall pay to Advisor the following fees:

☐ **a)** **COMPREHENSIVE FINANCIAL PLANNING:** The fee for providing comprehensive financial planning is based on the time required to prepare the financial plan. The Advisor's rate is $ _____ per hour. The financial analyst's rate is $ _____ per hour. The Fee for this service is estimated to be $ _____.

☐ **b)** **SPECIFIC FINANCIAL PLANNING:** The fee for providing specific financial planning is based on the time required to prepare the analysis. The Advisor's rate is $ _____ per hour. The financial analyst's rate is $ _____ per hour. The fee for this service is estimated to be $ _____.

☐ **c)** **HOURLY FINANCIAL CONSULTATION:** The fee for an hourly consultation is based on the time required to review the Client's situation. The Advisor's rate is $ _____ per hour. The financial analyst's rate is $ _____ per hour.

☐ **d)** **PORTFOLIO MANAGEMENT:** The fee depends on the type of assets managed. The fee will be billed _____ and the annual fee will be $ _____.

☐ **e)** **PORTFOLIO MONITORING:** This is a flat fee and the amount depends on the frequency and extent of the reports produced. Your fee will be $ _____ billed.

These fees are due and payable after services are rendered, but no later than 30 days after receipt of the analysis by the Client. The fees charged by the Advisor are solely for the preparation of your comprehensive financial plan, specific financial plan, portfolio management, or financial consultation, and do not include any commissions which might be generated upon implementation of any securities or insurance recommendations. The investment advisor shall not be compensated on the basis of a share of capital gains upon or capital appreciation of the funds or any portion of the funds of the client.

9. Termination Either party may terminate this Agreement upon thirty (30) days written notice to the other by certified or registered mail to the address set forth herein. Client may terminate this Agreement for any reason within five (5) business days after entering into this Agreement unless Client has received the Advisor's Form ADV, Section II, not less than forty-eight (48) hours prior to entering into this Agreement.

10. Required Disclosures Advisor is an investment adviser registered with the Securities Exchange Commission under the Investment Advisers Act of 1940. Advisor has delivered to Client information providing disclosures regarding Advisor's background and business practices in Form ADV, Section II. The Client acknowledges receipt of Form ADV, Section II.

11. Arbitration This Agreement shall be interpreted in accordance with the laws of the District of Columbia. At the sole and exclusive option of the Advisor, any controversy or claim arising out of this Agreement, or any breach thereof, or arising out of the services provided by Advisor and its employees hereunder, shall be settled by arbitration in accordance with the Commercial Rules of the American Arbitration Association, before one arbitrator in Washington, D.C., and judgment upon the award rendered by the arbitrator shall be final and may be entered in any court having jurisdiction. No punitive or non-compensatory damages shall be awarded. If any provision of this Agreement is held by any court or in any arbitration to be invalid, void, or unenforceable, the remaining provisions shall nevertheless continue in full force and effect.

12. Miscellaneous

a) This Agreement shall be applicable only to financial advice contained in the financial analysis or investment recommendation individually prepared for Client and shall not relate to any advice given by any person or persons not specifically designated by Advisor in writing to perform such services. Advisor is not responsible for the act, omissions or insolvency of any agent, broker, or independent contractor selected to perform any action for the Client's account.

b) Neither party hereto may assign, convey, or otherwise transfer any of its rights, obligations, or interests herein without prior express written consent of the other party.

c) Subject to the provision regarding assignment, this Agreement shall be binding on the heirs, executors, administrators, legal representatives, successors, and assigns of the respective parties.

d) This disclosure document represents the complete Agreement of the parties with regard to the subject matter and supersedes any prior understanding or agreements, oral or written.

e) This Agreement may be amended or revised only by an instrument in writing signed by the Client and by an officer of Advisor.

f) No provision hereof or breach of any provision may be incurred or discharged except by a written agreement of the party from whom the waiver or discharge is sought. No waiver of any breach of this Agreement shall in any way be construed to be a waiver of any future or subsequent breach.

g) Any provision of this Agreement which is prohibited or unenforceable shall be ineffective as to the extent of such prohibition or unenforceability without invalidating the remaining provisions hereof.

h) The validity of this Agreement and of any of its terms or provisions, as well as the rights and duties of the parties to the Agreement, shall be governed by the laws of the District of Columbia.

i) This Agreement may be executed in several counterparts each of which shall be deemed an original. **THE UNDERSIGNED HAS/HAVE CAREFULLY READ THIS ENTIRE DOCUMENT AND THE UNDERSIGNED AGREES TO ALL THE TERMS AND CONDITIONS HEREIN, AND ACKNOWLEDGES RECEIPT OF A COPY OF THIS CONTRACT.**

Advisor and Client have each caused this agreement to be executed on _____

This agreement shall remain in effect unless modified or terminated in writing by either the Advisor or the Client.

	Armstrong, Welch & Mavintyre, Inc. 1155 Connecticut Avenue, NW, Suite 250
Client Signature(s)	Washington, D.C. 20036

Agreed and Accepted:

X _____
(Client Signature)

By: _____
(Client Name)   (Financial Planner's Signature)

X _____
(Client Signature)

By: _____
(Client Name)   (Financial Planner's Signature)

The author wishes to thank Alexandra Armstrong, CFP and Chairman of Armstrong, Welch & MacIntyre for allowing this form to be reprinted here.

Financial Planning Agreement

THIS AGREEMENT is effective as of _____ _____ , 19____ and is entered into by and between Abens Financial Services, Inc. (hereinafter called "the Advisor") and _____ (hereinafter called "the Client"). (Collectively referred to herein as "the parties".) In consideration of the mutual benefits to be derived from the Agreement, it is understood and agreed as follows:

1. Services. The Advisor shall provide the Client the financial planning services indicated below:

☐ **Prepare a Financial Plan,** and furnish recommendations as to the allocation of present financial resources among different types of assets including investments, savings, and insurance with a view toward better correlating the assets with the Client's financial planning objectives.

☐ **Prepare a Plan** to assist the Client in defining personal financial planning goals and objectives to be pursued in various relevant areas which may include business planning, pension consulting, children's education, retirement planning, disability protection, estate planning, tax planning, and investments, and to supply analysis and recommendations as to the actions and investment strategies necessary to attain these goals and objectives.

2. Client's Responsibilities. The Client recognizes that the value and usefulness of the financial planning services described herein will be dependent upon information that he/she provides and upon his/her active participation in the formulation of financial planning objectives and in the implementation of plans to attain those objectives. The Client will complete a detailed questionnaire provided by the Advisor. The Client will also provide copies of insurance policies, wills and trust agreements, tax returns, and other documents as the Advisor may reasonably request in order to permit complete evaluation and prepare his or her recommendations to the Client.

3. Compensation. The Client shall pay to Abens Financial Services, Inc. for financial services provided a fee of $ _____ . Half of this fee is payable upon signing this Agreement and the balance upon delivery of the agreed upon services. Further, this is an annual retainer contract, meaning it will automatically renew annually on its anniversary date for a fee no higher than that listed in this paragraph 3.

4. Implementation. Client understands that personnel of Advisor are licensed with Royal Alliance Associates, Inc. ("Royal Alliance"), a registered broker/dealer. If the Client executes investment transactions through such personnel, such personnel will share in commissions received by Royal Alliance. The Client is under no obligation to execute any investment transactions through such personnel or Royal Alliance.

Client understands that personnel of Advisor are agents for various insurance agencies and that such personnel will earn a commission or other compensation for transactions implemented for or on behalf of the Client with these insurance companies.

5. Legal and Accounting Services. It is expressly understood and agreed between the parties of this Agreement that the Advisor will not provide accounting or legal advice nor prepare any accounting or legal documents for the implementation of the Client's financial, business, or estate plans. The Client is urged to work closely with his/her attorney in implementing the recommendations contained in the financial plan. Implementation of any portion of the plan is entirely at the Client's discretion.

6. Termination. Either party may terminate this Agreement at any time by providing written notice to the other via certified mail. A refund of any unearned fees will be made based on the time and effort expended by the Advisor before termination with the exception that a full refund of any fees paid will be made if the contract is terminated within five business days of its effective date.

7. Assignment. This Agreement may not be amended, transferred, assigned, sold, or in any manner hypothecated or pledged by the Client. This Agreement may not be amended, transferred, assigned, sold, or in any manner hypothecated or pledged by the Advisor without the consent of the Client.

8. Governing Law. Investment advisory services performed by the Advisor shall be in compliance with the Investment Advisers Act of 1940, as amended; rules and regulations thereunder; and applicable state laws regulating the services provided under this Agreement.

9. Acknowledgment. The Client acknowledges receipt of Part II of the Advisor's ADV registration form filed pursuant to the Investment Advisers Act of 1940, as amended, or a similar disclosure document.

_____

Client(s)   **Date**

_____

Title or Capacity

_____

Client(s)   **Date**

_____

Title or Capacity

Abens Financial Services, Inc.

_____

By   **Date**

_____

Title or Capacity

Distribution:
Original – Abens Financial Services, Inc. RIA File
Copy – Client
Copy – AFS, Inc. Client File

The author wishes to thank Arnold D. Abens, Jr., a Registered Representative of Royal Alliance Associates, Inc., and President of Abens Financial Services, Inc., Registered Investment Adviser, for allowing this form to be reprinted here. Mr. Abens uses this agreement with some fee clients and, depending on the particular circumstances of each client's case, in conjunction with other agreed upon forms, disclosures, or written clarifications as may be warranted.

Financial Planning/ Investment Adviser Agreement

I. SERVICES TO BE PERFORMED I will prepare a written Personal Financial Plan for you which will involve an analysis of your present financial position. It will include specific recommendations for investment and insurance for you to review.

I will also study and analyze your financial and investment situation in light of your goals and investment temperament. If appropriate, I may suggest repositioning certain assets to better fit your personal financial goals.

Although I will be making recommendations, you will make all the final decisions relating to my advice. Since this is your plan, the ultimate decision on how to implement the plan, and which products to purchase, is entirely yours.

II. SERVICES NOT TO BE PERFORMED I will not be reviewing your property and casualty coverage, nor will I be providing you any tax or legal advice.

III. CONFIDENTIALITY and all data you submit to me will be treated on a strictly confidential basis.

IV. FEE STRUCTURE The fee for my services will be $_____, which will be payable _____. This fee covers a twelve-month period from today's date.

This fee is compensation for my services in preparing your financial plan and does not include any commissions which might be generated upon the purchase of any securities or insurance products through my firm. The initial fee shall be paid within forty-eight hours after delivery and execution of this agreement. You may request an annual update of your Personal Financial Plan. The maximum fee for this service will be _____ . Your signature on this Agreement in no way obligates you to this periodic update.

V. DISCLOSURES

A. Fees/Commissions I am a registered representative of ABC Securities, Inc.

I am also employed as an independent insurance broker. However, you are free to implement your Financial Plan and purchase insurance or investments through the services of any other broker or representative.

B. Conflicts I do not know of any conflicts at this time. If a conflict should arise, I will disclose it to you at that time.

VI. BROCHURE/FORM ADV PART II DELIVERY

By signing this agreement, you acknowledge that you have received a copy of my Form ADV-II, which describes my philosophy of planning, important relationships I have with third parties, and other important information about my business. Your signature also acknowledges that you have fully read and understood the contents of Form ADV-II prior to entering into this agreement.

VII. MARRIED CLIENTS

As you are a married couple, I consider you one client. Therefore, any information given to me by one partner may be shared with the other. Authorization to trade by one partner will bind both of you.

VIII. ASSIGNMENT

No assignment of this agreement shall be permissible without your express written authorization.

IX. MEDIATION

If a dispute arises out of our engagement and cannot be settled through negotiation, the parties agree to first try in good faith to settle the dispute by mediation administered by the American Arbitration Association, the NASD, or another suitable group, before resorting to arbitration, litigation or some other dispute resolution procedure.

X. GUARANTEES Although none of our investments will have any guarantees as to performance, there is one guarantee I can make to you: something that we do will lose money! That is a natural part of investing; what goes up can also come down.

_____

Date:

Signatures:

_____

Signature

_____

Signature

_____

Name of Client

_____

Name of Financial Planner/Investment Adviser

_____

Name of Client

_____

Name of Firm

This form was drafted by the author.

Asset Monitoring Investor Agreement

THIS AGREEMENT is effective as of _____
_____ , 19____ and is entered
into by and between _____
("Investor") and Abens Financial Services, Inc., a
Minnesota corporation ("Advisor"), with whom
_____ is a registered
investment advisory affiliate ("Advisory Affiliate").
By this agreement, Investor retains Advisor to provide asset monitoring and investment management services to Investor on the following terms:

Section 1. Investment Program. Advisor is registered with the Securities and Exchange Commission under the Investment Advisers Act of 1940,
as amended ("Advisers Act") as an Investment
Advisor. Advisor will render investment advice and
various other advisory services under this agreement, and exercise the investment authority/trad-
ing discretion granted below, by and through Advisory Affiliate. In servicing Investor in an
investment program, Advisory Affiliate will use various techniques which may include, but may not be
limited to, asset allocation models, timing services
and selection of money managers, to attempt to
minimize losses during a declining market and to
capture gains in a rising market. Mutual funds and
variable annuities will be the primary but not necessarily the exclusive investment vehicles used in
the management of Investor's assets under this
agreement ("Investor's Account"). Depending on
Investor's preferences and Advisory Affiliate's recommendations and willingness, other types of
investments may be utilized which may include, but
may not be limited to: stocks, bonds and/or other

investment interests apart from mutual funds and variable annuities, certificates of deposit, 401(k) plans and company retirement plans.

Advisory Affiliate shall have the authority to direct the investment and reinvestment of the assets in Investor's Account in accordance with long term buy/sell signals as determined by Advisory Affiliate. Investor understands this is a long term investment program requiring at least three to five years to develop properly. Investor agrees to complete Advisory Affiliate's Investment Policy & Objective-Setting Questionnaire. Investor agrees to promptly inform Advisory Affiliate if any information provided in this Questionnaire becomes materially inaccurate, and of any significant changes in Investor's financial circumstances and investment objectives that might affect the manner in which Investor's Account should be managed. Investor also agrees to annually consult with Advisory Affiliate to provide Advisory Affiliate with updated information and such additional information as Advisory Affiliate may request from time to time to assist it in managing Investor's Account.

Section 2. Trading Discretion. Investor grants Advisory Affiliate the following trading discretion:

☐ **NO TRADING DISCRETION.** Although Advisory Affiliate shall retain the aforementioned authority to direct the investment and reinvestment of assets in Investor's Account, Advisory Affiliate shall gain approval from Investor beforehand.

☐ **LIMITED TRADING DISCRETION.** Advisory Affiliate shall have the authority and ability to determine asset class selection, pricing, and timing of exchanges within a family of mutual funds or a variable annuity, and to direct the investment and reinvestment of any such assets in Investor's Account, all without the prior approval of Investor. The general idea is to safeguard or increase the performance of the managed assets by changing asset classes or allocations within asset classes. This includes the authority to direct the investment and reinvestment of any assets in Investor's Account upon the prior approval of Investor.

☐ **FULL TRADING DISCRETION.** In addition to possessing Limited Trading Discretion described above, Advisory Affiliate shall have the authority to direct the investment and reinvestment of the assets in Investor's Account by making changes of and between all investment types and classes, all without the prior approval of the Investor. This includes, but shall not be limited to, buying and selling stocks, and moving from one fund family to another fund family.

Section 3. Custodial Arrangements. Advisor and Advisory Affiliate will not have custody of any assets in Investor's Account. Custody of assets will be maintained with Pershing, a division of Donaldson, Lufkin, Jenrette Securities Corp.; the custodian bank of a mutual fund group; or any other acceptable depository. Investor will be solely responsible for paying all fees or charges of a custodian. In accordance with the above granted trading discretion, Investor authorizes the Advisor and Advisory Affiliate to give custodians instructions for the purchase, sale, conversion, redemption, exchange or retention of any security, cash or cash equivalent or other investment for Investor's Account.

Section 4. Confidentiality. All information, recommendations and advice furnished by Advisor and Advisory Affiliate to Investor under this agreement shall be regarded as confidential by Investor and shall not be disclosed to any person, firm, or corporation without prior written or oral consent of Advisor or Advisory Affiliate.

Section 5. Investment Advisory Fees. Investor shall pay Advisor, Abens Financial Services, Inc., for services rendered under this agreement, an annual fee calculated according to the fee schedule set forth below. Fees shall be paid quarterly in advance based on the market value of the account on the last trading day of the previous quarter. Fees for partial quarters at the commencement or termination of this agreement will be prorated based on the number of days Investor's Account was open during the quarter. Fees will be offset by commissions earned by Advisory Affiliate as a result of transactions placed for Investor by Advisory Affiliate; provided that, fees will not be offset by such commissions earned by Advisory Affiliate resulting from variable annuity and other insurance product transactions. Quarterly fee adjustments for additional assets received into Investor's account during a quarter or for partial withdrawals will also be provided on the above prorata basis. Investor's Account being managed for liquidation will be included at the initial account date valuation for fee purposes. Investor understands that Investor's Account assets invested in shares of mutual funds or other investment companies ("funds") will be subject to additional fees and expenses, as set forth in the prospectuses of those funds, paid by the funds but ultimately borne by Investor.

Advisor's fee schedule is as follows:

ANNUAL ADVISORY FEE
_____ % of assets under management
NOTE: All accounts in a family, e.g., husband, wife, children, are combined for fee purposes.

Advisor shall not be compensated on the basis of a share of capital gains or capital appreciation of the funds or any portion of the funds of Investor. Refunds of fees may be available upon cancellation of this agreement as herein provided. If this agreement is canceled within 5 business days of its effective date, the Investor will be given a full refund of fees. If this agreement is canceled more than 5 business days after its effective date, refunds may be given on a prorated schedule, based on the date of cancellation.

In addition, a Solicitor, Advisory Affiliate or Representative of Advisor may receive a portion of the fees paid on this agreement. Advisor wishes to state that at times, the fee charges may be higher or lower than normally charged in the industry, and it is possible the same, similar or significantly different services may be available from other investment advisors at higher or lower rates.

Section 6. Valuation. Advisor and Advisory Affiliate will value securities in Investor's Account that are listed on a national securities exchange or on Nasdaq at the closing price, on the valuation date, on the principal market where the securities are traded. Other securities or investments in Investor's Account will be valued in a manner determined in good faith by Advisor and Advisory Affiliate to reflect fair market value.

Section 7. Other Investment Accounts. Investor understands that Advisor, by and through its Advisory Affiliates, provides investment management services for other clients and will continue to do so. Investor also understands that Advisor and its Advisory Affiliates may give advice or take action in performing their duties to other clients, or for their own accounts, that differ from advice given to or action taken for Investor. Advisor and its Advisory Affiliates are not obligated to buy, sell or recommend for Investor any security or other investment that Advisor or its Advisory Affiliates may buy, sell or recommend for any other Investor or for their own accounts. Investor also understands that transactions in a specific security may not be accomplished for all Investors' Accounts at the same time or at the same price.

Section 8. Risk Acknowledgment. Advisor and Advisory Affiliate do not guarantee the future performance of Investor's Account or any specific level of performance, the success or accuracy of any investment decision/determination or strategy that Advisor or Advisory Affiliate may use, or the success of Advisor or Advisory Affiliate's overall management of Investor's Account. Investor understands that investment decisions made for Investor's account by Advisor and Advisory Affiliate are subject to various market, currency, economic, political and business risks, and that those investment decisions will not always be profitable. Except as may otherwise be provided by law, neither Advisor nor Advisory Affiliate will be liable to Investor for (a) any loss that Investor may suffer by reason of any investment decision made or other action taken or omitted in good faith by Advisor and Advisory Affiliate with that degree of care, skill, prudence, and diligence under the circumstances that a prudent person acting in a fiduciary capacity would use; (b) any loss arising from Advisor's or Advisory Affiliate's adherence to Investor's instructions; or (c) any act or failure to act by a custodian, any broker or dealer to which Advisor or Advisory Affiliate directs transactions for Investor's Account, or by any other third party. The federal and state securities laws impose liabilities under certain circumstances on persons who act in good faith, and therefore nothing in this agreement will waive or limit any rights that Investor may have under those laws.

Section 9. Proxy Voting. Proxy voting will depend on whether Investor's assets are considered "ERISA" or "Non-ERISA" assets, as these terms are defined in this Section. (a) ERISA Assets: Unless otherwise required, Advisor will not vote or give advice about how to vote, proxies for ERISA assets held in Investor's Account. Advisor will only be required to vote proxies for ERISA assets if the applicable plan's "named fiduciary" cannot, according to the documents establishing and governing the applicable plan (the "plan documents"), reserve to itself or to another named fiduciary the right to direct a plan trustee regarding the voting of proxies. If, according to the plan documents, the "named fiduciary" can reserve said right to itself or someone other than Advisor, it must do so. If Advisor is required to vote proxies for ERISA assets Advisor may delegate this responsibility to Advisory Affiliate, provided Advisor is permitted to do so pursuant to the plan documents and applicable law. (b) Non-ERISA Assets: Advisor and Advisory Affiliate will not vote, but may give advice about how to vote, proxies for non-ERISA assets held in

Investor's Account. As used in this Section, "ERISA assets" refers to assets of an ERISA plan to and for which Advisor has been appointed an Investment Manager by the plan's trustees or "named fiduciary" in accordance with the plan documents. "Non-ERISA assets" refers to all other assets.

Section 10. ERISA Accounts. If Investor's Account is subject to the provisions of the Employee Retirement Income Security Act of 1974, as amended ("ERISA"), Investor represents that employment of Advisor, and any instruction that Investor have given Advisor with regard to Investor's Account, is consistent with applicable plan and trust documents. Investor agrees to furnish Advisor with copies of such governing documents. Investor acknowledges that it is a "named fiduciary" with respect to the control and management of the assets held in Investor's Account, and shall notify Advisor promptly of any change in the identity of the named fiduciary with respect to Investor's Account. If Investor's Account contains only a part of the assets of the plan, Investor understands that Advisor will have no responsibility for the diversification of all of the plan's investments, and that Advisor will have no duty, responsibility or liability for Investor assets that are not in Investor's Account.

Section 11. Brokerage Placement. Investor acknowledges that a Solicitor, Advisory Affiliate and/or personnel of Advisor, may be registered as a Representative of a broker dealer as indicated in Part II of Advisor's Form ADV or similar disclosure document (currently said broker dealer is Royal Alliance Associates, Inc.), and as such, may receive commissions and/or income from any brokerage placed through such broker/dealer by such persons.

Section 12. Termination. This agreement shall remain in effect until such time as the parties execute another contract intended to supersede this agreement, or until terminated by either party by written notice delivered to the other. Termination of this agreement will not affect (a) the validity of any action previously taken by Advisor and Advisory Affiliate under this agreement; (b) liabilities or obligations of the parties from transactions initiated before termination of this agreement; or (c) Investor's obligation to pay advisory fees (pro rated through the date of termination). Upon the termination of this agreement, Advisor and Advisory Affiliate will have no obligation to recommend or take any action with regard to the securities, cash or other investments in Investor's Account. If Investor is a natural person, the death, disability or incompetency of Investor will not terminate or change the terms of this agreement. However, Investor's executor, guardian, attorney-in-fact or other authorized representative may terminate this agreement by giving written notice to Advisor or Advisory Affiliate.

Section 13. Binding Agreement. This agreement will bind and be for the benefit of the parties to the agreement and their successors and permitted assigns, except that this agreement may not be assigned (within the meaning of the Advisers Act) by either party without the prior consent of the other party. This agreement shall supersede all other Asset Monitoring Investor Agreements, if any, previously entered into between the parties.

Section 14. Governing Law. This agreement will be governed by and construed in accordance with the laws of the State of Minnesota without giving effect to any conflict or choice of law provisions of that State, provided that nothing in this agreement will be construed in any manner inconsistent with the Advisers Act, any rule or order of the Securities and Exchange Commission under the Advisers Act and, if applicable to the Account, ERISA and any rule or order of the Department of Labor under ERISA.

Section 15. Miscellaneous. "Investor", as used in this agreement, may include more than one individual or entity, if more than one Investor signs below. If any provision of this agreement is or should become inconsistent with any law or rule of any governmental or regulatory body having jurisdiction over the subject matter of this agreement, the provision will be deemed to be rescinded or modified in accordance with any such law or rule. In all other respects, this agreement will continue and remain in full force and effect. No term or provision of this agreement may be waived or changed except in writing signed by the party against whom such waiver or change is sought to be enforced. Advisor's failure to insist at any time upon strict compliance with this agreement or with any of the terms of the agreement or any continued course of such conduct on its part will not constitute or be considered a waiver by Advisor of any of its rights or privileges.

Section 16. Disclosure. Investor acknowledges the receipt of Advisor's Form ADV, Part II or similar disclosure document.

If more than one Investor, all principals to the

Account must sign. If any signatory is a fiduciary, the capacity in which he or she is acting should be indicated.

Investor   **Date**

Title or Capacity

Investor   **Date**

Title or Capacity

Abens Financial Services, Inc.

By   **Date**

Title or Capacity

Distribution:
Original – Abens Financial Services,
Copy – Client
Copy – AFS, Inc. Client File
Copy – Advisory Affiliate File

Advisory Affiliate Acknowledgment:

                                               Date

The author wishes to thank Arnold D. Abens, Jr., a Registered Representative of Royal Alliance Associ-

ates, Inc., and President of Abens Financial Services, Inc., a Registered Investment Adviser, for allowing this form to be reprinted here. Mr. Abens uses this agreement with some fee clients and, depending on the particular circumstances of each client's case, in conjunction with other agreed upon forms, disclosures or written clarifications as may be warranted.

INVESTMENT POLICY STATEMENT

ABC Endowment Fund
January 1995
Financial Planner & Associates, Financial Advisors

THIS TEMPLATE SERVES only as an example of a type of investment policy statement. It should not be used as a substitute for a tailored IPS that is specifically geared to the needs and circumstances of a specific plan, as determined by the decision makers.

INVESTMENT POLICY DISCUSSION Prepared by Financial Planner & Associates, Financial Advisors.

WHAT IS AN INVESTMENT POLICY? An investment policy outlines and prescribes a prudent and acceptable investment philosophy and defines the investment management procedures and long-term goals for the investor.

THE NEED FOR A WRITTEN POLICY Requirements to which company retirement plans were subject originally created the need for written investment policies, as described below. We have found the process so useful for companies that we have expanded the concept and now make use of written investment policies for all investment management clients, including individuals.

With the enactment of ERISA in 1974, plan fiduciaries became liable for breaches in prudence and diversification standards. ERISA 402(b)(1) states, "Every employee benefit plan shall provide a procedure for establishing and carrying out a funding policy and method consistent with the objectives of the plan and requirements of this title."

A written investment policy allows clients, whether they be individual or plan fiduciaries, to clearly establish the prudence and diversification standards which they want the investment process to maintain. Plan sponsors should develop a written policy whether or not they take an active role in the investment of pension assets or delegate the task to outside investment managers or provide the participants with the right to direct their own accounts. Likewise for individuals. The net effect of the written policy is to increase the likelihood that the plan will be able to meet the financial needs of the investor and, if applicable, the plan beneficiaries through the development of specific objectives.

INVESTMENT MANAGER PERFORMANCE EVALUATION Measuring the time-weighted return is not enough; the risk of each investment portfolio should also be considered. A portfolio that slightly underperforms the S&P 500 but carries only half the overall risk is superior on a risk-adjusted basis to a portfolio that slightly outperforms the S&P 500 but carries a full amount of market risk. Deciding when to replace a portfolio manager is often subjective as much as objective. Just because a manager had a down year or two is not a valid reason for replacement. This document lays out the procedures to be followed in order to create a system for making such decisions.

INTRODUCTION The purpose of this Investment Policy Statement (IPS) is to establish a clear understanding between the trustees of the ABC Endowment Fund ("Investor") and Financial Planner & Associates, Financial Advisors ("Advisor") as to the investment objectives and policies applicable to the Investor's investment portfolio. This Investment Policy Statement will:

◆ establish reasonable expectations, objectives and guidelines in the investment of the Portfolio's assets

◆ set forth an investment structure detailing permitted asset classes and expected allocation among asset classes

◆ encourage effective communication between Financial Planner & Associates, Financial Advisors and the Investor

◆ create the framework for a well-diversified asset mix that can be expected to generate acceptable long-term returns at a level of risk suitable to the Investor

This IPS is not a contract. This IPS is intended to be a summary of an investment philosophy that provides guidance for the Investor and Financial Planner & Associates, Financial Advisors.

OVERVIEW OF THE CURRENT SITUATION The ABC Society is a 501(c)(3) tax-exempt organization founded in 1960 whose purpose is to provide educational programs for children about the history of America. The ABC Society is headquartered in Anytown, Florida and occupies a museum space which is leased from the county. The ABC Society has an annual budget which consists of revenues from memberships, admissions and grants from the county, state, and private foundations. In the past, the expenses have been fully covered by these sources of revenue. Several years ago, the Society established an Endowment Fund in connection with its planned giving program. The Endowment Fund's purpose is to provide 1) revenue to the Society in case of a deficit, 2) future funds for building expansion, and 3) special projects identified by donors with specific bequests.

There are no anticipated operating deficits within the near future, nor building plans. A recent bequest of $500,000 to the general fund has been made. The trustees are aware of the donor's desire to provide ongoing visits to the museum for inner city children. The annual budget for this purpose is estimated to be $30,000. The donor did not make this program mandatory, and the trustees are free to use the money as they determine appropriate. They intend to make every effort to see that such a program is created and successfully operated.

Trustees have sought the assistance of Financial Planner & Associates, Financial Advisors with regards to the management of the Investor's investment accounts primarily as a result of not having sufficient investment expertise and the Endowment Fund Investment Committee requires the services of a "prudent expert."

CLIENT INFORMATION
ABC Endowment Fund
Abraham Lincoln, Executive Director
One Main Plaza,
Anytown, Florida 33131

ACCOUNT INFORMATION
Investment Account

Custodian	Chuck Fidelity & Co.
Account Number	1234-4444
Tax ID Number	65-000000
Authorized Decision Maker	
	Endowment Fund Investment Committee majority vote
	Members of the Committee
	Joan Smith
	Stuart Friend
	Juan Ramirez
	Susan Helms
	Randy Block
	Current Value of Endowment Fund $3,000,000

Investment Advisor
John Jones & Company
123 Main Street Anytown, AL 99999
(444) 444-4444

Tax Preparer
Tom Thompson, CPA
138 Main Street
Anytown, AL 99999
(444) 444-5555

ECONOMIC OUTLOOK The Investor is modestly positive about the U.S. economy over the longer term. The Investor believes inflation will increase from its current rates.

The ABC Society has successfully provided for its operating budget each year for the past seven years as a result of museum tickets, bookstore sales, special events and annual fund raising. The Committee believes it is likely for the foreseeable future that operating budget requirements will continue to be satisfactorily met through normal Society activities. To provide for an inner city children's program, the Endowment assets will be expected to provide an annual income supplement to the operating budget of $30,000.

INVESTMENT OBJECTIVES Although the fund should seek to provide an annual income of at least $30,000 (or 1% of the principal value) growing in line with inflation, the primary investment objective for the fund's assets is to seek growth of principal over time. The Investor expects to need a small amount of income immediately and therefore will only accept minimal short-term volatility in those assets providing income, however, the majority of assets are to be invested for the long term, and volatility in these assets is to be expected and accepted. The investment objectives for these assets shall be to achieve an average annual rate of return of the Consumer Price Index plus 4% for the aggregate investments under this Investment Policy Statement evaluated over a period of five years.

As soon as a building program is identified and approved by the Board of Trustees, the Investment Policy will be revised to ensure adequate liquidity is available for the cost of building. It is anticipated that any building program would take at least three years to complete.

TIME HORIZON For the purposes of planning, the time horizon for investments is to be in excess of ten years. Capital values do fluctuate over shorter periods and the Investor should recognize that the possibility of capital loss does exist. However, historical asset class return data suggest that the risk of principal loss over a holding period of at least three to five years can be minimized with the long-term investment mix employed under this IPS.

RISK TOLERANCE The Investor is viewed as a moderate risk taker with regard to these investment assets. The Investor rates its own risk tolerance as moderate. The Investor recognizes that higher returns involve some volatility and has indicated a willingness to tolerate declines in the value of this portfolio of between 0% and 5% in a given year. The Investor would accept losses as often as two out of ten times to achieve higher returns.

The Portfolio will be managed in a manner that seeks to minimize principal fluctuations over the established horizon and is consistent with the stated objectives. Financial research has demonstrated that risk is best minimized through diversification of assets, including international investments.

ASSET ALLOCATION Academic research suggests that the decision to allocate total assets among various asset classes will far outweigh security selection and other decisions that impact portfolio performance. After reviewing the long-term performance and risk characteristics of various asset classes and balancing the risks and rewards of market behavior, the following asset classes were selected to achieve the objectives of the Investor's Portfolio.

No guarantees can be given about future performance, and this IPS shall not be construed as offering such a guarantee.

ASSET ALLOCATION

Asset Category	Initial Target Allocation		Acceptable Range
Cash	2.0%	2.0%	2 - 10%
Fixed Income	30.0%		20 - 45%
U.S. Government Bonds		15.0%	
Foreign Bonds		5.0%	
U.S. Corporate Bonds		10.0%	
Mortgage-Backed Securities		0.0%	
Stocks	58.0%		35 - 70%
Large U.S. Stocks		15.0%	
Mid-Cap U.S. Stocks		8.0%	
Small Company Stocks		15.0%	
Foreign Stocks		20.0%	
Real Estate	10.0%	10.0%	10 - 25%
TOTAL		100.0%	

It should be recognized that the Portfolio will invest in actively managed mutual funds, that the actual weightings of these mutual funds can and will vary and, as a result, actual returns can be higher or lower than those presented below.

For illustrative purposes, solely, a portfolio of assets (exclusive of any funds which may be managed elsewhere) combined in a manner consistent with the normalized weightings suggested above and using standardized figures for each represented asset class based on historical norms and adjusted for today's environment suggests that 95% of the time, performance results can be reasonable projected as follows:

For Investor's Allocation Based on Asset Class Categories

	One Year	Ten Year
Maximum for Period	26.13%	14.89%
Estimated Average	9.69%	9.69%
Minimum for Period	-6.76%	4.49%
"Worst Case Conditions"	-11.29%	3.05%

All return calculations herein include price appreciation/depreciation, income distributions and capital gains distributions. Above figures based on 95% statistical likelihood, except for those of "Worst Case Conditions," which returns are expected to exceed all but ½% of the time.

This portfolio design can be expected to experience losses one in eight times, and in such cases should take an average of somewhat more than nine months to recover such losses. Over a five-

For Investor's Allocation Based on Asset Class Categories

	One Year	Ten Year
Large U.S. Stocks	9.75%	15.63%
Small Company Stocks	11.00%	19.21%
Mid-Cap U.S. Stocks	10.00%	13.96%
Foreign Stocks	11.00%	14.66%
U.S. Government Bonds	6.50%	5.20%
U.S. Corporate Bonds	7.50%	5.75%
Foreign Bonds	7.50%	6.90%
Real Estate	9.50%	8.41%
Cash	4.80%	0.74%

year period, such a portfolio's performance should exceed inflation in all but ⅟₁₆ of the time.

UPDATED ALLOCATIONS From time to time it may be desirable to amend the basic allocation policy or calculations. When such changes are made, updates will be attached to this Investment Policy Statement as Appendix A and will be considered part of this Investment Policy Statement.

REBALANCING PROCEDURES From time to time, market conditions may cause the Portfolio's investment in various asset classes to vary from the established allocation. To remain consistent with the asset allocation guidelines established by this IPS, each asset class in which the Portfolio invests shall be reviewed on a quarterly basis by Financial Planner & Associates, Financial Advisors and rebalanced back to the recommended weighting if the actual weighting varies by 3% or more from the recommended weighting (e.g., from 10% to between 7% and 13% of total assets).

ADJUSTMENT IN THE TARGET ALLOCATION The approved asset allocation displayed previously indicates both an initial target allocation and a range for each broad investment category. From time to time, based on changing economic circumstances and the various relative investment opportunities as perceived by Financial Planner & Associates, Financial Advisors, it may be desirable to make changes in the target allocation. Financial Planner & Associates, Financial Advisors may determine such changes, as long as they are within the acceptable ranges, also listed previously. Subsequent investment changes, which you must approve prior to any changes actually being put in place, will reflect the updated allocation, about which Financial Planner & Associates, Financial Advisors will keep you fully informed.

LIQUIDITY Trustees have determined that sufficient dependable income and liquidity are personally available from other sources such that the Investor does not need to maintain cash balances among these assets, except as may be dictated for investment reasons.

However, as previously stated, as soon as a building project is identified and approved by the Board of Trustees, adequate liquidity must be maintained to ensure the funds are available when needed.

MARKETABILITY OF ASSETS Due to the Investor's relatively long-term investment horizon but with potential for changes, Trustees have determined that, as appropriate, up to 20% of the assets under this Investment Policy Statement can be invested in illiquid, long-term investments to include but not be limited to deferred annuities, private real estate investment trusts, limited partnerships and bank certificates of deposit with extended maturities.

DIVERSIFICATION Investment of the Trust funds shall be limited to the following categories:

A. Permitted Investment Categories
1. Cash and cash equivalents, including money market funds
2. Fixed income assets
   a) Bonds (corporate, U.S. government, or foreign government)
   b) Bank certificates of deposit

c) Secured bank loans, pooled accounts (commonly known as prime rate trusts)

d) Mortgages backed securities/promissory notes

e) Fixed rate deferred annuities

3. Stocks (U.S. and foreign-based companies)

4. Real estate

B. Excluded Categories for Investment

1. Equipment leasing

2. Natural resources

3. Precious metals

4. Venture capital

C. Investment Concentration

At all times there must be a minimum of three investment categories represented among the plan assets. There shall be no maximum limit to the number of categories.

Bond maturities shall average no more than 10 years. No more than 20% of bonds in the portfolio shall have maturities at any time of greater than 20 years.

Most of the portfolio will be invested in mutual funds. No single mutual fund shall represent more than 30% of the entire value of the portfolio. No individual security held shall represent more than 5% of the total portfolio.

SELECTION AND RETENTION CRITERIA

A. Cash Equivalent Vehicles The Trustees have determined that all cash equivalent investments shall be pooled investment vehicles, such as money market funds, where a fund's share price is intended to remain constant and the fund's yield is comparable with the current risk-free rate of return. Also permitted in this category shall be United States agency-guaranteed bank certificates of deposit (purchased directly from banks or indirectly through brokerage accounts) or short-term U.S. government securities.

The Trustees have established the following criteria for selecting and retaining any pooled investment vehicle serving as a Cash Equivalent investment:

1. The fund will have an investment track record of no less than three years.
2. The fund's average annualized yield, net of fund level expenses, over a three-year period will be no less than 0.5% below that of the average of all other funds sharing a similar investment objective for an equivalent period.

The Advisor, in conjunction with the Investor, will review the performance of each Cash Equivalent vehicle on a quarterly basis. The investment vehicle's total returns will be compared with the average returns for all other cash equivalent funds with a similar investment objective for the previous one, three-, and five-year periods.

In the event a selected fund underperforms the returns established by such averages by more than 0.5% for the prior three-year period, such fund(s) will be placed on probation for the subsequent twelve months. If over the subsequent one year period the fund's average annual return remains 0.5% below that earned by the applicable average, the Advisor, in conjunction with the Investor, will make a determination as to whether the fund continues to be a prudent and appropriate investment.

B. Common Stocks The Trustees have determined that any selected Common Stock Funds shall be pooled investment vehicles, such as a publicly traded open or closed-end mutual fund, providing daily asset valuations. Such investments may include focus on any size domestic or non-U.S. stock.

The Trustees have established the following criteria for the selection and retention of any pooled common stock investment vehicles:

1. The fund will have an investment track record of no less than three years.
2. The fund's average annualized returns net of fund level expenses, over a three year time period or more, will be no less than 20% below the average returns for equivalent pooled investment vehicles sharing the same investment objective.
3. The fund will incur investment risk no more than 20% above that incurred by publicly traded funds with the same investment objective, as measured by the fund's standard deviation.

The Advisor, in conjunction with the Investor, will review the performance of each Common Stock Fund on a quarterly basis. Each fund's total returns will be compared against the average returns for equivalent pooled investment vehicles sharing the same investment objective for the previous one, three, and five-year periods.

In the event any selected fund underperforms the applicable averages by more than 20% for a period of three years, the selected fund will be placed on probation for the subsequent twelve months. If over the subsequent 12 months the average for the applicable three-year period remains 20% below that earned by the average equivalent pooled investment vehicle sharing the same investment objective, the Advisor, in conjunction with the Investor, will make a determination as to whether the fund continues to be a prudent and appropriate investment.

The relative risk of the selected investment vehicle will also be reviewed on a quarterly basis, as measured by the fund's standard deviation, over the most recent one-, three-, and five-year periods. The fund's relative risk is to be calculated by independent fund evaluation services, such as Lipper Analytical Services, Inc. or Morningstar, Inc.

In the event the level of risk assumed by the fund exceeds that incurred by the average for equivalent pooled investment vehicles sharing the same investment objective by more than 20% over any previous three-year period, the Advisor, in conjunction with the Investor, will determine whether the fund continues to be a prudent and appropriate investment.

C. Bond Funds and Other Fixed Income Vehicles

The Trustees have determined that any selected diversified bond fund shall be a pooled investment vehicle, such as a publicly traded mutual fund, providing net asset valuations published on a daily basis.

The Trustees have established the following criteria for selecting and retaining such diversified bond funds:

1. The fund will have an investment track record of no less than three years.
2. The fund's average annualized returns net of fund level expenses, over a three-year time period or more, will be no less than 2% below the returns generated by the average of all diversified bond funds sharing the same investment objective.
3. The fund will incur investment risk no more than 20% above that incurred by publicly traded funds with the same investment objective, as measured by the fund's standard deviation.
4. The fund will invest in no fewer than twenty income producing securities representing at

least twenty corporate issuers or a comparable number of securities backed by the full faith and credit of the U.S. government or one of its agencies or a combination thereof.

The Advisor, in conjunction with the Investor, will review the performance of the selected investments on a quarterly basis. The investment vehicle's total returns will be compared with the average returns of all diversified bond funds sharing the same investment objective for the previous one-, three-, and five-year periods.

In the event any selected fund underperforms the applicable averages by more than 2% for a period of three years, the selected fund will be placed on probation for the subsequent twelve months. If over the subsequent 12 months the fund's average return for the applicable three-year period remains 2% below that earned by the average equivalent pooled investment vehicle sharing the same investment objective, the Advisor, in conjunction with the Investor, will determine whether the fund continues to be a prudent and appropriate investment.

The relative risk of the selected investment vehicle will also be reviewed on a quarterly basis, as measured by the vehicle's standard deviation, over the most recent one-, three-, and five-year periods. The fund's relative risk is to be calculated by independent fund evaluation services such as Lipper Analytical Services, Inc. or Morningstar, Inc.

In the event the level of risk assumed by the fund exceeds that incurred by the average for equivalent pooled investment vehicles sharing the same investment objective by more than 20% over any previous three-year period, the Advisor, in conjunction with the Investor, will determine whether the fund continues to be a prudent and appropriate investment.

D. Balanced Funds The Investor may determine it desirable to employ the use of one or more Balanced Funds, which shall be pooled investment vehicles, such as a publicly traded mutual fund publishing net asset valuations on a daily basis.

The Trustees have established the following criteria for selecting and retaining investment vehicles serving as Balanced Funds:

1. The fund should have at least a three-year track record.

2. The fund's average annualized returns, net of fund level expenses, over a three- year time period or more, should be no less than 2% below the returns generated by the average balanced fund as compiled by Lehman Brothers, Standard & Poor's, or Morningstar, Inc.

3. The fund should incur risk no more than 20% above that incurred by the publicly traded funds with the same investment objective, as measured by the fund's standard deviation.

4. No less than 20% of the fund's assets should be invested in U.S. government securities or investment grade corporate bonds or a combination thereof at all times.

The Advisor, in conjunction with the Investor, will review the performance of the selected investments on a quarterly basis. The investment vehicle's total returns will be compared with the average returns of all diversified balanced funds sharing the same investment objective for the previous one-, three-, and five-year periods.

In the event any selected fund underperforms the applicable averages by more than 2% for a period of three years, the selected fund will be placed on probation for the subsequent twelve months. If over the subsequent 12 months the fund's average return for the applicable three-year period remains 2% below that earned by the average equivalent pooled investment vehicle sharing the same investment objective, the Advisor, in conjunction with the Investor, will determine whether the fund continues to be a prudent and appropriate investment.

The relative risk of the selected investment vehicle will also be reviewed on a quarterly basis, as measured by the vehicle's standard deviation, over the most recent one, three, and five-year periods. The fund's relative risk is to be calculated by independent fund evaluation services such as Lipper Analytical Services, Inc. or Morningstar, Inc.

In the event the level of risk assumed by the fund exceeds that incurred by the average for equivalent pooled investment vehicles sharing the same investment objective by more than 20% over any previous three-year period, the Advisor, in conjunction with the Investor, will determine whether the fund continues to be a prudent and appropriate investment.

E. Additional Investments, If Any The Trustees have established the following criteria for selecting and retaining other investment vehicles the Investor may wish to hold.

When determined to be appropriate by both the Investor and Advisor, such investments may include direct investments, either publicly available or limited in scope and, therefore, not available to the general public. Such vehicles may or may not provide daily valuations.

The selection and use of such vehicles shall be restricted by the following criteria:

All such vehicles, in the aggregate, shall be no more than 15% of the Investor's portfolio.

The proposed manager(s) of such vehicles, if any, shall have a proven and successful track record of at least five years in endeavors sharing a similar investment process.

Use of such vehicles shall be determined appropriate based on the needs of the overall portfolio, such that each such vehicle will be expected to help increase the overall portfolio return while not significantly increasing overall risk, or each such vehicle will be expected to help decrease the overall portfolio risk while not significantly decreasing overall returns.

INVESTMENT MONITORING AND CONTROL PROCEDURES
Reports

1. Custodian shall provide the Investor with a report no less than monthly that lists all assets held by the Investor, values for each asset and all transactions affecting assets within the portfolio, including additions and withdrawals.

2. Investor shall receive no less frequently than on a quarterly basis and within 30 days within the end of each such quarter the following management reports:

   a) Portfolio performance results over the last quarter, year, 3 years, and 5 years
   b) Performance results of each individual manager for the same periods
   c) Performance results of comparative benchmarks for the same periods
   d) Performance shall be reported on a time-weighted and a dollar-weighted rate of return basis

e) End of quarter status regarding asset allocation—current versus policy

Duties and Responsibilities Financial Planner & Associates, Financial Advisor

Financial Planner & Associates, Financial Advisors is responsible for assisting the Investor in making an appropriate asset allocation decision based on the particular needs, objectives, and risk profile of the Investor.

Financial Planner & Associates, Financial Advisors is a Registered Investment Advisor and shall act as the investment advisor to the Investor until the Investor decides otherwise.

Financial Planner & Associates, Financial Advisors shall be responsible for:

1. Advising the Investor about selecting and allocating of asset categories
2. Identifying specific assets and investment managers within each asset category
3. Providing the Investor with the current prospectus for each investment proposed for the portfolio
4. Monitoring the performance of all selected assets
5. Recommending changes to any of the above
6. Periodically reviewing the suitability of the investments for the Investor
7. Being available to meet with the Investor at least twice each year, and being available at such other times within reason as the the Investor requests
8. Preparing and presenting appropriate reports

Financial Planner & Associates, Financial Advisors will not take title to any assets nor shall Financial Planner & Associates, Financial Advisors exercise discretionary control over any of the Investor's assets. Financial Planner &

Associates, Financial Advisors shall be responsible only to make recommendations to the Investor and to implement investment decisions as directed by the Investor.

The Investor The Investor must provide Financial Planner & Associates, Financial Advisors with all relevant information on financial condition, net worth, and risk tolerances and must notify Financial Planner & Associates, Financial Advisors promptly of any changes to this information. The Investor should read and understand the information contained in the prospectus of each investment in the Portfolio.

INVESTMENT MANAGEMENT Investment managers (including mutual funds, money managers, and limited partnership sponsors) shall be chosen using the following criteria:

◆ Past performance, considered relative to other investments having the same investment objective

◆ Consideration shall be given to both performance rankings over various time frames and consistency of performance

◆ The historical volatility and downside risk of each proposed investment

◆ The investment style and discipline of the proposed manager

◆ How well each proposed investment complements other assets in the portfolio

◆ The current economic environment

◆ The likelihood of future investment success, relative to other opportunities

ADOPTION Adopted by the below signed Investor at _____

_____ this _____

day of _____ , 199 ___ .

_____

_____

_____

_____

This sample Investment Policy Statement was included in this book due to the generosity of Linda S. Lubitz, CFP, and Norman M. Boone, CFP. More information on investment policy statements and sample documents can be found in their publication, The Investment Policy Statement Guidebook *(Ibbotson Associates, 1996; 800-758-3557).*

FORMS EXPLAINING INVESTMENTS

Explanation of Investment: General Form

PLEASE READ THE prospectus carefully, as it contains details of the investment. Your financial advisor is required to review your investment with you. By signing this application and checking each statement that pertains to your investment, you acknowledge the following:

Adequate information. You have received the current prospectuses for the investments applied for.

Investment objectives. You understand the investment objectives and risks of the investment(s) for which you are applying.

There can be no assurance that such objectives will be achieved. Your specific objectives must be indicated.

Goals and Objectives:

☐ Aggressive Growth   ☐ Growth with Income
☐ Tax-Free Income   ☐ Tax Deferral
☐ Growth   ☐ Preservation of Principal
☐ Income   ☐ Other:

Charges and fees. You understand that you may have

to pay sales or surrender charges on certain investments, and that your financial advisor receives fees as explained in the prospectuses. For this and other reasons, most investments should be held for a number of years.

Value of shares. You understand that the value of your shares may go up or down, and that when you redeem your shares, you may receive more or less than you paid for them.

Fluctuating yield. You understand that the dividends and interest may also fluctuate up or down, and that the amount is not guaranteed.

Limited partnerships. You understand that:

◆ Since no secondary market is likely to develop for your Limited Partnership(s), you may not be able to liquidate your limited partnership prior to termination of the partnership.

◆ The partnership will terminate upon the sale of all assets or other events specified in the prospectus.

◆ Your financial advisor is a distributor of Limited Partnership offerings and does not participate in selecting, managing, or selling real property or other investments, except as may be described in the prospectus.

◆ This offer is limited to investors who meet the financial suitability standards described in the prospectus.

Client's Signature   Date

Joint Owner's Signature   Date

Explanation of Investment: Mutual Funds

Royal Alliance Associates, Inc.
Member NASD/SIPC

I understand the following disclosures regarding the material features of the mutual fund investment(s) listed below. These factors have been reviewed and explained to me and were considered in my decision to invest.

Investment Goals: I understand the investment goals of the mutual fund investment(s) listed below are as follows: (Check all that apply:)

- ☐ Aggressive Growth
- ☐ Preservation of Capital
- ☐ Income
- ☐ Other:
    - ☐ Conservative Growth
    - ☐ Tax Advantage
    - ☐ Tax Free
    - ☐ International Growth

Value of shares: I understand the value of my shares may fluctuate. Depending on the net asset value at the time I redeem my shares, I may receive more or less than what I paid for them.

Cost of purchase: I understand a percentage of my purchase price may include sales charges. I acknowledge the following investment has not been represented to me as a no-load (offered without sales charges) mutual fund. I have also been made aware of the pricing alternatives which may be available (i.e., the different classes of shares — A, B, C, etc.) and that these alternatives may affect the amount and/or nature of the charges assessed.

Reduced sales charges: I am aware I may be able to obtain a reduced sales charge through volume purchases or through agreements to purchase larger amounts over a set period of time.

Clarifications of distributions: I am aware there is no advantage to buying shares in anticipation of a stock dividend or capital gains distribution. Any subsequent distribution is actually part of the offering price and thus becomes a refund of part of my investment.

Tax aspects: I understand my investment activity may affect the amount of tax I owe.

Acknowledgment of Receipt of Prospectus I hereby acknowledge receipt of the prospectus for each of the following mutual fund investment(s):

Mutual Fund	Date Prospectus Rec'd	Client Initials	Fund Objective
_____	_____	_____	_____
_____	_____	_____	_____
_____	_____	_____	_____
_____	_____	_____	_____

Investor Name(s): _____

Social Security Number: _____

Investor Signature(s) _____
(both must sign for joint account)

Registered Representative's Signature: _____

Rep. No: _____

Registered Representative's Name (please print): _____

The author wishes to thank Arnold D. Abens Jr., a Registered Representative of Royal Alliance Associates, Inc., and President of Abens Financial Services, Inc., a Registered Investment Adviser, for allowing this form to be reprinted here.

Letter of Understanding
Re: Change In Portfolio

Client: _____

Investment to be sold: _____

Investment to be purchased: _____

Your financial advisor has recommended the above change in your investment portfolio because he/she feels your investment goals and objectives will be better served by doing so. It is not the practice of Financial Partners, Ltd. to recommend such a change lightly. At Financial Partners, we feel that an educated investor is our best client. The following information may be helpful to you:

1. The original investment was made approximately _____ years ago.

2. The objective of the old investment was _____ .

The objective of the new investment is _____ .

3. As a result of the exchange, risk is
   ☐ increased,
   ☐ decreased,
   ☐ about the same.

4. A sales charge will be paid to move funds into the new investment and/or out of the old one. The sales charge will be calculated as follows.

5. An approximate capital gains liability of $ _____ will be incurred when funds are moved from the previous investment.

6. Your financial advisor has recommended this switch for the following reason:

Please indicate that you have read and understand this letter by signing below:

Client's Signature   Date

Client's Signature   Date

Financial Advisor's Signature   Date

Supervising Principal's Signature   Date

1. Material facts upon which I based my recommendation to liquidate the original investment:
2. Material facts upon which I based my recommendation for the new investment:

The author wishes to thank Nancy J. Johnson, CFP, formerly of Long Grove Trading Company, and now of Cambridge Investment Research, Inc., Fairfield, IA, for allowing this form to be reprinted here.

RECEIPT FORMS

Prospectus Receipt #1

Investments In Contingent Differed Sales Load Funds

I have received, from my Registered Representative, a prospectus for _____ . Although there is no up front sales charge to this mutual fund purchase, I understand that upon liquidation of this investment there may be a charge on a declining percentage basis annually, and this charge may be reduced to zero after a stated number of years. This investment is not to be construed as a no-load mutual fund.

_____

Signature of Applicant   **Date**

_____

Signature of Co-Applicant   **Date**

_____

Signature of Registered Representative   **Date**

Prospectus Receipt #2

Client _____

Address _____

Zip _____ Phone (____) _____

I (we) acknowledge receipt of the current Prospectus for the purchase of _____
_____ .

I (we) have been advised by my Registered Representative, _____ , of the sales charge in connection with this purchase, and of the risks involved in this investment.

_____
Client Signature   **Date**

The author wishes to thank Richard Young, FSC Securities Corp., Atlanta, GA, for allowing the receipt forms to be reprinted here.

SEC AUDIT REQUEST

United States
Securities and Exchange Commission
Office of Compliance Inspections and Examinations
450 Fifth Street, N.W.
Mail Stop 9-1
Washington, D.C. 20549

EXAMINATION RECEIPT (We) hereby acknowledge receipt of SEC Form 1661 (9-89), "Supplemental Information for Regulated Entities Directed to Supply Information Other Than Pursuant to a Commission Subpoena" and SEC Form 2389 (2-95), "Inspection Informational Brochure" from

_____ , _____

on _____ , 19 _____ .

_____

_____

Registrant   Signature and Position

File No. _____

_____

_____

Street Address   Signature and Position

_____

_____

City, State, Zip Code   Signature and Position

_____

(_____) _____

Telephone Number   Signature and Position

INVESTMENT ADVISER EXAMINATION LIST OF BOOKS AND RECORDS REQUESTED FOR REVIEW

Instructions: Please furnish the information and number of copies indicated below for the above entity during the examination. Where necessary, furnish responses on Registrant's letterhead. Unless otherwise indicated, please provide the requested records for the time period January 1, 1994 to Date.

I. Copies of Information for Examiners' Use

1. A list or lists of current clients featuring for each the name, its custodian, type of account (e.g. equity, balanced, or fixed), whether or not Registrant has discretionary authority, and the current balance of its assets under management. Also, provide a total of all assets managed on this list.

2. A list of clients obtained during this period, their inception dates, and the identity of any third party consultant instrumental in Registrant's obtaining a particular account.

3. A list of clients lost during the period, their effective dates of termination, and the reason for the termination.

4. A list of current and former clients which have or had wrap fee arrangements governing their compensation of Registrant, featuring for each the client's name, its custodian/sponsor broker-dealer, and the terms of the arrangement, including the terms of Registrant's compensation.

5. A list of all client accounts which have instructed Registrant to direct a portion or the entirety of their brokerage to particular broker-dealers, including the name of the brokerage firm and the client's purpose for such direction, if known.

6. A list of all client accounts which are directly or indirectly related to Registrant or any of its related persons, featuring the names of the accounts, their account number, and the party related to.

7. A copy of Form ADV Part II currently furnished clients and/or any alternative disclosure document given in conjunction with or in lieu of Part II.

8. A copy of each of Registrant's standard advisory contracts or agreements currently in use.

9. A copy of powers of attorney or discretionary authority if not incorporated directly in the contracts specified in Item 8 above.

10. A copy of Registrant's fee schedule currently in use, if not stated in the contracts specified in Item 8 above.

11. A copy of Registrant's standard commission schedule currently in use, if not stated in the contracts specified in Item 8 above.

12. A copy of each of Registrant's financial statements dated _____; and most current year to date.

13. A copy of Registrant's general ledger chart of accounts.

14. A copy of the trial balances underlying the financial statements in Item 12 above.

15. A copy of Registrant's organization chart, employee list, and a schedule or chart of all affiliated entities.

16. The names and addresses of Registrant's current auditor or accountant and Registrant's legal counsel.

17. A list of litigation to which Registrant has been a party to in the period, including a brief description of any dispute and its current status, as well as a list and brief description of any out of court settlements made during the period.

18. A copy of written policies and procedures adopted pursuant to Section 204A of the Investment Advisers Act of 1940 and the Insider Trading and Securities Fraud Enforcement Act of 1988 and any written Chinese Wall policies and procedures.

19. A copy of any Code of Ethics or policies governing the personal securities transactions of Registrant's employees.

20. A list of all employees reporting personal securities transactions to Registrant pursuant to Rule 204-2(a)(12) under the Investment Advisers Act.

21. Any lists of approved broker-dealers currently in use by Registrant trading staff.

22. Any written trading department policies and procedures, including order entry and execution allocation policies.

23. A list of pricing services, quotation services, and externally acquired portfolio accounting systems utilized by Registrant including a description of whether such items were paid for with hard or soft dollars or combination.

24. A list of all proprietary trading or investment accounts of Registrant.

25. A list of affiliated broker-dealers featuring their

affiliation and a description of their clearing arrangements.

26. A list of securities which Registrant or any affiliate underwrote or with respect to which it participated in such securities' underwriting as underwriting manager or member of a purchase group (syndicate) or selling group during the period which were purchased by any client portfolios and the approximate date of such underwritings.

27. A list of the securities in which Registrant or an affiliate was a market maker during the period.

28. A list of trading errors (e.g. bought rather than sold, entered limit order at wrong price, entered for wrong account, etc.) that occurred in client or proprietary accounts during the period featuring the transaction date, the security, the account and broker-dealer involved, and a summary of the error and its ultimate disposition, including the conditions of any financial settlement.

29. A list of cross transactions which took place during the period between client and/or proprietary or affiliated accounts.

30. A list of all securities of a public offering that were invested in by client or proprietary accounts at that offering or in the aftermarket which traded at a premium over the public offering price whenever their secondary markets began ("hot issues").

31. A list of all broker-dealers, affiliated or unaffiliated, that, to Registrant's knowledge, received order flow payments or rebates related to executing transactions for client portfolios.

32. A copy of any promotional brochures, pamphlets, or other materials routinely furnished prospective clients.

33. A copy of any composite or representative performance reports, data, or graphs currently disseminated to clients or prospective clients.

34. A copy of any advertisements (e.g. newspaper or magazine ads, radio scripts, etc.) used to inform or solicit clients during the period.

35. A copy of any newspaper or magazine article reprints disseminated to clients or prospective clients during the period.

36. A list of all parties to whom cash referral fees were paid during the period.

37. For each investment partnership, trust, and any other pooled investment vehicle formulated or offered by Registrant or its officers, directors, or employees to clients or prospective clients. On the list please indicate the following:

- ◆ the general partners, trustees, or others as applicable;
- ◆ whether the instruments are registered with the Commission and if not, the exemption relied upon;
- ◆ names and addresses of clients invested in each partnership, trust or other pooled investment vehicle and the number of shares or units owned and the amount of money invested.

RECORDS TO PREPARE FOR EXAMINER ACCESS DURING EXAMINATION

Records to Be Furnished at Examination Inception

1. A cross reference, stock record, or securities position record of all client securities holdings as of December 31, 1995 and most recent date.

2. A record of all securities held in client portfolios (aggregate position totals for all securities) as of December 31, 1995 and most recent date.

3. Registrant's trading blotter or purchase and sales journal for the period, preferably feating the following fields of information in chronological order:

   a) Trade date;
   b) Buy or sell.
   c) Number shares or principal amount;
   d) Security name;
   e) CUSIP number;
   f) Price;
   g) Total commission;
   h) Commission in cents Per share;
   i) Fees;
   j) Accrued interest;
   k) Net amount to/from client;
   l) Client name;
   m) Client account number; and
   n) Broker or dealer name.

RECORDS TO BE FURNISHED AT EXAMINERS' REQUEST

1. Access to a record of client securities holdings by client as of _____ and most recent date.

2. Access to all order memoranda or trade tickets for the period.

3. Access to all brokerage account statements and transaction confirmations for all proprietary trading or investment accounts.

4. Access to all records of employee personal securities transactions during the period kept pursuant to Rule 204-2(a)(12) under the Investment Advisers Act.

5. Access to any investment committee meeting minutes made during the period.

6. Access to any written agreements concerning soft dollar arrangements.

7. Access to any separate ledgers and journals recording trading in client accounts to satisfy soft dollar commitments.

8. Access to any sub-advisory agreements or other contracts with wrap fee program sponsoring broker-dealers.

9. Access to Schedule 13G or 13D filings made for the period.

10. Access to the general ledgers and any subsidiary ledgers which form the basis of the financial statements specified in Section I, Item 12 above.

11. Access to the general, cash receipts, cash disbursements and any other journals which form the basis of the ledgers specified in Section II, Part B, Item 10 above.

12. Access to all bank statements, canceled checks, deposit slips, and check registers for all bank accounts open during the period.

13. Access to all loan agreements and notes payable.

14. Access to all notes receivable.

15. Access to all bills and statements, paid or unpaid, presented to or issued by Registrant.

16. Access to any correspondence with the staff of the Commission, particularly any no-action interpretations granted to Registrant by the Commission.

17. Access to any correspondence with any other regulatory agencies or self-regulatory organizations.

18. Access to any correspondence with or reports from public accounting firms during the period.

19. Access to files of client complaints during the period.

20. Access to Board of Directors meeting minutes, Articles of Incorporation, Corporate Bylaws, and stock transfer records or partnership agreements, as applicable.

21. Access to any newsletters sent to clients during the period.

22. Access to records and workpapers supporting the performance data described above in Section I, Item 33 above.

23. Access to any agreements executed with any third party solicitors, any correspondence with such solicitors, and any separate disclosure documents disseminated by such solicitors.

24. During the examination the examiners will review Registrant's records pertaining to certain clients. Be prepared to furnish the following records for review for each client indicated:

    a) Contracts.
        Correspondence.
        Documentation of annual offers pursuant to Rule 204-3 under the Investment Advisers Act.
    b) New account information forms.
    c) Account statements internally generated, from client custodians, and from broker-dealers as well as any written reconciliations between such.
    d) Performance appraisals.
    f) Trade confirmations.
    g) Fee invoices.
    h) Custodial or trust agreements.

Author's note: The foregoing is a copy of an actual SEC audit request provided by a recently audited adviser.

Knowing the Alphabet

1 Phyllis Bernstein, Personal Financial Planning Director, AICPA, supplied the information contained in this section.

2 Dick Young, General Counsel, CFP Board of Standards, supplied the information contained in this section.

3 Ibid.

4 Susan Farmer, Public Relations, American Society of CLU and ChFC, supplied the information contained in this section.

5 Ibid.

6 Julie Sewing, Administrative Director, IARFC, supplied the information contained in this section.

7 Margery Wasserman, Executive Director, NAPFA, supplied the information contained in this section.

CHAPTER I

The Financial Planner

1 Investment Advisers Act Release No. IA-1092 (October 8, 1987).

2 32 M.R.S. § 9752 (1995).

3 MD. Corps. & Ass'ns. Code Ann. § 11-101 (f) (1) (ii) (3).

4 Minn. Stat. § 45.026 and Minn. Rule 2875.105.

5 News Release from Minnesota Commerce Department, May 22, 1990.

6 Jacquelin H. Hallihan and Robert Stirling, "Financial Planning: 'Gray Areas' Regarding Investment Adviser Registration," *CFP Today* (October 1995): 11-12.

7 Ibid.

8 Bill E. Carter, "Study Forecasts Broad Future for Financial Planning," *Journal of the American Society of CLU & ChFC* (January 1996): 77.

9 International Association for Financial Planning, *Profile,* undated.

10 Ibid.

11 *Code of Ethics and Professional Responsibility,* Certified Financial Planner Board of Standards, Inc. (1997): 8.

12 John P. Moriarty and Curtlan R. McNeily, *Regulation of Financial Planners,* Vol. 19, Securities Law Series (New York: Clark Boardman Callaghan, 1996), 2-6.

CHAPTER 2

The Investment Adviser

1 Investment Advisers Act of 1940 § 217.

2 Section 202(a)(11).

3 Section 202(a)(11)(A) through (F).

4 Section 203(b).

5 Investment Advisers Act Release No. IA-1092 (October 8, 1987).

6 Thomas P. Lemke and Gerald T. Lins, *Regulation of Investment Advisers* (New York: Clark Boardman Callaghan, 1996), 1-5.

7 Ibid., 1-4.

8 Investment Advisers Act Release No. IA-1092 (October 8, 1987).

9 Lemke and Lins, 1-6.

10 Ibid.

11 Eli P. Bernzweig, *The Financial Planner's Legal Guide* (Englewood Cliffs, N.J.: Prentice-Hall,1986), 30.

12 Ibid.

13 Ibid., (citing *SEC v. T.W. Howey Co.,* 328 U.S. 293 (1946)).

14 Ibid., 34.

15 Lemke and Lins, 1-8.

16 *Lowe v. SEC,* 472 U.S. 181 (1995).

17 Mr. Alfred A. Zurl, 1995 SEC No-Action letter; and Mr. Hugh A. Hoffman, 1995 SEC No-Action letter.

18 Investment Advisers Act Release No. 1092 (October 8, 1987).

19 Ibid.

20 Bernzweig, 35.

21 Lemke and Lins, 1-9 (citing IA Release No. 471 (1975)).

22 Bernzweig, 36 (citing FPC Securities Corp., [1974-75 Transfer Binder] Para. 80,072, CCH Federal Securities Law Reporter (September 9, 1974)).

23 The author is grateful to John McGovern, formerly of Nathan & Lewis Securities, for providing assistance with this section.

24 Investment Advisers Act of 1940 § 203(b)(1).

25 John P. Moriarty and Curtlan R. McNeily, *Regulation of Financial Planners,* Vol. 19, Securities Law Series (New York: Clark Boardman Callaghan, 1996), 2-2.

26 Investment Advisers Act Release No. 1092 (October 8, 1987).

27 MD. Corps. & Ass'ns. Code Ann. Section 11-101(f)(1)(ii)(3).

28 Dennis M. Groner and Mary B. Petersen, *Compliance: The Life Insurance Practitioner's Practical Survival Guide* (Bryn Mawr, Pa.: Leimberg Associates Books,

1995), 48.

29 Moriarty and McNeily, 4-5.

30 Blue Sky Law Reports, p. 475 (Par. 21).

31 Moriarty and McNeily, 4-5, 4-6.

32 "Frequently Asked Questions about Changes in the Regulation of Investment Advisers," in SEC Web site (5/15/97): http://www.sec.gov/rules/othem/advfaq. htm.

33 § 275. 203A-3.

34 Dale E. Brown, IAFP, interview by author, 19 May 1997.

CHAPTER 3

The Fiduciary

1 Andrea Rock, "Financial Advice You Can Trust," *Money* (November 1989): 80 ff; *Financial Services Week* (May 28, 1996): 32.

2 *Black's Law Dictionary*, 6th ed. (St. Paul: West Publishing Co., 1991),432.

3 John P. Moriarty and Curtlan R. McNeily, *Regulation of Financial Planners*, Vol. 19, Securities Law Series (New York: Clark Boardman Callaghan, 1996), 5-7.

4 375 U.S. 180 (1963).

5 *Johnston v. Cigna Corporation*, 916 P. 2d 643 (Colo. App. 1996).

6 *Paine, Webber, Jackson & Curtis, Inc. v. Adams*, 718 P. 2d 508 (Colo. 1986).

7 Eli P. Bernzweig, *The Financial Planner's Legal Guide* (Englewood Cliffs, N.J.: Prentice-Hall, 1986), 96.

8 *Kohler v. Kohler Co.*, 319 F. 2d 634, 642 (7th Cir. 1963).

9 *Johnston v. Cigna Corporation*, 916 P. 2d 643, 646 (Colo. App. 1996).

10 *Kohler v. Kohler Co.*, 319F. 2d 634, 642 (7th Cir. 1963).

CHAPTER 4

Other Financial Professionals

1 The Uniform Securities Act Sec. 401(c), 1 Blue Sky L. Rep. (CCH), (par. 5541).

2 John P. Moriarty and Curtlan R. McNeily, *Regulation of Financial Planners,* Vol. 19, Securities Law Series (New York: Clark Boardman Callaghan, 1996), 4-19.

3 *Black's Law Dictionary.* (St. Paul: West Publishing Co., 1968), 945. Citing *Pacific Fire Ins. Co. v. Bowers,* 163 Va. 349, 175 S.E. 763.

4 Bloomberg L.P.

5 *Black's Law Dictionary.* Citing *McKinney v. Alton,* 41 Ill.App. 512; *State v. Accident Ass'n,* 67 Wis. 624, 31 N.W. 229.

6 Paul A. Argenti, ed., *The Portable MBA Desk Reference* (New York: John Wiley & Sons, 1994), 19.

7 Available from National Association of Enrolled Agents electronic bulletin board, http://www.naea.org/.

CHAPTER 5

The Competency Factor

1 Catherine Newton, "The Compliance Quandary," *CFP Today* (April 1992): 18.

2 "One in Four Investors Hold Low Opinion of Brokers," *Financial Planning* (January 1996): 14.

3 John P. Moriarty and Curtlan R. McNeily, *Regulation of Financial Planners,* Vol. 19, Securities Law Series (New York: Clark Boardman Callaghan, 1996), 1-5.

4 Amy S. Friedman, "Push Begins for Planner Competency Standards," *National Underwriter* (November 13, 1995): 69.

5 Ibid.

6 "CFP Board Pushes State Competency Testing of Financial Planners," *CFP Today* (December 1995): 18.

7 Ibid.

8 Ibid.

9 Dick Young, General Counsel, CFP Board of Standards, supplied the information contained in this section.

10 Susan Farmer, Public Relations, American Society of CLU and ChFC, supplied the information contained in this section.

11 Julie Sewing, Administrative Director, IARFC, supplied the information contained in this section.

12 Margery Wasserman, Executive Director, NAPFA, supplied the information contained in this paragraph.

13 "NAPFA Seeks to Mollify Critics," *Financial Planning* (April 1997), 14.

14 Phyllis Bernstein, Personal Financial Planning Director, AICPA, supplied the information contained in this section.

CHAPTER 6

Insurance Regulations

1 Dennis M. Groner and Mary B. Petersen, *Compliance: The Life Insurance Practitioner's Practical Survival Guide* (Bryn Mawr, Pa.: Leimberg Associates Books, 1995): 2.

2 Ibid., 3 (quoting from the *Bulletin of the New York State Insurance Department* (May 1994)).

3 John P. Moriarty and Curtlan R. McNeily, *Regulation of Financial Planners,* Vol. 19, Securities Law Series (New York: Clark Boardman Callaghan, 1996), 4-21, 8-49.

4 Groner and Petersen, 217 (citing NYIL § 2602(a)).

5 Moriarty and McNeily, CA-9.

6 Ibid., 8-48.

7 Groner and Petersen, 94–95.

8 Ibid.

9 Ibid., 95.

10 Ibid.

11 Moriarty and McNeily, 4-21.

12 Cynthia Crosson, "NAIC Support for Commission Disclosure is Building Slowly," *National Underwriter* (January 2, 1995): 36.

13 *Introduction to the Life Insurance Illustration Questionnaire (IQ)*, American Society of CLU and ChFC, white paper, revised (April 1996).

CHAPTER 7

Broker-Dealer Regulations

1 Thomas P. Lemke and Gerald T. Lins, *Regulation of Investment Advisers* (New York:Clark Boardman Callaghan, 1996), 2-63.

2 Ibid.

3 NASD Notice to Members 94-44, (May 15, 1994): 245.

4 Lemke and Lins, 2-63.

5 "NASD 94-44 Stirs Interest at Retreat," *CFP Today* (August 1995): 17, 20.

6 Donald R. Fischer and Robert N. Veres, *The Liability Handbook* (Atlanta: International Association for Financial Planning, 1990).

7 Dale E. Brown, IAFP, interview by author, 19 May 1997.

CHAPTER 8

Investment Adviser Regulations

1 Investment Advisers Act of 1940, Rule 206(4)-1.

2 Thomas P. Lemke and Gerald T. Lins, *Regulation of Investment Advisers* (New York: Clark Boardman Callaghan, 1996) (citing Investment Advisers Act Rule 206 (4)-1(b)), 2-47.

3 Ibid.

4 Ibid.

5 Ibid.

6 Ibid., 2-50 ff.

7 John P. Moriarty and Curtlan R. McNeily, *Regulation of Financial Planners,* Vol. 19, Securities Law Series (New York: Clark Boardman Callaghan, 1996), 3-16.

8 Lemke and Lins, 2-49 (citing Investment Advisers Act Rule 206 (4) -1(a)(2)).

9 Ibid., 2-47, 48 (citing Investment Advisers Act Rule 206(4)-1).

10 Ibid., (citing Stalker Advisory Services, SEC No-Action letter (January 18, 1994); Kurtz Capital Management, SEC No-Action letter (December 18, 1987)).

11 Jeffrey Kelvin, Financial Planners Assistance, interview by author, 15 July 1996.

12 Gallagher and Associates, Ltd., SEC No-Action letter (July 10, 1995).

13 Amherst Financial Services, SEC No-Action letter (May 23, 1995) and Multi-Financial Securities Corporation, SEC No-Action letter (November 9, 1995).

14 Investment Advisers Act of 1940, Rule 204-3(b).

15 Ibid. at Rule 204-3(c).

16 Moriarty and McNeily, 1-5, 1-6.

17 Ibid, 3-10.

18 Form ADV, Part II, Item 14.

19 Moriarty and McNeily, 3-10 (citing fn. 2).

20 Investment Advisers Act Release No. IA-1092, p. 6 (October 8, 1987).

21 Moriarty and McNeily, 3-11 (citing fn. 1 to 3).

22 Ibid.

23 Investment Advisers Act of 1940, Rule 204-2(g).

24 Lemke and Lins, 2-6, 2-7.

25 Ibid.

26 William R. Meck, speech to IAFP, 13 May 1995.

27 Investment Advisers Act of 1940, Rule 206 (4)-3.

28 Ibid.

29 Moriarty and McNeily, 3-17.

30 Eli P. Bernzweig, *The Financial Planner's Legal*

Guide (Englewood Cliffs, N.J.: Prentice-Hall,1996), 42.

31 Ibid.

32 Investment Advisers Act of 1940, Reg. § 275.205-3(b)(1), (b)(2).

33 Investment Advisers Act of 1940, § 208(c).

34 Ibid, § 208 (a), (b).

35 Tracey Longo, "Put to the Test," *Financial Services Week* (November 2, 1992): 17 ff.

36 John McGovern, formerly Compliance Director, Nathan & Lewis Securities, interview by author, 19 September 1996.

CHAPTER 9

Other Laws

1 Dennis M. Groner and Mary B. Petersen, *Compliance: The Life Insurance Practitioner's Survival Guide* (Bryn Mawr, Pa.: Leimberg Associates Books, 1995), 11–12.

2 "ADVERTISEMENT—For the purpose of this section and any interpretation thereof, 'advertisement' means material published, or designed for use in the newspaper, magazine or other periodical, radio, television or tape recording, videotape display, signs or billboards, motion pictures, telephone directories (other than routine listings), or other public media." Groner and Petersen, 13 (citing Art. III § 35(a) of the NASD Rules of Fair Practice, NASD Manual, NASD (July, 1994)).

3 Ibid., 113.

4 Art. III, § 35(b)(2) of the NASD Rules of Fair Practice, NASD Manual, NASD (July, 1994).

5 "Financial Advisers and the Internet," *Planning Matters* (August 1996): 6. Using electronic media for delivery purposes is discussed at great length in SEC Release No. 337233 (October 6, 1995).

6 NASD Notice to Members 95-74 (August 9, 1995).

7 "Financial Advisers and the Internet," *Planning Mat-*

ters (August 1996): 6.

8 Anthony L. Kimery, "Financial Fraud on the Internet," *Financial Planning* (April 1995): 121.

9 NASD Regulatory & Compliance Alert, Ask the Analyst about Electronic Communications, p. 5 (April 1996).

10 Ibid., 4.

11 Ibid., 5.

12 Ibid.

13 Ibid.

14 "Regulators Grapple with Internet," *Journal of Financial Planning* (August 1996): 88.

15 "Financial Advisers and the Internet," 6.

16 NASD, Ask the Analyst, 5.

17 Ibid.

18 The Consortium's Hot Line Service (June 22, 1996): 2.

19 "Financial Advisers and the Internet," 6.

20 Ibid. Using electronic media for delivery purposes is discussed at great length in SEC Release No. 337233 (October 6, 1995).

21 Laura Begley, "Living-Will [sic] Sales Are Target of State Order," *Minneapolis Star and Tribune* (September 7, 1990): 4D.

22 Donald J. Korn, "Sued If You Don't," *Financial Planning* (December 1994): 33.

23 National Conference of Commissioners on Uniform State Laws, Uniform Prudent Investor Act, prefatory note and comments, p. 1 (drafted July 29–August 5, 1994).

24 Ibid., 3.

25 Ibid.

26 Ibid.

27 Korn, 34.

28 "'Do-Not-Call' Lists Mandated," *Financial Planning* (August 1995): 14.

29 "Can You Trust Your Broker?" *Business Week* (Feb-

ruary 20, 1995): 70.
30 Ibid.
31 Ibid.
32 Korn, 34.

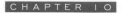

Product and Service Providers

1 Arnie Abens, Abens Financial Services, Inc., interview by author, Edina, Minn., 30 May 1997.

CHAPTER 11

The First Client Meeting

1 Press Release IAFP, Atlanta (May 20, 1993). Other responses were: Accessibility/Availability, 8%; Experience, 7%; Reputation, 7%; and Professional Qualifications, 6%.
2 *Financial Services Week* (May 28, 1990): 32.
3 Steve Moeller, "From Profiles to Profits," *Dow Jones Investment Advisor* (April 1996): 32.
4 Ibid.
5 Ibid.

CHAPTER 12

Subsequent Client Meetings

1 Linda S. Lubitz and Norman M. Boone, *The Investment Policy Guidebook* (Ibbotson, 1996), 6.
2 Ibid.
3 Melissa Gitter, "An Ounce of Prevention," *Financial Planning* (February 1996): 92.
4 Lubitz and Boone, 4.
5 Gitter, 92, 95 (quoting Eric Sippel, an attorney with a San Francisco law firm).
6 Ibid.
7 Gitter, 96, and Reinhardt Werba Bowen Advisory

Services, *The Prudent Investor's Guide to Beating the Market* (Irwin Professional Publishing, 1996).

CHAPTER 13

The Importance of Feedback

1 Panel discussion by Douglas Henderson and David Paulukaitis, 1993 IAFP Broker-Dealer Conference.
2 Amy Stevens, "Lawyers' Annoying Misdeeds Targeted," *The Wall Street Journal* (September 9, 1994): B1.
3 947 F. 2d 257 (7th Cir. 1991).
4 Lecture in Annapolis, Md., 10 July 1996.

CHAPTER 14

The Unhappy Client

1 Rod Mason, Chandler & Mason, Ltd., interview by author, 19 July 1996.

CHAPTER 15

When Clients Sue

1 J. Michael Dryton, Esq., Tips for Securities Professionals on Avoiding/Winning Litigation, white paper (1992).
2 444 U.S. 11 (1979).
3 Gary Irwin, Counsel, IDS Financial Services, interview by author, 17 September 1992.
4 Dryton, Tips for Securities Professionals.
5 Dale E. Brown, "Regulating the Financial Planning Industry," *Life Insurance Selling* (September 1989): 144ff.
6 Eli P. Bernzweig, *The Financial Planner's Legal Guide* (Englewood Cliffs, N.J.: Prentice-Hall, 1986), 95.
7 *Cash v. Frederick & Company, Inc.* 57 F.R.D. 71 (E.D. Wis. 1972).
8 Bernzweig, 95.

9 Ibid., 100.

10 *Hanley v. SEC,* 425 F. 2d 589 (2d Cir. 1969).

11 Code of Federal Regulations, § 240.10b-5.

12 Bernzweig, 99.

13 Ibid., 106ff.

14 Gretchen Morgenson, "Inviting the Cat to Take Care of the Canaries," *Forbes* (June 25, 1990): 252.

15 Donald Jay Korn, "Protecting the Protector," *Financial Planning* (September 1995): 127.

16 Ibid., 127ff.

17 Ibid., 127.

18 *IDS Financial Services, Inc. v. Smithson,* 843 F. Supp. 415 (N.D. Ill. 1994).

19 William B. Shearer, Jr., "Your Legal Exposure" (Financial Planners Liability Seminar, International Association for Financial Planning, Atlanta, 1987), 26.

20 Richard D. Young, Compliance Specialist, FSC Securities Corporation, interview by author, 25 November 1992.

CHAPTER 16

Common Complaints

1 Thomas Kostigen, "Suitability Emerges as a New Concern for Compliance Pros," *Financial Planning* (May 1992): 26, 27.

2 Bayard Bigelow, "Loss Prevention and the Greening of the Financial Planning Profession," Financial Service Mutual Insurance Company, white paper (1995).

3 Kostigen, 26, 27.

4 NASD Manual, "Rules of Fair Practice," Art. III, § 2(a) (July, 1994).

5 Eli P. Bernzweig, *The Financial Planner's Legal Guide* (Englewood Cliffs, N.J.: Prentice-Hall, 1986), 147.

6 Bigelow, 3.

7 W.A. Jackson, The Broker/Dealer Program Claim-Handling Experience, Lancer Claims Services, Inc.,

Cal-Surance Assoc., Inc., white paper, pp. 2–3 (August 28, 1992).

8 Gregory Bresiger, "Shearson Memo Urges Reps to Use Care in Selling LPs, Cites Arbitration Case," *Financial Services Week* (December 24, 1990): 8.

9 Jackson, pp. 2–3.

10 Kostigen, 26.

11 Jackson, 1.

12 John McGovern, formerly Compliance Director, Nathan & Lewis Securities, interview by author, 26 October 1992.

13 Karen Slater, "Conflict Issues Cloud Financial Planning," *Wall Street Journal* (March 22, 1990): C1.

14 Larry Dignan, "Sharper Image?" *Financial Planning* (January 1996): 46, 47.

CHAPTER 17

Errors and Omissions Coverage

1 Michael Murray, "So Sue Me," *Financial Planning* (November 1995): 134.

2 Bayard Bigelow, "Loss Prevention and the Greening of the Financial Planning Profession," white paper, p. 2(1993, 1995).

3 Murray, 134.

4 "Ruder Report," Report of the Arbitration Security Task Force to the Board of Governors, National Association of Securities Dealers Inc., Securities Arbitration Reform (January 1996): 7.

5 Dennis M. Groner and Mary B. Petersen, *Compliance: The Life Insurance Practitioner's Practical Survival Guide* (Bryn Mawr, Pa.: Leimberg Associates Books, 1995), 65.

CHAPTER 18

Mediation

1 National Association of Securities Dealers, Inc., NASD Mediation, An Alternate Path to Resolving Securities Disputes, p. 3 (October 1995).

2 Ibid., p. 6.

3 Amy Dunkin, "Battling Your Broker? Tell It to a Mediator," *Business Week* (May 27, 1996): 148.

4 National Association of Securities Dealers, Inc., pp. 7 ff.

5 "Ruder Report", Report of the Arbitration Policy Task Force to the Board of Governors, National Association of Securities Dealers, Inc., Securities Arbitration Reform (January 1996): 49.

6 American Arbitration Association, *A Guide to Mediation for Financial Planning Disputes,* p. 6 (March 1996).

7 Ibid, pp. 6 ff.

8 McEldowney Financial Services, SEC No-Action letter; also Fed. Sec. L. Rep. pp. 78, 373. (October 17, 1986).

9 Dunkin, 148.

10 Ibid.

11 Trident Holdings, *Mediation—A Newly Emerging Form for Resolving Accountancy Disputes,* No. 5, p. 1, white paper (1994).

CHAPTER 19

Arbitration

1 486 U.S. 220 (1987), reh'g denied, 483 U.S. 1056 (1987).

2 "Ruder Report," Report of the Arbitration Task Force to the Board of Governors, National Association of Securities Dealers, Inc., *Securities Arbitration Reform* (January 1996): 6.

3 Ibid., 7.

4 Deborah Masucci, Vice President, Dispute Resolution, NASD, The Changing Landscape of Dispute Resolution in the Securities Industry, white paper (April 1996).

5 "Ruder Report," 6.

6 "Ruder Report," App. 4-1.

7 Ibid.

8 Ibid., 22 ff.

9 Ibid., 24.

10 Ibid.

11 Ibid., App. 4-2.

12 Ibid., App. 4-3.

13 Ibid., 78.

14 Ibid., App. 4-3.

15 Ibid., App. 4-4.

16 Ibid., App. 4-4, 4-5.

17 Ibid., App. 4-5.

18 Eli P. Bernzweig, *The Financial Planner's Legal Guide* (Englewood Cliffs, N.J.: Prentice-Hall, 1987), 119 ff.

19 Ibid.

20 28 F. 3d 704 (7th Cir. 1994).

21 Terrence J. Fleming, "The Trouble with Arbitration," *The Hennepin Lawyer* (March-April 1996): 17 (citing *Federal Commerce & Navigation Co. v. Kanematsu-Gosho, Ltd.*, 457 F. 2d 387, 389 (2d Cir. 1972)).

22 Ibid., 16 ff.

23 Ibid.

24 Michael Burnett, Report of the United States General Accounting Office on Securities Arbitration, Securities Arbitration, Vol. 1, Practicing Law Institute (1992): 54.

25 Fleming, 16 ff.

26 "Ruder Report," 140.

27 Fleming, 16 ff.

28 Ibid.

29 Ibid., 18.

30 Ibid., 17 (citing *Federal Commerce & Navigation Co. v. Kanematsu-Gosho, Ltd.,* 457 F. 2d 387, 389 (2d Cir. 1972)).

31 Ibid. (citing 49 F. 3d 347 (8th Cir. 1995)) .

32 Ibid. (citing *Bavarati v. Josephthal, Lyon, and Ross, Inc.,* 28 F. 3d 704 (7th Cir. 1994)).

33 "Ruder Report," *Arbitration Reform* (1996).

34 Stan Hargrave, telephone interview by author, 23 September 1996.

35 Terry Fleming, Lindquist and Vennum, interview by author, 23 September 1996.

CHAPTER 20

SEC and State Audits

1 John P. Moriarty and Curtlan R. McNeily, *Regulation of Financial Planners,* Vol. 19, Securities Law Series (New York: Clark Boardman Callaghan, 1996), 1-4, 1-5.

2 Kevin G. Salwen, "The SEC Proposes Tightening Reins on 17,000 Advisers," *Wall Street Journal* (January 24, 1992): C1.

3 Nancy J. Johnson, formerly Senior Vice President, Long Grove Trading, interview by author, 3 September 1996.

4 William R. Meck, speech to IAFP, 13 May 1995.

5 645 F. 2d 310 (5th Cir. 1981).

6 Investment Advisers Act of 1940, Rule 204-2(g).

7 Thomas P. Lemke and Gerald T. Lins, *Regulation of Investment Advisers* (New York: Clark Boardman Callaghan, 1996): 2-105.

8 Richard D. Marshall, Surviving an Inspection of an Investment Company or Adviser: Insights from a Former Inspection Chief, white paper, pp. 729, 730.

9 Moriarty and McNeily, 6-8.

10 According to Nancy J. Johnson, CFP, formerly Senior Vice President of Long Grove Trading, it is important to disclose and disclose again. She notes the case in which the SEC did not feel the RIA had disclosed his broker-dealer affiliation and his fee and commission arrangements enough times. The RIA was required to disclose it more than once in order to be clear. Interview by author, 3 September 1996.

11 Lemke and Lins, 2-91.

12 Moriarty and McNeily, 6-10.

13 Ibid., 6-11.

14 Ibid., 6-12.

15 Ibid., 6-7.

16 Ibid. In one case, the SEC sanctioned an adviser for inadequate insider trading procedures, even though there was no wrongdoing and no misuse of material, nonpublic information. The SEC appeared to be concerned that the procedures in place were not adequately adhered to and did not include objective review.

17 The author would like to thank Alexandra Armstrong of Washington, D.C. for this excellent suggestion.

18 William R. Meck, speech to IAFP, 13 May 1995.

19 Moriarty and McNeily, 2-106.

20 Carl Sullivan, "How to Survive SEC Scrutiny," *Financial Planning* (September 1995): 101, 105.

21 Moriarty and McNeily, 6-17, 6-18, fn. 4.

22 Ibid.

23 Ibid., 6-19.

Appendix A

1 Individual members in the Practitioner Division (those who have met the necessary requirements of the Division and have signed the Practitioner Division Certificate) may use fact of membership in the following manner:

Member, Practitioner Division
International Association for Financial Planning

Members of the Practitioner Division should contact the compliance department of their broker-dealer to make sure any state or NASD regulatory concerns are addressed before using fact of membership for commercial purposes.

2 Companies in the IAFP's Corporate and Broker-Dealer Divisions may use fact of membership as follows:

Member, Corporate Division
International Association for Financial Planning

Member, Broker-Dealer Division
International Association for Financial Planning

PERMISSIONS CREDITS

GRATEFUL ACKNOWLEDGMENT is made to the following for permission to reprint material copyrighted or controlled by them. This constitutes a continuation of the copyright page.

◆ Investment Policy Statement. Reprinted by permission of Linda Lubitz, CFP, Woolf Lubitz & Foldes, Miami, FL., and Norman M. Boone, MBA, CFP.

◆ Individual Compliance Checklist, Master Compliance Checklist, Recordkeeping Audit Checklist, Client Attitude/Experience Survey, Information Gathering Session Agenda, and Information Gathering Session Notes. Reprinted by permission of Edwin P. Morrow, ChFC, CFP, RFC, Financial Planning Consultants, Inc., Middletown, OH. 513-424-1656 ©FPC.

◆ Quarterly Survey courtesy of J. Floyd Swilley. Reprinted by permission.

◆ Letter of Understanding Re: Change in Portfolio courtesy of Nancy J. Johnson, CFP. Reprinted by permission of Nancy J. Johnson, CFP, formerly of Long Grove Trading Company, and now of Cambridge Investment Research, Inc., Fairfield, IA.

◆ Asset Monitoring Investor Agreement, Explanation of Investment, Financial Planning Agreement, and Investment Policy & Objective Setting Questionnaire. Reprinted by permission of Arnold D. Abens, Jr., a Registered Representative of Royal Alliance Associates, Inc., and President of Abens Financial Services, Inc., a Registered Investment Advisor.

◆ "Eight Steps to Establishing An IPS," adapted from material published in *Financial Planning*, February 1996, courtesy of John J. Bowen, Jr. Reprinted by permission of John J. Bowen, Jr., McGraw Hill-Companies, Inc., and *Financial Planning*.

◆ For portions of the article "An Ounce of Prevention," by Melissa Gitter in *Financial Planning*, February 1996. Reprinted by permission of *Financial Planning*.

◆ Engagement Letter and Financial Planning/Advisory Disclosure Agreement courtesy of Alexandra Armstrong, CFP. Copyright 1996 Alexandra Armstrong, Armstrong, Welch & MacIntyre. Reprinted by permission of Alexandra Armstrong, CFP, Chairman of Armstrong, Welch & McIntyre, Inc.

◆ FSC Prospectus Receipts. Reprinted by permission of Richard Young, FSC Securities Corp., Atlanta, GA.

◆ Haiker Letter Series and Financial Planning Checklist courtesy of H. Fred Haiker. Reprinted by permission of H. Fred Haiker, CFP, Financial Network Investment Corporation.

◆ Rybka Life Insurance Plan Letter courtesy of Lawrence Rybka. Reprinted by permission of Lawrence Rybka, Vice President of Executive Insurance.

◆ Material for the Difficult Client Profile courtesy of Steven Moeller. Reprinted by permission of Steve Moeller, President of American Business Visions.

◆ For material quoted extensively by Bud Bigelow. Reprinted by permission of Bayard Bigelow III.

About Bloomberg

Bloomberg Financial Markets is a global, multimedia-based distributor of information services, combining news, data, and analysis for financial markets and businesses. Bloomberg carries real-time pricing, data, history, analytics, and electronic communications that is available 24 hours a day and is currently accessed by 200,000 financial professionals in 92 countries.

Bloomberg covers all key global securities markets, including equities, money markets, currencies, municipals, corporate/euro/sovereign bonds, commodities, mortgage-backed securities, derivative products, and governments. The company also delivers access to Bloomberg News, whose more than 400 reporters and editors in 70 bureaus worldwide provide around-the-clock coverage of economic, financial, and political events.

To learn more about Bloomberg—one of the world's fastest-growing real-time financial information networks—call a sales representative at:

Frankfurt:	49-69-920-410
Hong Kong:	852-2521-3000
London:	44-171-330-7500
New York:	1-212-318-2000
Princeton:	1-609-279-3000
São Paulo:	5511-3048-4500
Singapore:	65-226-3000
Sydney:	61-29-777-8686
Tokyo:	81-3-3201-8900

About the Author

Katherine Vessenes, J.D., CFP, is America's best-known authority on legal, compliance, and ethics issues for financial advisers. She frequently conducts seminars for professional organizations such as American Express Financial Advisors and Chubb and is the author of IAFP's *The Compliance and Liability Handbook* (1992), which this new book supersedes. She is president of Vestment Consulting, of counsel to the law firm of Chandler & Mason Ltd., and lives in the Minneapolis area. She may be contacted at (612) 896-0166 or by fax at (612) 831-5898.

About the IAFP

The International Association for Financial Planning is a professional membership association dedicated to advancing the financial planning process. Founded in 1969, IAFP is the oldest and largest nonprofit organization of its type in the world. The IAFP represents more than 16,500 individuals and institutions in all 50 states and abroad who are committed to furthering the financial planning process as the foundation for smart decision making. Its members, primarily financial advisers, are from all backgrounds and disciplines.

Katherine!
Send **HELP!!!**

I have no time to create forms that protect my practice!

☐ **SEND PYP: DocuMate**—The digital companion to *Protecting Your Practice*. Offers forms, checklists, contracts, letters surveys and much more, *already entered into MicroSoft Word™!* Absolutely indispensible. Save time and money; no need to retype these crucial practice management tools. **$124.95**

☐ **SEND YOUR Audio Tapes**—*A Marketing Approach to Improving Client Relations and Avoiding Litigation.* 6 Audiocassettes of Katherine's most popular seminars about turning compliance into profits. **$149.95**

☐ **SEND MORE INFORMATION**—About your products and services

___**PYP: DocuMate**	$124.95	Total $_____	
___**6 Audiocassettes**	$149.95	Total $_____	
___**Buy Both, Save $25**	$249.90	Total $_____	
	Shipping & Handling $		7.00
MN Residents please add 6 1/2% Sales Tax: $_____			
Prices subject to change		TOTAL $_____	

Name (please print)

Address

City/State/Zip

Phone   Fax

☐ Visa   ☐ M/C   ☐ AMEX   Exp. Date _____

Cardholder Name

Card Number

Authorized Signature

For faster service, fax this form to 612-831-5898
For more information call 1-800-999-9958

Mail this card today!

BUSINESS REPLY MAIL
FIRST-CLASS MAIL   PERMIT NO 27335   MINNEAPOLIS, MN

POSTAGE WILL BE PAID BY ADDRESSEE

VESTMENT CONSULTING
70 NORMAN RIDGE DR
BLOOMINGTON MN 55437-9927

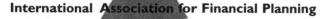

For faster service call
1-800-945-4237

≡IAFP

International Association for Financial Planning

**Please send me more
information from IAFP
that will help my
business GROW!**

☐ Products & Services Catalog
    •Books •Tapes •Logo Items

☐ Prospective Client Brochures
    •Sample Set

☐ Audio/Edutapes Brochures

☐ IAFP Member Application

☐ Consumer Referral Program

☐ Fax-On-Demand Table of Contents
    Call 1-888-IAFP-FAX

Name (please print)

Company   **Title**

Address

City

State   **Zip**

Phone Number

Fax   **E-mail**

**Visit our Web site at http://www.iafp.org
For faster service call 1-800-945-4237**

Mail this card today!